Neue Arbeits- und Tätigkeitsformen

New Forms of Work and Activity

Nouvelles formes de travail et d'activités

COLLOQUIUM/COLLOQUE
Brussels, 25.4.1986

Documentation/Dokumentation

herausgegeben von/edited by/préparé par
Ralf Dahrendorf
Eberhard Köhler
Françoise Piotet

Europäische Stiftung zur Verbesserung der Lebens- und Arbeitsbedingungen
Loughlinstown House, Shankill, Co. Dublin, Irland. Telefon: 826888 Telex: 30726 EURF

Fondation européenne pour l'amélioration des conditions de vie et de travail
Loughlinstown House, Shankill, Co. Dublin, République d'Irlande.
Téléphone: 826888 Telex: 30726 EURF

European Foundation for the Improvement of Living and Working Conditions
Loughlinstown House, Shankill, Co. Dublin, Ireland.
Telephone: 826888 Telex: 30726 EURF

Luxembourg: Office for Official Publications of the European Communities
ISBN: 92-825-6418-5
Catalogue number: SY-46-86-775-3A-C
Cataloguing data can be found at the end of this publication.

© Copyright: THE EUROPEAN FOUNDATION FOR THE IMPROVEMENT OF LIVING AND WORKING CONDITIONS, 1986. For rights of translation or reproduction, application should be made to the Director, European Foundation for the Improvement of Living and Working Conditions, Loughlinstown House, Shankill, County Dublin, Ireland.

Printed by the European Foundation.

Contents

PREFACE by Clive Purkiss, Director, European Foundation — i

INTRODUCTION by Eberhard Köhler, Project Manager, European Foundation — iii

STATEMENT by F. Staedelin, Secrétaire, Confédération Européenne des Syndicats, Bruxelles — ix

STATEMENT by F.J. Kador, Geschäftsführer, Bundesvereinigung der deutschen Arbeitgeberverbände — xiii

1. EMPLOYMENT FLEXIBILITY AND INTERNAL AND EXTERNAL LABOUR MARKETS
   John Atkinson, Institute of Manpower Studies, University of Sussex, Brighton — 1

2. ISSUES IN JOB SHARING
   Joyce Epstein, freelance social researcher, London — 39

3. TELEWORK
   Attitudes of the Social Partners and the Labour Force and the potential for Decentralized Electronic Work in Europe
   Empirica, Berlin — 89

4. TELEWORK
   Women and Environment
   Rosalyn Moran and Jean Tansey, Irish Foundation for Human Development, Dublin — 101

5. LES CONSEQUENCES DES FORMES NOUVELLES D'EMPLOI SUR LA VIE FAMILIALE ET L'ORGANISATION SOCIALE
   Françoise Piotet, Institut de Sociologie, Sorbonne, Paris — 107

6. AUSWIRKUNGEN VON NEUEN ARBEITSFORMEN AUS BETRIEBSPSYCHOLOGISCHER SICHT
   Otto Renda & Hans-Jürgen Reuter, Institut für Angewandte Betriebspsychologie, Berlin — 139

7. LEGAL AND CONTRACTUAL LIMITATIONS TO WORKING TIME
   Roger Blanpain, Faculty of Law, University of Leuven — 193

8.	LES CONSEQUENCES DES FORMES NOUVELLES D'EMPLOI SUR LE DROIT DU TRAVAIL ET DE LA SECURITE SOCIALE Yota Kravaritou-Manitakis, Faculty of Law, University of Thessaloniki	205
9.	NEUE WEGE DER ARBEITSORGANISATION Erfahrungen aus selbstverwalteten Betrieben - Acht Thesen Lothar Gretsch, Institut für Sozialforschung und Sozialwirtschaft, Saarbrücken	261
10.	LIFESTYLE, ECONOMIC STRUCTURE AND TIME USE Jonathan Gershuny, School of Humanities and Social Studies, University of Bath	267

TENTATIVE CONCLUSIONS AND FURTHER WORK   213

ANNEXES:

Programme of Colloquium   325
List of Participants at Colloquium   333

Preface

This volume contains the documentation of the Colloquium on New Forms of Work and Activity, held by the European Foundation on 25 April 1986 in Brussels under the chairmanship of Professor Ralf Dahrendorf.

This subject is of fundamental importance to the work of the Foundation on issues of living and working conditons. But it is a broad subject, so the Foundation, including its Administrative Board, saw the need for some preliminary work to make clear the issues on which we can most usefully work and develop our understanding through research in a practical way.

For this purpose, the Foundation has established an Advisory Committee, consisting of representatives of the social partners and the governments of the Member states of the European Community, augmented by experts from various scientific disciplines. The Foundation is grateful to Professor Dahrendorf for making his expertise and knowledge in this field available to the Advisory Committee by agreeing to act as its honorary chairman.

In order to structure and assist the deliberations of this Advisory Committee, the Foundation had commissioned a number of issue papers relating to this project which served as a vehicle for a first broad debate in the course of the Colloquium on 25 April 1986. These issue papers are presented in this volume together with a summary of the contributions to the colloquium by the participants. The Foundation had thought it important that from the outset we should have the guidance of those who are concerned with effecting policy in this area. Therefore, it was of great significance that **Mr. Michael Welsh,** Chairman of the European Parliament's Committee on Social Affairs and Employment, **Mr. Jean Degimbe,** Director-General for Employment, Social Affairs and Education of the Commission of the European Communities, who is at the same time chairman of the Administrative Board of the European Foundation, and **Dr. Enrico Kirschen,** chairman of the Section for Social Questions of the Economic and Social Committee of the European Communities were able to attend and to contribute formally to the debate of the Colloquium. Their main points are also contained in the introductory chapter of this volume.

As an indication of the degree of political agreement or controversy in the assessment of the problems and issues at hand, the introductory contributions of the social partners - Mr. François Staedelin's statement on behalf of the European Trade Union Confederation (ETUC) and Dr. Fritz-Jürgen Kador's statement on behalf of the Union of Industries of the European Community (UNICE) - are reproduced in their entirety. At the end of this documentation, first tentative conclusions emanating from the second meeting of the Foundation's Advisory Committee, held on 27 June 1986, are recorded which point a way forward towards a constructive transformation of this first phase of the project into concrete and useful research avenues in the coming years.

Finally, the European Foundation acknowledges the important contributions to the Colloquium from all participants, among them several Members of the European Parliament, experts and researchers from many organisations with a common concern for the issues and problems under investigation.

Clive Purkiss
Director of the European Foundation

July 1986

Einleitung: Die Spannweite der Problematik

von Eberhard Köhler, Forschungsleiter, Europäische Stiftung

Neue Organisationsweisen der Arbeit zur Anpassung an eine veränderte Nachfrage nach Produkten und Dienstleistungen, veränderte Verhaltensweisen und eine anhaltende technologische Entwicklung gekoppelt mit beängstigend hohen Arbeitslosenzahlen zwingen zu einer Neueinschätzung des Arbeitsmarktes und damit einer Neudefinition von Arbeit. Für eine Vielzahl von Personen hat "Arbeit" ihre herkömmliche Bedeutung im Sinne von Vollzeitbeschäftigung gegen Bezahlung verloren.

Zum besseren Verständnis dieser Veränderungen startete die Stiftung 1985 ein Forschungsprogramm über neue Arbeits- und Tätigkeitsformen. Dieses Programm untersucht die Art und Weise, in der der Arbeitsmarkt auf diese veränderten Bedingungen reagiert sowie die neuen Arbeitsformen, die zunehmende Beachtung finden und bewertet die sozialen und wirtschaftlichen Auswirkungen hiervon. Zu diesen neuen Arbeitsweisen gehören solche, die Flexibilität in die räumliche Dimension der Arbeits-/Wohnsituation von Arbeitnehmern einbringen, wie etwa Heimarbeit oder Telearbeit sowie jene, die auf einer andersartigen Nutzungsweise von Zeit fußen, wie etwa Wochenendarbeit, 12-Stunden-Schichtarbeit, Arbeit "auf Abruf" und wiederum Telearbeit.

Auch außerhalb des formellen Arbeitsmarktes finden grundlegende Änderungen statt. Je schwieriger es wird, eine bezahlte Arbeit zu finden, desto mehr Personen wenden sich anderen Tätigkeitsformen zu, die gewöhnlicherweise nicht den gleichen Stellenwert einnehmen, wie z. B. gemeinnützige Arbeit, Familienfürsorge oder Bürgerinitiativen im Umweltschutz, um nur einige Beispiele zu nennen. In einer Gesellschaft, in der sich der soziale Status lange Zeit aus der Arbeit ergab, bedürfen diese Tätigkeiten einer Neubewertung.

Die Stiftung hat veranlaßt, dieses Thema aus verschiedenen Perspektiven zu umreißen. Sie versucht damit, zu einem umfassenderen Verständnis der einzelnen Faktoren zu gelangen, die diese Entwicklung charakterisieren. Die bisher geleistete Arbeit umfaßt folgende Bereiche:

. Externe und interne Arbeitsmärkte und Beschäftigungsflexibilität

. Entwicklung von Job-sharing

. Entwicklung von Telearbeit

. Auswirkungen auf Familien und soziale Organisationen

. Psychische Auswirkungen neuer Arbeits- und Tätigkeitsformen

. Rechtliche und vertragliche Arbeitszeitbestimmungen

. Arbeitsrechtliche und sozialversicherungsrechtliche Fragen

. Arbeitsorganisation in kooperativen Unternehmen

. sich verändernde Strukturen der Zeitnutzung

Zu diesen Themenkomplexen wurden Arbeitspapiere erstellt, die im folgenden abgedruckt sind. Um die Diskussion um diese Problematik in ihrer weiteren politischen und gesellschaftlichen Bedeutung zu begreifen, wurden dem Kolloquium kurze Stellungnahmen aus der Sicht der Kommission, des Europäischen Parlaments, des Wirtschafts- und Sozialausschusses, der Arbeitgeber und Arbeitnehmerseite und - last but not least - aus der Sicht des politisch interessierten Wissenschaftlers Ralf Dahrendorf vorangestellt.

Jean Degimbe, Generaldirektor für Beschäftigung, soziale Fragen und Bildung und Vorsitzender des Verwaltungsrates der Europäischen Stiftung, betonte das große Interesse der Kommission an den aufgeworfenen Fragen. Sowohl der Präsident der Kommission, Jacques Delors, als auch Vizepräsident Manuel Marin Gonzales, zuständig für diesen speziellen Politikbereich, messem dem Problem der Arbeitslosigkeit größte Bedeutung bei. In dem scheinbaren Widerstreit zwischen wirtschaftlicher Realität und gesellschaftlichen Notwendigkeiten, Wünschen und Erwartungen muß versucht werden, durch gemeinsame Anstrengungen aller Beteiligten gemeinsam tragbare Lösungen zu erarbeiten. Aus diesem Wunsch resultieren auch die Bemühungen, durch die Neubelebung bzw. Intensivierung des "sozialen Dialogs" zwischen Gewerkschaften und Arbeitgebern auf allen Ebenen die Einsicht zu vertiefen, daß nur durch gemeinsames Vorgehen eine evolutionäre

Anpassung des Arbeitsmarktes an veränderte Rahmenbedingungen zu erreichen sein wird. In diesem Bezugsfeld fällt auch der Erarbeitung wissenschaftlich fundierter Kenntnisse und Einsichten erhöhte Bedeutung zu, eine Aufgabe, zu deren Lösung die Europäische Stiftung laut Satzung und Selbstverständnis einen wichtigen Beitrag leisten sollte und kann.

Michael Welsh als Vorsitzender des Ausschusses für soziale Angelegenheiten und Beschäftigung des Europäischen Parlamentes wies auf die enge thematische Verflechtung hin, die zwischen dem Arbeitsfeld der Stiftung und den Sorgen seines Ausschusses bestehen. Während wir und in den Ländern der Europäischen Gemeinschaft einerseits auf einem nie dagewesenen Niveau absoluten materiellen und gesellschaftlichen Wohlstandes befinden, ist großen Teilen der Bevölkerung, etwa den Arbeitslosen, der direkte Zugriff zu diesem Wohlstand verwehrt. Nach Meinung von Welsh ist das Phänomen der Arbeitslosigkeit kein vorübergehendes Ärgernis in unseren Gesellschafts- und Wirtschaftssystemen, sondern ein strukturelles Problem des Arbeitsmarktes, das nur durch massive Veränderungen in der Werte- und Erwartungshaltung der Bürger der Europäischen Gemeinschaft angepackt werden kann. Aus diesem Grunde sollten verschiedene Arten und Formen von Arbeit und Aktivität nicht mehr hierarchisch klassifiziert und definiert werden, sondern als absoluter Wert, als Kontinuum gesehen werden, so daß eine gesellschaftliche Diskriminierung "atypischer" Arbeitsformen erst gar nicht entsteht bzw. sich nicht weiter ausbreitet. So muß einer neuen "Klassenbildung" entgegengewirkt werden, vor allem der Gefahr der Entwicklung einer neuen Unterschicht, bestehend aus gering oder nicht ausreichend ausgebildeten Menschen, die in einem stärker kompetitiven Arbeitsmarkt chancenlos abseits stehen müßten. Diese Gefahr zu erkennen und ihr entgegenzuwirken, sei es durch Anpassung und Flexibilität auf allen Seiten, ist eine der großen Aufgaben der heutigen Politik, denn nach Welsh ist eine Gesellschaft, die ihre schwächeren Mitglieder nicht sinnvoll in das Gesamtgefüge ihrer sozialen Organisation einbinden kann, eine Gesellschaft ohne Zukunft. In diesem Sinne erhofft sich Welsh durch die enge Zusammenarbeit zwischen der Europäischen Stiftung und dem Parlaments-Ausschuß, dem er vorsitzt, wissenschaftlich fundierte Impulse zur politischen Bewältigung des Problems einer notwendigen Neubelebung und Neuorientierung des Arbeitsmarktes. Auch außerhalb des Rahmens des Kolloquiums, das in diesem Band dokumentiert ist, wird diese Zusammenarbeit intensiv und beiderseits fruchtbar vorangebracht.

Enrico Kirschen unterstrich im Namen des Wirtschafts- und Sozialausschusses der Europäischen Gemeinschaft die gegenseitige Abhängigkeit und Bedingung sozialer und wirtschaftlicher Entwicklungen. Das in den Ländern der Europäischen Gemeinschaft erreichte allgemeine Niveau sozialer Sicherheit dürfte nicht leichtfertig aufs Spiel gesetzt werden. Wenn etwa technologisch bedingte Neuerungen in der Produktion zu kostspieligen Investitionen führen, die wiederum aus betriebswirtschaftlichen und aus Kostengründen zu einer Reorganisation von Arbeit, auch im Sinne von Arbeitszeit führen, um die neuen Produktionsanlagen höher auszulasten, so sollte dies nicht zu einer Verschlechterung der Arbeitsbedingungen derjenigen führen, die solche extensive Nutzung ermöglichen. Das heißt, daß Teilzeitarbeit oder zeitlich befristete Arbeit nicht diskriminiert werden sollte, d. h. auch, daß Fragen von Sicherheit und Gesundheitsschutz am Arbeitsplatz möglicherweise neu überdacht werden müssen. Mit anderen Worten, der gesellschaftliche Aspekt der tatsächlich stattfindenden elektronisch-technologischen Entwicklung darf nicht hintangestellt werden im Vergleich zu den makro-ökonomischen Aspekten eines weltweit stattfindenden Wettbewerbs. Diese Sichtweise fand ihren Niederschlag auch in wichtigen Arbeiten des Wirtschafts- und Sozialausschusses, etwa in dem Bericht über "Europa und die neuen Technologien: Forschung, Industrie, Gesellschaft", der im Juni 1986 der Öffentlichkeit vorgestellt wurde. Innerhalb dieses Szenarios wird der Europäischen Stiftung eine wichtige Rolle zugewiesen, indem sie dazu beitragen sollte, die gesellschaftlichen Konsequenzen technischer Entwicklung deutlicher zu machen. Nach Meinung der Stiftung ist das hier dokumentierte Forschungsfeld geeignet, sich an die Herausforderungen eines solchen Anspruches, einer solchen Aufgabe heranzuarbeiten und damit einen Beitrag zu leisten zu einer gesamtgesellschaftlich akzeptablen Entwicklung technischer Neuerungen.

Schließlich spannte Ralf Dahrendorf, der sowohl Vorsitzender dieses Kolloquiums als auch einer hochrangigen Expertengruppe war, die von der OECD einberufen worden war, den Bogen zwischen den weltweiten Problemen und den EG-spezifischen Lösungsmöglichkeiten, die auf breiter Basis erörtert werden müssen. In der Sorge um die anhaltend hohe Arbeitslosigkeit ist es notwendig, die Zukunft der Arbeit in einem weitestmöglichen Kontext zu bedenken. Die strukturellen Probleme des Arbeitsmarktes sind supplementär zu den globalen makro-ökonomischen Gegebenheiten zu verstehen. Nach Dahrendorf, der sich hierbei auch auf seine

Arbeit mit der oben erwähnten Expertengruppe im Rahmen der OECD berufen konnte, und deren Ergebnisse im Mai 1986 unter dem Titel "Labour Market Flexibility" veröffentlicht wurden, siedelt sich die Frage der Arbeitsmarktflexibilität bzw. der Umorientierung und Umorganisation des Arbeitsmarktes zwischen vier Problemfeldern an, die alle miteinander verbunden sind, aber doch separat definiert werden können:

1) Die Notwendigkeit wirtschaftlicher Anpassungsfähigkeit an einen global stattfindenden Wettbewerb, sei es auf den Finanzmärkten, Gütermärkten, Servicemärkten;

2) Die Notwendigkeit fortschreitender technologischer Neuerung unter Berücksichtigung der Möglichkeiten neuer Arbeitsorganisation und neuer gesellschaftlicher Organisationsformen;

3) Die Notwendigkeit, sich neu auftretenden sozialen Problemen zu stellen und mit ihnen fertig zu werden, etwa mit den komplizierten Aspekten der Entwicklung einer neuen "Unterklasse" im Zuge langanhaltender Arbeitslosigkeit;

4) Die Notwendigkeit, die Qualität des Lebens allgemein zu verbessern als Folge veränderter Erwartungshaltungen der in unseren Gesellschaften lebenden Menschen.

Laut Dahrendorf gibt es kein Allheilmittel für diese Probleme, nicht wenn man sie einzeln angeht, geschweige denn als Gesamtkomplex. Es muß allerdings möglich sein, die Umrisse gewisser Veränderungsstrategien aufzuzeigen, die zu einer Lösung führen könnten, ohne allerdings die von vielen ersehnte globale Wundermedizin zu sein. Dazu gehört zu erkennen und anzuerkennen, daß es gar kein Allheilmittel geben muß, das überall und gegen alles wirkt, sondern daß in einer Vielfalt von möglichen, teils unterschiedlichen Lösungen ein Reiz liegt; daß Unterschiede nicht unbedingt überwunden werden müssen, sondern vielleicht sogar gepflegt werden sollten; daß wir uns nicht nach einer US-Lösung oder Japan-Lösung sehnen sollten, sondern eine spezfisch europäische Lösung möglich sein muß, die etwa Flexibilität mit Absicherung "sozialer Menschenrechte", wie sie für Europa typisch und gut sind, verbindet; eine europäische Lösung, die die Wettbewerbsfähigkeit auf globalen Märkten aufrecht erhält oder gar verstärkt, ohne die geschichtlichen, kulturellen, wirtschaftlichen, politischen und institutionellen Rahmenbedingungen zu sprengen.

Diese Balance zu finden, wird auf jeden Fall schwierig, sicher auch schmerzhaft werden, aber es darf nicht unmöglich sein, sie zu suchen.

Die Europäische Stiftung will durch Erarbeitung und Bereitstellung wissenschaftlich fundierten Wissens dazu beitragen, daß die dazu berufenen Entscheidungsträger, auf welcher Ebene auch immer, in die Lage versetzt werden zu erkennen, was auf der Suche nach balancierten Lösungen gesellschaftlich und wirtschaftlich wünschenswert, erstrebenswert und machbar ist; um damit die notwendigen Umwälzungen und Veränderungen ohne schwerwiegende Verwerfungen innerhalb der Europäischen Gemeinschaft und innerhalb der Mitgliedsländer einleiten, begleiten und durchführen zu können.

In der ersten Phase der Arbeit ging es jedoch zuerst einmal um die Definition und die Vermessung des Problems. Die dazu im Auftrag der Stifung erarbeiteten Positionspapiere, die auf den folgenden Seiten wiedergegeben sind, sollen ein erstes "Vorfühlen" in die Problemvielfalt ermöglichen. Dies ist ergänzt durch die Problemsicht der Arbeitgeber- und Arbeitnehmerseite. Wie sich die konkrete Forschungstätigkeit der Europäischen Stiftung weiter gestalten könnte, wird schließlich im letzten Kapitel zur Diskussion gestellt, in dem auch die Ergebnisse einer zweiten Sitzung des Beratenden Ausschusses der Stiftung, die am 27. Juni 1986 stattgefunden hat, verarbeitet sind.

COLLOQUE

DE LA FONDATION EUROPEENNE POUR L'AMELIORATION DES
CONDITIONS DE VIE ET DE TRAVAIL

NOUVELLES FORMES D'ORGANISATION DE TRAVAIL

Intervention de F. Staedelin au nom de la
Confédération Européenne des Syndicats

Les membres représentant les organisations syndicales dans le Conseil d'Administration de la Fondation de Dublin ont largement oeuvré pour que ce projet d'études soit retenu dans le programme de travail. En effet, de plus en plus, les formes traditionnelles de répartition de travail dans le temps (2 vacations journalières, semaine de 5 jours, journée de 8 heures) ne sont plus la règle. L'organisation du travail, surtout depuis l'introduction de formes nouvelles de production, a subi des changements considérables, qui dans beaucoup de cas sont imposés par la conception de la technologie et par le souci de productivité et de compétitivité.

Il ne faut pas négliger dans ce constat, la pression des travailleurs qui aspirent, de plus en plus, à ne pas se déplacer deux ou plusieurs fois par jour pour se rendre au travail. Ils préfèrent n'effectuer qu'un seul trajet journalier pour se déplacer du lieu d'habitation au lieu de travail. Ceci est dû en grande partie à l'allongement du temps de transports, mais aussi au fait que dans beaucoup d'entreprises et de services, il est possible de restaurer sur place grâce à l'aménagement de cantines et de réfectoires.

Il est important que la Fondation fasse des études de cas pour dresser le constat de la situation actuelle, en observant non seulement les effets négatifs ou positifs dans l'entreprise, mais aussi les retombées que l'organisation du travail produit sur l'ensemble de la vie sociétale et familiale.

Nous ne voulons pas nier que les problèmes que pose l'organisation du travail sont grandement conflictuels et il appartient aux acteurs sociaux de rechercher des compromis à travers la négociation et au législateur d'empêcher des abus dommageables pour la qualité de la vie.

Bien sûr, nous sommes conscients que les investissements dans les entreprises coûtent de plus en plus chers. Bien sûr, nous savons que des installations doivent être utilisées au maximum pour devenir ou rester rentables et compétitives. Pour autant, nous ne saurions souscrire à des formes d'organisation du travail dont la seule finalité serait la production au détriment de la qualité de vie et des aspirations humaines.

C'est pourquoi, les nouvelles formes d'organisation du travail, dont certaines ne sont d'ailleurs pas nouvelles, mais un simple retour en arrière, doivent être étudiées avec toutes leurs conséquences et sous tous les aspects.

Ce que dans le langage syndical nous appelons les formes de travail atypiques - travail temporaire, travail à temps partiel, sous-traitance, contrat de travail à durée déterminée, travail à domicile, travail de week-end, travail de nuit, contrainte à domicile, partage du travail, etc. - ne sont tolérables et acceptables qu'à plusieurs conditions, dont voici quelques-unes:

- ne pas nuire à la santé
- être soumis à la négociation collective
- avoir un effet positif sur l'emploi
- bénéficier de la protection sociale
- respecter les droits fondamentaux de la vie sociétale et familiale
- garantie de salaires et de traitements
- droit aux congés annuels et repos hebdomadaires
- limitation de la durée de travail
- qualification des postes de travail permettant aux travailleurs leur expression personnelle.

Ne cachons pas que cet ensemble de problèmes relève d'un débat fondamental sur l'organisation d'une société démocratique. Il nous faut trouver l'équilibre entre une société de production et de services et le droit des personnes à l'amélioration constante de la qualité de la vie collective et individuelle. Que serait la société la plus compétitive, la plus performante, si en même temps ce qui fait la qualité de la vie était négligé?

L'étude que la Fondation vient d'entreprendre doit, à partir de données réelles, permettre aux acteurs sociaux de ne pas se tromper de choix. Les décideurs, qu'il s'agisse des entrepreneurs, des syndicats ou des gouvernements, doivent obtenir le maximum d'informations sur les conséquences de leurs décisions. Si le travail entrepris par la Fondation pouvait servir à cela, si à partir des résultats un véritable débat communautaire pouvait s'instaurer, si des décisions pouvaient ensuite être prises, notre engagement dans cette étude n'aura pas été inutile.

KOLLOQUIA

der Europäischen Stiftung zur Verbesserung der
Lebens- und Arbeitsbedingungen

<u>Neue Arbeits- und Aktivitätsformen aus Sicht der unternehmerischen Wirtschaft</u>

von Dr. Fritz-Jürgen Kador
Geschäftsführer der Bundesvereinigung der Deutschen Arbeitgeberverbände

Bei meinen folgenden Ausführungen geht es um den Versuch einer ersten Einschätzung zum Thema, die zweifellos mehr Fragen aufwerfen als gefestigte Positionen darstellen werden. Auf einem hohen Abstraktionsniveau erscheint der Befund ziemlich klar:
Die technische, wirtschaftliche und soziale Entwicklung verändert die Arbeit in inhaltlicher, zeitlicher und räumlicher Hinsicht. Die Beispiele hierfür sind geläufig: Verlagerung von Tätigkeiten, die bislang gegen Arbeitsentgelt ausgeführt werden, in den Bereich der Freizeit; neue und flexible Formen der Arbeitszeitgestaltung, die Verlagerung von beruflicher Arbeit aus zentralen Betriebsstätten in dezentrale Einheiten oder gar in die eigene Wohnung. Solche neuen Arbeits- und Aktivitätsformen haben vielfache Ursachen und Konsequenzen. Sie bieten Chancen und Risiken für Arbeitnehmer wie für Arbeitgeber. Im übrigen lassen sich die gegenwärtigen Arbeitsmarktprobleme realistisch und zutreffend überhaupt nur unter Einbeziehung der komplexen Problematik neuer Arbeitsformen diskutieren.

Die Gruppe der Arbeitgeber im Verwaltungsrat der Europäischen Stiftung zur Verbesserung der Lebens- und Arbeitsbedingungen hat das umfangreiche Projekt, über das in diesem Kolloquium zu diskutieren ist, eingehend beraten. Sie identifiziert sich mit dem Ziel der Forschungsaufgabe, mehr Klarheit in das teilweise unübersichtliche Feld der neuen Arbeits- und Aktivitätsformen zu bringen und damit die Sozial- und Betriebspartner dialogfähiger zu machen und sie in die Lage zu versetzen, den Strukturwandel sowohl wirtschaftlich wie menschengerecht zu gestalten.

Die neuen Erscheinungsformen der Arbeit sind so vielfältig und differenziert, daß sie kaum zu überblicken geschweige denn in ein System einzuordnen sind. Sie begegnen naturgemäß einer Vielzahl unterschiedlicher Einstellungen und Interessen, die sich keineswegs auf die klassischen Dimensionen der Arbeitgeber-Arbeitnehmerbeziehungen reduzieren lassen.

Aus Sicht der Wirtschaft stehen dabei folgende Aspekte im Vordergrund:

- Senkung der Produktionskosten und damit Steigerung der Wettbewerbsfähigkeit und Sicherung der Beschäftigung

- Rationelle Nutzung der immer kapitalintensiveren Produktionsanlagen

- Entkoppelung von Arbeitszeit und Betriebszeit

- Flexible und kostengünstige Anpassung der Beschäftigung an Markt und Nachfrageveränderungen sowie betriebsbedingten unterschiedlichen Arbeitsanfall

- Motivation der Mitarbeit durch stärkere Berücksichtigung ihrer Arbeitserwartungen im Rahmen einer mitarbeiterorientierten Arbeitsgestaltung.

Auch aus Sicht der Arbeitnehmer haben die verschiedenen neuen Arbeits- und Tätigkeitsformen positive Aspekte, wie beispielsweise

- Sicherung der Arbeitsplätze durch Erhöhung der Wettbewerbsfähigkeit

- Größerer Spielraum für individuelle Arbeitszeitgestaltung und damit bessere Abstimmung zwischen beruflichen und privaten Interessen

- Sinnvolle Nutzung wachsender Freizeit.

Natürlich werfen neue Arbeits- und Tätigkeitsformen auch Probleme auf. Aus Sicht der unternehmerischen Wirtschft sind dies z.B.

- Kosten- und Organisationsprobleme

- Hoher Verwaltungsaufwand

- Probleme der Mitarbeiterkontrolle

- Neue Konkurrenzbeziehungen.

Aus der Sicht der Arbeitnehmer werden häufig befürchtet

- Benachteiligung bei Entlohnung oder sozialen Leistungen

- Geringere soziale Sicherheit

- Soziale Isolierung.

Die Arbeitgeberseite nimmt auch solche Befürchtungen von Arbeitnehmern und Gewerkschaften ernst. Sie erwartet von dem Projekt der Europäischen Stiftung mehr Aufschluß über die Berechtigung von Hoffnungen und Befürchtungen aller Beteiligten. Vor allem aber erwartet sie die konkrete Gestaltungshinweise für die Einführung und Praktizierung neuer Arbeits- und Aktivitätsformen, denn es kann nicht darum gehen, neue Entwicklungen wegen möglicher Gefahren oder negativer Auswirkungen bereits in ihren Anfängen zu blockieren oder im Keim zu ersticken, sondern sie so zu implementieren, daß ihr Nutzen für alle Beteiligten möglichst groß und ihre Risiken möglichst gering sind. Daß dies in der Praxis mit Schwierigkeiten verbunden ist, braucht nicht besonders betont zu werden. Im Kern geht es darum, mögliche Entwicklungen nicht zu blockieren, sondern sinnvoll zu gestalten.

Eine Bewertung der zum heutigen Kolloquium vorgelegten Positionspapiere ist im einzelnen kaum möglich. Darum nur einige allgemeine Anmerkungen:

- Es handelt sich um Ausarbeitungen, die sich in Struktur und Inhalt stark voneinander unterscheiden. Es wird daher wichtig sein, ein Raster von Fragen zu entwickeln, das vergleichbare Forschungsergebnisse ermöglicht.

- Als Voraussetzung hierfür ist eine Systematik neuer Arbeits- und Tätigkeitsformen zu entwickeln.

- Unverzichtbar erscheint eine Beratung und Abstimmung dieser Forschungsfragen, -hypothesen sowie Methoden und Forschungsfelder zwischen den Sozialpartnern. Ein solcher Konsens über den Forschungsansatz hat grundsätzliche und praktische Bedeutung. Grundsätzlich ist er die Voraussetzung für verwertbare Forschungsergebnisse, praktisch öffnet er den Weg für eine erfolgsversprechende Durchführung der Forschungsarbeit.

Im übrigen möchte ich mich der Einschätzung des Vorsitzenden im Hinblick auf die Erwartungen an das Forschungsprojekt anschließen. Das Feld, das hier betreten werden soll, ist über weite Strecken Neuland. Es ist bestimmt von nationalen, regionalen sowie branchenabhängigen Unterschieden. Es sollten also keine Modelle mit dem überhöhten Anspruch auf Übertragbarkeit erwartet werden, sondern eine Vielzahl differenzierter Lösungsansätze.

Im übrigen möchte ich die Erwartungen auch in einem anderen Aspekt auf ein realistisches Maß zurückführen. Bei allem Bestreben, Friktionen und Konflikte bei den absehbaren Wandlungsprozessen der Arbeit zu verringern, sollte man die die Tatsache berücksichtigen, daß Strukturwandel nie ohne Probleme und Konflikte vor sich geht.

EMPLOYMENT FLEXIBILITY IN INTERNAL AND EXTERNAL LABOUR MARKETS

John Atkinson

Institute of Manpower Studies
University of Sussex

Brighton,
MARCH 1986

Preface

This report is a contribution to the Colloquium on 'New Forms of Work and Activity' organised by the European Foundation for the Improvement of Living and Working Conditions. It sets out the issues raised for public, corporate and individual actors in European labour markets by the current concentration on the theme of flexibility. The term itself is extremely flexible, and is widely used to denote a very broad range of labour market policy, at several different levels in the labour market, and with various anticipated outcomes.

This report concentrates on several aspects of flexibility; emerging contractual relationships, new working time patterns, changing job content, changing pay systems, new spatial patterns, precarious forms of employment, labour mobility and flexibility of pay levels. Its aim is not to describe or document these aspects of flexibility, nor to identify particular national or trans-national trends. Rather the aim is to establish how these separate aspects combine to enhance labour market flexibility, and to identify the issues so raised.

The research was conducted through a review of secondary sources and through a series of interviews with researchers, academics and labour market actors, between December 1985 and March 1986.

Chapter 1 : Changing Perspectives on Flexibility

Introduction

For some years now flexibility in the labour market has been a central theme in corporate and government approaches to employment policy throughout Europe. The origins of this concern can be traced to the impact of the oil price shocks of 1973 and 1978, the resulting downturn in economic activity, and the widespread failure of the traditional instruments of economic fine-tuning to accommodate them. The current preoccupation with flexibility may well contain an element of over-reaction, to the extent that it derives from the particularly unstable and (since 1945) unprecedented market conditions experiences in recent years. As yet there is little evidence to suggest that all of this turbulence is likely to become a permanent feature of economic life. Nevertheless, if the last decade can be characterised as a period of transition for European economies, then it was surely a transition to economic and social configurations that will permanently embody many of the features of that transition; for example, greater competitiveness in product markets, an increased rate of technological change embodied in both product and process innovation, and greater immediacy between the recognition of market opportunities (or pressures) and the need to respond to them. Thus, while we may not know the nature of the changes with which we will be faced in coming years, it seems certain that the pace of such change has permanently increased. As a result, the current concern with flexibility, and the responsiveness of the labour market to change, is not just a flash in the pan.

Flexibility is not a very precise term. There are several reasons for this; firstly, the range of subjects which might be drawn within its ambit is substantial; secondly, it means vastly different things to different constituencies; and thirdly, its use is often blatantly ideological, reflecting our cultural disposition to value flexibility (in the abstract) over inflexibility. Thus the term should be used with some care. In particular, we should take care to distinguish between static and dynamic aspects of flexibility. By dynamic aspects of flexibility we mean changes to institutional, cultural and other social or economic regulations or practices which permanently increase the capacity to respond to change; by the static aspects we mean one-off accommodations to particular pressures. The reduction of retirement age to (say) 55 as a response to unemployment would be an example of the latter, while the introduction of a five-year age band from 55 to 60 during which workers could retire at any time would be an example of the former. In this paper we will be concerned with the dynamic aspects of flexibility.

Perspectives of the Social Partners

It is important to note at the outset that there are major differences between the perspectives of European governments, employers and workers on the question of labour market flexibility. By and large these tend to be more marked than differences within each of these constituencies, and more marked (in general terms) than differences between member states. therefore, we will begin by briefly delineating these different orientations between social partners in terms of goals, subjects and means of implementation.

1) Government Perspectives

The principal goal for European governments in seeking greater labour market flexibility is the reduction of unemployment. This is pursued through a policy of simultaneously reducing the financial costs of job creation at a given level of output, while reducing administrative or legal impediments to such job creation. The means of implementation are to reform wage bargaining in such a way as to permit market forces to influence the outcome more directly, and deregulation of legally and administratively established conditions of employment. The extent of such initiatives, and the balance between the two policy thrusts clearly varies greatly from state to state, according to the ideological position of the government and the institutional and legislative framework of the labour market.

2) Employer Perspectives

The principal goal for European employers in seeking greater labour market flexibility is to promote optimal cost-effectiveness in the deployment of their workforces. This is pursued through the reorganisation of their internal labour markets, and in particular the contractual, working time, job content and payment system aspects of those internal labour markets. The means of implementation is the division of the internal labour market into fixed and variable components, the former being the source of functional flexibility (the reorganisation of competences so that workers can deploy them over a wider range of tasks), and the latter being the source of numerical flexibility (the ability to adjust the volume of labour inputs in line with changes in output). There is considerable variation in the extent, novelty and conscious articulation of such a reorganisation according to sector, size of firm and the labour market context in which it is placed.

3) Trade Union Perspectives

The principal goal for European trade unions is to secure the terms and conditions of their members where public or corporate flexibility initiatives threaten them. This is pursued at the level of the enterprise (and in some cases nationally) through collective bargaining, and nationally through the promotion of protective legislation. The only area where unions have taken widespread initiatives is on the flexibility of working time. Apart from this their role has been defensive.

From this brief overview it is evident that the social partners have substantially different priorities within the general ambit of flexibility, and that the prospects for change through consensus on this matter are restricted. In effect we can observe two radically opposed views of flexibility.

The Social Solidarity View

This approach to labour market flexibility has been dominant in most sectors of the economy throughout Europe until recently. It holds that productivity advance is best secured through co-operation between the social partners. Government's role is to steer the economy and control economic aggregates to provide a context in which labour can actively participate in such advance. The rewards of productivity growth are distributed by a combination of collective bargaining and welfare provision. Priority is given to the establishment of social and labour market conditions which permit and encourage mutuality in the labour process, through improved pay and working conditions, training provision, compensation for redundancy, unemployment benefit, job placement etc. The full use of the productive potential of the workforce is encouraged through high employment, no underemployment and high participation rates.

In effect the versatility and adaptability of the workforce is seen as central to the positive acceptance of change. Flexibility in the face of change is secured through a combination of social and corporate schemes to protect workers from the costs of accepting change, and the provision of the skills and aptitudes needed to operate effectively in a changing environment. A secure, skilled and committed workforce is seen as of equal or greater importance to growth and adaptability than managerial dynamism or entrepreneurial vigour.

The Market Adjustment View

This approach has eclipsed the social solidarity view to a greater or lesser extent in most of Europe since the mid 1970s. In this view the unrestrained market mechanism is seen as the principal guarantor of efficiency and adaptability in both product and labour markets. Thus impediments to such forces (whether public, trade union or employer derived) are seen as potential or actual constraints on adaptability rather than instrumental in securing it. As a result, they are relegated to the provision of minimum standards and conditions of employment. Risk-bearing is seen as a matter for individual firms and workers rather than for collective action. A two-fold process is envisaged; first, a cathartic shock to attitudes schooled in the social solidarity approach, and secondly, an energised response to change guided by market efficiency and the unencumbered flow of economic resources.

In effect this model gives priority to supply-side adjustments. Removing constraints here both provides for static improvements in productivity and dynamic adjustment to change. Managerial and entrepreneurial initiatives are held to embody such adjustments; the role of labour is to follow.

From Social Solidarity to Market Adjustment

Broadly speaking the trade union movement in Europe adheres strongly to the social solidarity perspective, primarily because it conceives such a model to provide the best immediate and longer term provision for workers, but also because it can see no role for itself in the market adjustment model. From a variety of different starting points, European governments have shifted towards the market adjustment model - in some cases energetically and wholeheartedly (UK), and in others reluctantly and tentatively (France).

In contrast to both these developments, it appears that the emerging pattern among employers is to embrace both models, applying each to different components of their workforces. This is the basis of the segmentation of the labour market which is now evident in Europe, and it is this duality which appears to be increasingly the source of internal labour market flexibility for European firms. We go on to consider the nature of such segmentation in the next chapter.

Chapter 2 : Flexibility in Internal Labour Markets

We have already noted that, with the exception of working time arrangements, trade unions have tended not to initiate flexibility moves, and that public policy has on balance shifted away from direct intervention within employing organisations. Thus, as might anyway be expected, the main agents of change within employing organisations have been the employers. Changes in the composition of internal labour markets intended to secure flexibility have therefore tended to be originated by, and implemented in the interests of, the employers. This chapter will therefore be largely concerned with their perspectives, and we need to begin by asking 'what do the employers mean by flexibility?', and thereby to question 'and how are they achieving it?'. We can then go on to identify the issues which arise as a result of these internal labour market changes, not only for the employers, but also for workers, their unions and government.

Employers' Flexibility Priorities

So far as European employers are concerned there appear to be four broad approaches to internal labour market flexibility. These are described below.

1) **Numerical Flexibility:** numerical flexibility is defined as the ability of firms to adjust the number of workers, or the level of worked hours, in line with changes in the level of demand for them. It is therefore concerned with employers' ability to adjust employment levels to workload, period by period. As that workload fluctuates, employers respond to it either by changing the number of workers deployed (ie the use of additional workers) or by changing the distribution of worked time (ie the use of existing workers). The main determinants of how they do this appear to be (a) the scale, frequency and predictability of these workload fluctuations, and (b) the legal and administrative possibilities for securing additional workers who will not enjoy continuity of employment. Of course, firms have always required numerical flexibility to some extent, to deal with workload fluctuations during the worked day, week or year, and to adapt to the changing relationship between output produced and labour required as technology changes.

It would appear, however, that the pressures on employers to be flexible in this sense have intensified recently, for one or more of the following reasons:

* output fluctuations have become larger, more frequent and/or more unpredictable;

* under increasing competitive pressure companies have become less able to bear the short term costs of not being numerically flexible; and

* the costs of becoming numerically flexible have themselves reduced.

We might also add that the opportunities to pursue numerical flexibility have also increased. Legal and administrative deregulation in some European states have increased the potential for using additional short term and/or part time and/or contract workers, while at the same time legal and collective bargaining initiatives have opened up wider possibilities for variation in working time of permanent workers. Thus, both forms of numerical flexibility have become moe accessible to employers.

2) **Functional Flexibility:** just as numerical flexibility is concerned with how employers adjust the numbers of people employed or the hours they work to changing workload levels, so functional flexibility is concerned with how they adjust the deployment of those people and the contents of their jobs to meet the changing tasks generated by that workload. Functional flexibility is defined as the ability of firms to reorganise the competences associated with jobs, so that the job holder can deploy such competences across a broader range of tasks. Such a redeployment may be sequential (eg redeployment out of redundant skills) or involve the simultaneous use of old and new skills; it may be permanent or temporary; it may involve working up into a higher skilled job, working down into a less skilled job or shifting between functions.

The need for greater functional flexibility can be attributed to one or more of the following factors:

* skill boundaries are being blurred by technological change and this is accelerating;

* cost pressures on headcount may lead to an increasing pressure to spread the available workforce over a larger number of tasks; and

* growing uncertainty in product markets and process may require a workforce which is capable of responding to as yet unknown changes in these dimensions.

The dominant pressures leading employers towards increasing their workforces' functional flexibility seem therefore to be technological and organisational. If jobs can be regarded, crudely, as collections of tasks, then new technology may render existing job boundaries obsolete, in the sense that the most efficient grouping of tasks into jobs are changed. The cost pressures on headcount, and the increasing volatility and uncertainty in workloads, are also important contributors to the perceived need for functional flexibility. Companies having demanned, and simultaneously facing fluctuating, uncertain workloads, need to be able to deploy their remaining employees across a wider range of tasks than previously.

3) **Distancing:** distancing is defined as the displacement of employment contracts by commercial contracts, as exemplified by sub-contracting. It is an alternative to flexibility, rather than another form of flexibility. Thus companies, faced with an apparent need for greater numerical or functional flexibility, may decide that it is easier in management terms, or more cost-effective, to make the achievement of that flexibility 'somebody else's problem'. What this generally involves is the displacement of an employment contract by a commercial contract as a means of getting a job done. Thus, rather than organise its own workforce flexibly to meet peaks in workload, a company may simply contract out those peaks to another individual or organisation. Similarly, if it finds that a particular in-house activity can be made cost-effective only by increasing the functional flexibility of the workforce in that activity, it may decide that the costs (financial, administrative, and industrial relations) to the organisation of achieving that flexibility exceed the costs of paying another organisation to provide the service in question. These are 'distancing strategies', and all organisations pursue them to some extent.

Distancing strategies appear to be increasingly prevalent for any or all of the following reasons:

* a desire to concentrate the organisation's resources on its areas of comparative advantage, leaving the other areas to those whose comparative advantage they are;

*   a consideration of the relative costs of undertaking an activity in-house and putting it out, when outsiders may be able to achieve economies of scale, exert monopsony buying power, achieve greater workforce flexibility, pay lower wages etc;

*   a desire to shift elsewhere the burden of risk and uncertainty, and the associated costs; and

*   a desire to reduce the organisation's total headcount and wage bill.

4) **Pay Flexibility:** pay flexibility is defined as the ability of firms to adjust pay structures to encourage functional flexibility, match market rates for scarce skills, and/or reward individual performance. It appears that, for the most part, changes to pay systems are intended to reinforce or pay for greater functional flexibility, and therefore the pressures for change coincide with those underlying the drive for greater functional flexibility described above. In so far as there are other pressures they appear to be threefold:

*   the traditional management desire to motivate and retain individual 'high performers', perhaps sharpened by smaller headcount and the drive for greater overall productivity;

*   the persistence of skill shortages in a few occupations, coinciding with oversupply of labour in others, may have increased companies' desire to distinguish between the two in pay terms; and

*   the displacement of wages by fees, as employment contracts are displaced by commercial contracts under a regime of distancing.

Shifts in the Structure of Internal Labour Markets

So broad and far-reaching are these overall aims that their potential impact on internal labour markets is at once massive and complex. The main effect is one of segmentation into different labour market regimes within individual firms, and the main reason for this is that employers have tended to seek numerical and functional flexibility from different groups of worker inside the firm, while simultaneously pursuing distancing, which pushes other workers outside the internal labour market altogether. The result is a growing actual and potential differentiation between groups of worker.

There appear to be three main segments emerging, as follows:

1) **Core Workers:** these are employees conducting what the firm regards as its most important and most unique activities. They tend to be male, full time, permanent, with long job tenures, and deploying skills which the firm cannot readily recruit outside. Their employment regime is still structured by the social solidarity model discussed in Chapter 1; this is because it is from these workers that the company seeks functional flexibility, and it requires their active compliance in achieving that end.

2) **Peripheral Workers:** these also are employees, but they conduct what the firm regards as its routine and mechanical activities. They are more likely to be female, part time, possibly temporary, with shorter job tenures, and deploying skills which are readily available on the external labour market. Their employment regime is increasingly structured by the market adjustment model discussed in Chapter 1; this is because the company seeks numerical flexibility from them; it requires only more or less of them at any given time and it needs only minimal compliance on their part to achieve this, provided that there is an excess supply in the external labour market.

3) **External Workers:** these are not employees at all (though they may be employed by other firms, employment agencies, sub-contractors, or be self-employed). They conduct those activities from which the firm has chosen to distance itself. These tend to be either highly specialist or very mundane activities, and these workers are likely therefore to demonstrate the greatest diversity of employment characteristics. They tend to be regarded by the firm itself as a second group of numerically flexible workers, but in some cases their actual employer might regard them as core workers. Thus again their experience is likely to be more varied than either of the other two groups.

A Model of Internal Labour Market Flexibility

It is useful here to consider the model of the 'flexible firm' developed a the Institute of Manpower Studies. The model is helpful, not because it describes the situation of any actual organisation, but because it contains all the main parameters of change observed in the research work to date. It draws into a simple framework the new elements in employers' manpower practices, bringing out the relationships between the various practices, and their appropriateness for different companies and groups of workers.

The 'flexible firm', then, has geared itself up to achieve the four types of flexibility identified earlier. Its essentials are summarised in the diagram below. It consists of a 'core' group of employees, surrounded by peripheral and external groups of workers who may or may not be employees. The peripheral groups, with appropriate contracts and conditions of service, provide numerical flexibility. Functional flexibility is achieved in the core, supported by appropriate incentives and rewards, possibly including enhanced employment security. In theory, this is possible because the peripheral groups soak up numerical fluctuations in demand. The core is the centre of the diagram; the surrounding ring is the periphery, whose ready expansion and contraction achieves numerical flexibility; and the outer ring (of commercial sub-contractors, specialist self-employed workers on project or fee-based contracts etc) represents the adoption of distancing strategies.

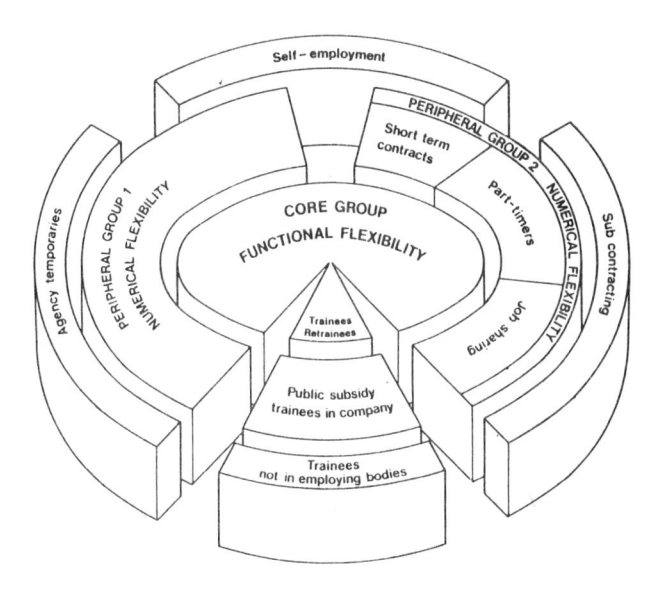

Source: IMS

Finally, we emphasise that the flexible firm is an analytical construct, which brings together into a common framework the changes which are occurring (often on a fragmented basis) and reveals their commonalities and the relations between them. It is presented neither as an example of a type of organisation which already exists, nor as an ideal for organisations to aim at. Indeed, we know that the segmentation of the internal labour market conforms to no set pattern between firms, within and between sectors, and across the different social and economic context of the community states. Given the impetus of increasingly competitive and uncertain product markets, the differing permissive factors, in particular variations in labour supply, protective legislation, and technology, combine to produce wide variations in the extent, the form and the composition of this new form of work organisation. Yet whatever form such developments take there appear to be common tendencies dividing Europe's workforce into core groups whose employment experience is structured by the long term logic of mutual commitment between worker and employer, and a variety of peripheral and external groups whose experience is structured by the short term logic of the market.

Internal Flexibility : What are the Issues?

It is around this division of the workforce that the issues for the social partners may conveniently be discussed. They fall into four distinct groups.

1) **The Extent and Dynamics of Segmentation**

Virtually all the evidence of the emergence of this segmentation springs from two sources; one-off nationally based case study research focussed on particular sectors, or relatively small numbers of firms; and macro-economic labour market analysis using aggregate data which proxy, but do not always accurately fit, the emerging forms of employment. Neither gives a reliable picture of the extent of change, nor the manner in which the two groups interact. The division into core and periphery is rarely overt; there is a multiplicity of different forms of peripheral employment; there may be movement of workers from one group to another over time; some forms of peripheral employment are certainly covert either because they are within the black economy or because they contravene collective agreements and/or legal provision. For these and other reasons it is quite simply not known how far this segmentation exists. This is a critical point, not only because it inhibits assessment of the importance of such developments for policy formulation, but also because it constrains prediction about how far, and under what circumstances, the segmentation may deepen and/or spread. However, it is also largely a methodological issue for researchers and thus we will not dwell on it here.

A second issue surrounds the permanency of observed changes. Are they simply a function of the combination of over-supply of labour with acute economic uncertainty? or are they rather derived from technological change which provides for such systematisation of some jobs that they increasingly do not require versatility and judgement from workers and thus can be manned up on a peripheral basis? It might be suggested that the widely observed growth of sub-contracting represents only a desire to export risk at a time of economic uncertainty, or alternatively that it represents a permanent re-division of labour intended to exploit specialisation.

A third issue is the motivation of employers in producing these divisions within the workforce. If their main motivation is to use peripheral labour because it is relatively cheap labour (almost always in terms of non-pay benefits and social costs, but often also in terms of hourly pay rates) then we might expect to see a consistent push towards increasing the proportion of such workers. If, on the other hand, they are primarily viewed as forming a buffer to protect core group workers from the uncertainty of the market, then we would expect employers themselves to limit and regulate their deployment of peripheral groups.

The motives of workers in entering peripheral jobs are also uncertain. There are any number of hypotheses, ranging from those which stress the positive attraction of such employment (eg part time jobs for workers with domestic, educational or other commitments; self-employment for the frustrated entrepreneur), through those which allude to an instrumental orientation (eg people who will take a temporary job in the hope of being transferred to permanent status) to those which stress the pressure of unemployment (eg a job on any terms is preferable to idleness). All are intrinsically logical explanations of behaviour over job-choice, but they are none the less only hypotheses; we simply do not know what motivates recruits to these types of job, and the answer is important if the supply of workers to them is affected by changes in the level of unemployment.

Thus the issues which we need to consider are how extensive has the segmented internal labour market become, how do we expect it to develop in the future, why have employers acted to create it, and how far does it enhance or inhibit worker choice?

2) Segmentation and Conditions of Employment

Differentiation between groups of worker on the internal labour market occurs around five main axes, contractual relations, working time patterns, job content, pay systems and spatial patterns, any or all of which may distinguish core from peripheral workers. Such widespread differentiation has major implications for conditions of employment, as follows:

Employment Security and Continuity: There are several issues to consider here; firstly, how far in practice does peripheral employment also imply precarious employment? There are clear cases, such as the use of temporary workers, where employment is explicitly insecure, and likely to result in relatively short job tenure. Is this true for part time workers, however? Clearly they are often less well protected by legislative and collectively bargained provision, and they also tend to have higher voluntary labour turnover rates than full timers, but it is not clear that such jobs need to be precarious, since they can provide the day to day numerical flexibility which employers seek without recourse to termination of employment. It may not be true for agency employees either, where their employment tenure (with the agency) might be long despite any number of short job tenures (with the agency's clients). **There are two issues here then; how precarious are these jobs in practice, and how necessary is such precariousness to their function of providing numerical flexibility?**

Secondly, and at the other end of the spectrum, we need to consider how far employment security might be a facet of core employment. Certainly such workers tend to have longer job tenures than peripheral workers, but it is unclear how far this simply reflects residual immobility combined with collectively bargained and legislative provision which fixes such workers in place, or on the contrary, how far it represents a deliberate provision by employers to trade off security of employment for acceptance of, and commitment to, functional flexibility at the core. To the extent that it is the former, security of employment could represent a constraint on flexibility, but to the extent that it is the latter, it can be the means to enhanced flexibility. The issue here is to assess how the balance between residual and explicit employment security might be changing for core workers, and how far this enhances their flexibility.

This raises a third issue; how far is the security of core workers conditional on the insecurity of peripheral workers? There are two ways of considering this issue; the first is to present peripheral workers as buffer groups of workers whose function is to soak up fluctuations in the level of output and thus create conditions which allow security for core workers. The second viewpoint is to stress the difficulties which employers face in securing numerical flexibility from core workers, and to present peripheral employment as an alternative way of achieving it. There appears to be no evidence whatever to provide an answer here as to which school of thought most accurately reflects the reality, but it does lead on to a fourth issue.

If employers were able to secure greater numerical flexibility from workers with stable levels of employment, then they ought to be less attracted to peripheral forms of employment which are less stable. Thus greater flexibility in the distribution of worked hours over time from core workers might be a means of minimising precarious forms of employment and the emergence of a secondary workforce. For example, the development of an obvious peripheral workforce appears to be most advanced in the UK, where there is relatively little flexibility in the distribution of normal working time. In both France and Germany there is now significantly more scope for variations in the pattern of working time; it may be that such possibilities will preclude, or at least inhibit, so extensive a shift to peripheral workers as is evident in the UK. The issue here therefore is to what extent can such changes in working time regimes be secured, and how far might they reduce the need for peripheral employment?

Job Content and Polarisation: One important area of differentiation between core and periphery is the content of the jobs of workers in each segment. Peripheral working tends to be associated with a restricted and precisely defined job content, capable of being met with the sort of skills that are readily available on the external labour market, and requiring little discretion or autonomy from the worker. When company-specific, or product-specific skills are required, then these are usually subsumed into technological or supervisory control systems to permit recruitment of peripheral staff. On the other hand, core jobs appear to be increasingly associated with the broad and relatively unconstrained definition of jobs which permit and encourage these workers to deploy their skills over a wide range of tasks and to perform them relatively autonomously. There appear to be two issues of importance here; the first is to question how the commitment of peripheral workers to the aims of the employer can be secured, since neither job nor working environment is likely to promote it. The second issue is to suggest that in view of this divergence of job content, the movement of workers from peripheral to core status may be constrained, and thus new rigidities created that may not have existed before. Both these issues turn on the possibility that in creating peripheral workforces, employers may be limiting the versatility, adaptability and commitment of part of their workforces.

Training Issues: Given their long job tenures, and requirement to provide functional flexibility, core group workers are increasingly at the centre of firms' training strategies. Peripheral workers are not. Thus, the first issue to arise concerns the extent of training and the source of provision. While it seems that firms are increasingly likely to treat training of their core workforces as an investment and to seek to increase the level of that investment, the opposite may be the case for peripherals. If peripheral workers are not a training priority for employers, then who is to be responsible for their training? The 'market adjustment' school of thought would suggest that the workers themselves should be responsible; the social solidarity school would look to the state.

Beyond the extent and provision of training, there is the issue of the type of training to be provided. For core workers it is clear that a new rationale for training is emerging and this provides for a new conception of training. Core worker training would therefore aim for a workforce with the knowledge, understanding and skill to perform their current jobs efficiently, and to perform efficiently the next jobs in the company to which they might move. At the same time, this would be a workforce which constantly seeks and implements new ways to improve efficiency and the quality of its products and services, and which takes the initiative in identifying and solving problems in day-to-day work. This should provide a workforce which stays with the company because of the stimulation and opportunities to develop which it is offered and which handles change well because it has the habit of learning, the skills of learning and the desire to learn.

Few of these aims are likely to attend the training of peripheral workers, and there is a serious contradiction between their employers' aim, which is likely to be the identification of quick, cheap and single skill training, and the workers' needs for skills that are transferable, either to other employers, or to other jobs within the existing employer.

Representation at Work: It is by no means clear that the traditional organisation and methods of trade unionism are appropriate for the effective representation of either core or peripheral workers. For the latter group this is immediately obvious; they are likely to be more difficult to recruit and retain as members, their interests are likely to be more diverse, their experience and commitment to unions may be less strong than core workers. But for core workers also the relevance of trade unions may be questioned; certainly unions will find themselves in great competition with employers for influence over this key group; certainly, where it exists, the old craft basis for union membership is increasingly questioned; certainly decentralisation and local autonomy within corporate structures may undermine national and sectoral level bargaining conventions. Further, core workers are less likely to be subject to authoritarian and hierarchical work disciplines, are more likely to enjoy staff conditions of employment, and are more likely to have some form of individual merit pay than in the past; all of these may make it more difficult for unions to represent them effectively.

The issue here is therefore to what extent, and how, might the representation of both groups of worker best be secured? An orientation towards protective legislation could be one means by which unions could defend the conditions of peripheral workers, but at the same time a more decentralised and localised approach to collective bargaining across a broader range of issues is likely to be needed to appeal to core workers.

Pay Levels and Segmentation: There is some evidence to suggest that segmentation is leading to greater variation in pay levels between core and peripheral workers. In part this results from legal deregulation, in part from differences in union strength among the two groups, and in part from varying employers' strategies for productivity advance from the two groups. There appear to be three questions at stake here. Firstly, if substantial pay differentials exist alongside non-pay differentials, then this could encourage the displacement of core status workers by peripheral groups as employers seek to reduce costs in the short term. This may result in configurations of core and peripheral workers which are sub-optimal in the longer term, with the functional flexibility of the workforce impaired. Secondly, this effect would be to increase competition between groups of workers, with the result that core workers could come to regard peripheral workers as a threat to their established pay rates and other conditions of employment, rather than as a buffer against insecurity. Finally, to add pay disadvantage to less than comparable non-pay benefits, and to a greater exposure to job loss, would be to multiply the disadvantages faced by peripheral workers in the labour market. In the long run, greater diversity in contracts and job tenures might be both economically more efficient and socially more acceptable if differences in contract terms were offset and evened out by differences in pay. In reality, they are not often so offset; they are accentuated. **The issue, therefore, is how far do such differentials exist, and where they do exist, what are their effects on labour flexibility?**

3) The Peripheral Worker and Segmentation

So far, the issues which we have identified have related to the extent and nature of segmented internal labour markets and thus have involved both core and peripheral workers. However, there are also a number of issues which are relevant to peripheral workers alone. Most atypical forms of employment involve some form of peripheral status, and so these partial issues are particularly worthy of note.

<u>Who are the Peripheral Workforce</u>? Comparable with our lack of data on the extent of peripheral employment is a related shortcoming on the composition of the peripheral workforce. Essentially **the issue here is how far is peripheral status randomly distributed throughout the workforce, or how far does it comprise certain social groups?** There is some evidence to suggest that peripheral working is indeed socially concentrated firstly among certain categories of person - mostly women and young people; and secondly, among certain skill and educational levels - mostly among relatively unskilled and under-educated groups. It may also be geographically influenced, firstly towards labour markets that are the least effectively regulated by law, and secondly towards the regions with the highest levels of unemployment, but there are quite clearly sectoral factors which also influence the distribution, as well as the type, of peripheral working. If these forms of employment are so distributed, then it would seem that new rigidities may be appearing in the labour market, and that these might effectively inhibit the

free flow of labour in line with changing economic pressures, in addition to limiting the life-chances of workers in those groups disproportionately represented among peripheral workers.

Mobility and the Peripheral Worker: In addition to an uneven static distribution of peripheral workers it seems evident that their distribution over time is also constrained. The emergence of segmentation appears to have the effect of reducing access to core status jobs for peripheral workers. By virtue of their training, their working time profiles, and their experience within any particular firm, these workers may be prevented from moving up the internal labour market into core jobs. This cannot of course apply to all peripheral labour, as some employers may choose to retain, say, temporary staff and make them permanent; similarly, in theory, jobsharers are held to enjoy access to core jobs often denied more orthodox part time labour; and of course an agency employee may be peripheral at the place of work, but core for his employer. Nevertheless, on balance, the effect of segmentation is to reduce mobility between these groups; for the core worker, then, mobility tends to mean mobility between jobs within a firm, while for the peripheral worker, it is more likely to mean mobility between firms, and while the core worker enjoys some form of career progression, the peripheral is locked in peripheral status work.

Not enough is known about the bridges in firms between these two segments of the internal labour market. The issue is, to what extent do they exist, how effective are they and are they susceptible to influence, from collective bargaining, legislation or human resource management within the firms themselves?

Non-Pay Benefits and Peripheral Workers: Most studies testify to the inferiority of the non-pay benefits of peripheral workers compared with core workers in similar enterprises, particularly in those states where legal provision of such conditions is inadequate. This differential provision is most often seen in terms of paid time off (sick, holiday, meal breaks etc), accumulated benefits, whether contributory or non-contributory (pensions, unemployment and lay off provision) and notice periods (call in, lay off or termination). Only in smaller enterprises does this differential sometimes extend to actual hourly pay rates, but differences over pay administration (particularly regarding overtime and shift premia) are common. **The issue here is how necessary is such discrimination and how far does it contribute to flexibility? Clearly many of these inferior conditions simply make peripheral** labour cheaper to employ and contribute nothing to internal flexibility. Others do appear to have a genuine contribution to flexibility. A related issue is how might protection of such conditions of employment be pursued without reducing the numerical flexibility of such workers; for example, can legislated provision be sufficiently subtle to distinguish between them? Can any such legislation operate effectively in any case without local union activities to police implementation? And finally, should this establishment of minimum conditions and benefits anyway be the proper role of legislation, or might it not be equally effective simply to limit either the extent of peripheral working or the duration of individuals in it?

Social Security and Other Public Benefits: Clearly the assumption which underpins much of Europe's social security provision is one of permanent employment, with the possibility of accumulating benefits and a clear cut distinction between employment and unemployment. With growing levels of peripheral working - particularly in casual work, self-employment, and the black economy - such assumptions become less tenable and such systems tend to be less well suited to the support of those who are likely to rely on it. The issue here is therefore on what central assumptions should benefit accumulation and payment be based if they are adequately to meet the needs of the peripheral worker.

Chapter 3 : Flexibility in External Labour Markets

Just as the employer is seen as the main agent of change in so far as the internal labour market is concerned, so governments have tended to make the running for external labour market flexibility. This means that changes which have been introduced are much more evident than those affecting the internal labour market, being usually national in scope, publically implemented and often subject to political debate. Less is known about the impact and the effects of such changes, however.

This chapter will therefore be largely concerned with two aspects of change, labour mobility (including regulations affecting job protection) and pay bargaining, as these seem to be the principal mechanisms through which external labour market flexibility is promoted.

Flexibility and Mobility

Mobility in the external labour market may involve any or all of the following; geographical mobility (which we will take as mobility requiring a change of residence), job mobility (involving a change of employer) and occupational mobility (involving a change of skill undertaken outside the employing organisation). There is some evidence of a decline in both job and geographical mobility in a number of European states, but such falls are in some cases marginal in extent and are heavily overshadowed by the substantial variation between countries and between different groups of worker within and between countries. This reflects the enormous range of influences on these form of mobility, which appear almost literally to be 'affected by everything'. The main influences, however, appear to be (a) institutional factors, like housing tenure, job protection legislation etc, (b) the overall level of economic activity and its regional and sectoral distribution, (c) the ease with which social and economic stimuli (mainly regional and job pay differentials) are generated and recognised by workers, and (d) the cultural readiness of the workers to respond to them. We might also add constraints on their readiness to respond, but we will discuss this later.

Geographical Mobility

There can be little doubt that the physical movement of Europe's labour force has declined in recent years. In Germany, for example, the proportion of population changing residence between Lander fell from 1.8 per cent in 1970 to 1.3 per cent in 1981, despite an emergent regional disparity between an expanding south and a declining north over this period. A similar fall occurred in the UK over the same period. This stagnation of the workforce is often compared with those of other states (USA, Canada, Japan, Australia), who tend to demonstrate both higher and constant levels of inter-regional mobility (though differences in data make this problematic to confirm) and a better economic performance than in Europe.

The critical issue here is to what extent low and/or falling mobility rates cause or contribute to a relatively sluggish economic performance, and to what extent they are themselves a by-product of that performance. A subsidiary issue is to question how important is the link between observed mobility trends and labour market efficiency in any case.

We have been unable to find research outputs which explicitly and conclusively address these issues. While a number of American studies are available which appear to demonstrate a clear and positive link between economic growth rates and mobility flows, there is no comparable European corpus of work. We may hypothesise that the positive attractions of job opportunities, expanding industry and higher wages may act as a more important 'pull' effect than a 'push' effect of long term and/or structural unemployment, but it is simply not known how far the availability of jobs, or their relatively higher pay, is the main determinant, or how far it is the contraction of local job opportunities.

This is obviously important from a policy point of view, as it critically influences who is most likely to be so influenced, those in employment or those who are unemployed. Given the orientation of public policy towards unemployment, it would seem that job availability in other regions, the information available to the unemployed about such jobs, and their practical opportunities to move are important factors. **Therefore, even if we were to conclude that declining mobility is more a consequence of economic stagnation than a cause, it would still be important to question how far such constraints on mobility exist, and might be lowered by public policy.**

Certainly a combination of regional house price differentials and a shift to home ownership is widely recognised in the UK to be an important constraint. Differences in tax rates and welfare provision between regions do not appear to be common in Europe and therefore they will be less important constraints. Educational provision may be important where either the level or the type of provision differs between regions. As far as the unemployed are concerned, access to jobs through mobility appears to be most constrained simply through the high cost of mobility relative to their low incomes, although public subsidy initiatives to offset such disadvantage do not appear to have been markedly successful. The unemployed are in any case only a small proportion of potential migrants.

Occupational Mobility

This kind of mobility is by far the hardest to assess or to compare between states because of differences in the definition of occupations between them. At the same time it is clearly the least socially disruptive approach to mobility. We are concerned here with ocupational mobility outside the firm, and so the main vehicles for effecting such mobility are (a) initial vocational and educational provision in so far as it provides for transferable skills and aptitudes, and (b) adult retraining provision. The issue of occupational mobility is riven with a clear contradiction: most movement between occupations occurs relatively early in workers' lives, but most of the job displacement which enforces such mobility is likely to affect adults.

The issues which arise here are, therefore, is subsequent occupational mobility affected by an initial education and vocational preparation which is oriented to particular specialisms, trades or sectors, or is it enhanced by a more generally based training; and secondly, how can adult retraining most effectively be conducted?

There does not seem to be any clear evidence on the former issue. The tendency of young people to demonstrate this type of mobility appears to be equally marked whatever the basis of their education and training. Retaining the readiness to change direction in adults seems to be largely a question of public provision. In no European economy is there a high level of self-provision of such occupational retraining among adults. A further question that arises here is the loss of extrinsic benefits (status, incremental pay etc) that adults may stand to invoke should they opt for a change of occupation in later life. While this loss can be somewhat accommodated within firms, it is difficult to see how it could be between them. Thus adults are faced not only with a cultural bias against self-provision of retraining, but the need to bear also the other costs associated with such a reorientation. A shift towards a 'market forces' approach to flexibility would surely accentuate these costs for individuals, as both firms and public authorities reduce the scope of their activities here. It is not at all clear that this could produce any tangible improvement in occupational mobility.

Job Mobility

It cannot be assumed that the higher is the level of job mobility through the external labour market, the more efficient is the labour market. Frequent job changes necessarily entail transitional costs which may lower total productivity, and produce employee resistance to accepting changes. Optimum performance clearly requires a balance between job tenures. In view of the (high) American level of job mobility and the (low) Japanese level, it is not prima facie clear whether Europe requires more or less.

What is clear is that the dominant thrust of public intervention has been to stimulate job mobility to remove legal and administrative support to long job tenures - essentially a strategy of letting the market decide the appropriate combination of individual short and long tenures. For example, the 1985 Employment Promotion Act in Germany opens up the possibility of shorter job tenures, as does the 1980 Italian legislation on fixed term contracts, and UK legislation of 1979, 1980, 1982 and 1985. In the Netherlands the more extended use of fixed term employees as a possibility. In France, on the other hand, there have been attempts to improve the position of temporary and short term employees.

Alongside such initiatives to alter the balance between short and long individual job tenures, there have been initiatives to reduce constraints on collective layoffs - once again in Germany, for example, the Works Constitution Act has been relaxed to permit higher levels of layoff without the need for extended consultation, while in Italy the hiring system has been liberalised in the case of takeovers to give employers greater discretion in such cases. Similarly, in the Netherlands dismissal procedures have been relaxed.

On balance, it appears that the impact of either the imposition of protective legislation designed to extend job tenures, or its removal to reduce them, is slow to take effect and marginal in impact, although the effects may be greater among small and non-union firms, who do not have the same recourse to the internal labour market as bigger ones.

The issues arising here are, therefore, where is the most appropriate balance between long and short job tenures, and how is this best to be achieved? In so far as employers are shifted from their perceived optimum position by social policy, are they to be compensated? If workers are similarly disadvantaged for economic reasons, are they too to be compensated? Should all firms be treated alike, or is there a case for treating small firms separately and differently?

Finally, we should note that the effect of reducing average tenures may hide a polarisation of tenures and encourage the tendencies towards segmentation which we described in the previous chapter. The available evidence is far from conclusive here; both opponents and proponents of greater job mobility lack hard empirical data to support their case. If governments are to base their intervention here less on intuitions and more on solid evidence, then we need answers to the following questions:

* what is the net cost of greater job security through longer job tenures to the employer?

* are these costs sufficient to inhibit recruitment?

* can such costs be offset through segmentation of the labour market?

* how far, if at all, can job security provision be relaxed without disadvantaging particular groups of worker?

Flexibility and Pay Bargaining

Many commentators have argued that a key factor underpinning labour market differences between Europe and the USA is the behaviour of real and nominal wages in the face of market shock. It is suggested that the failure of real wages to accommodate to oil price shocks is at the root of Europe's slow job generation since the mid 1970s; and conversely that the growth of employment in the USA has resulted from the fact of wage flexibility. In other words, the level of employment is critically influenced by whether the labour market response to such a shock is in terms of volume or price, in terms of rising unemployment or falling real pay.

This contention is a controversial one, about which little consensus exists, but there can be no doubt that the issues raised here are of great importance to the flexibility debate. It is important to establish at the outset that to consider the level of real wages to be an influence on the level of employment is not necessarily to consider it to be either the dominant influence, or one readily susceptible to external manipulation. There appears to be some consensus behind the view that the acceleration of employment costs during the 1970s did indeed play a part in pushing up unemployment in most parts of Europe. After 1978/79, and the subsequent downturn in activity nominal, wage growth levelled off while unemployment continued to climb. This indicates either a lagged effect of the wage inflation, or, more likely, the impact of other factors, most obviously stagnant, and in some cases falling, output, and a collapse of business confidence. Certainly, after 1979, any consensus on the role of wage costs disappears.

The issue arising here is the extent to which real wage behaviour influences employment levels, compared with other factors, and whether this changes over time.

There does seem to be some positive correlation between the growth of unemployment and the rigidity of real wages ..... particularly when comparisons are made between economies that in other respects are quite differently structured. There is less evidence matching similar economies, or indeed similar regions. In addition, it is one thing to cite pay rigidity as causing unemployment to rise; it is quite another to go on to assert pay flexibility as therefore causing unemployment to fall. In particular, it could be that different elasticities of demand for labour would require substantial cuts in pay levels to produce modest job gains.

The issue arising here, therefore, is the extent to which extrinsic downward pressure on real pay is likely to produce an increase in employment; and how much do real pay levels have to fall for a given increase in employment? On this issue there is no conclusive empirical evidence, despite the centrality of the question to current labour market policy formulation.

In addition to this empirical question, there is the entire subject of how such extrinsic pressure might best be applied to achieve such an end; what operational tools are available to effect this influence? Incomes policies have been widely applied at the national level in the past to achieve it, though the consensus seems now to be that such aggregate national approaches themselves tend to inflexibility and rigidity when they are applied, and that they are problematic to maintain in place for more than short periods. An alternative approach is one that stresses the role of labour market flexibility itself in reducing undue pay pressure; at one end of the political spectrum this involves the implicit undermining of union bargaining strength, at the other it asserts that changing the structure of pay systems (towards merit pay, productivity incentives and fees) will reduce, or at least dissipate, across-the-board upwards pressure. A third approach (Italy) focusses on marginal reductions in pay indexation in order to moderate upward pressures. It is evident that the appropriate vehicle to implement such a policy is likely to differ from state to state, and that there is no uniform blueprint.

Nor can it be assumed that such pressures are best directed at wage bargaining. Taxes and other forms of non-pay cost are high in Europe; there is every reason to propose that cost reductions in these areas might have precisely the same effect as downwards pay pressure. They are furthermore widely regarded as a less socially divisive mecahnism, and in theory ought to be more susceptible to control and implementation. It is also suggested that such an approach could have a positive multiplier effect on demand provided other taxes were not raised to compensate, whereas pay reductions would have a reverse multiplier effect in the absence of expansion elsewhere.

The issues here, then, are what form of intervention might be most apprpriate to achieve the desired end of reduced real pay levels, and how far similar effects might be more readily generated by cuts in payroll taxes rather than real pay costs?

An alternative view of pay flexibility is that of adjustments in relative pay levels. By changing the relative employment costs of particular groups of worker - most often young workers - it is often argued that (a) their employment can be increased at the expense off other workers, and, less often, that (b) it can be increased without affecting other workers. Action on pay structures to increase differentials is one approach here; others would be displacing wages altogether by (lower) training allowances, introducing wage subsidies or recruitment subsidies, selectively reducing non-pay overheads. All of these might have the effect of locking such workers into low pay, insecure and low productivity jobs, however.

Looked at in theory, the proponents of pay flexibility have not demonstrably proven the case. There appears to exist a number of likely leakages between pay restraint and job creation, and in practice these are almost impossible to seal up. In practice, a sensitive and consensual form of introducing such pay restraint is not immediately evident. There thus exist serious question marks, both in theory and practice. Nevertheless, it would be a mistake to conclude that the issue of pay flexibility should not be pursued. It clearly deserves more effort to analyse and articulate its dynamics and potential. Whether it is wise to allow practice to forge ahead of such analysis is another matter.

Chapter 4 : Social and Economic Divergence

The realisation that greater flexibility in the labour market is a necessary component of competitiveness and economic growth for the future is widespread across Europe. Only the most extreme proponents regard it as a sufficient component to achieve this end, however, and many are concerned that the social costs of achieving such flexibility will outweigh the economic benefits. For this reason, it is worthwhile raising as relevant issues the tension between these social and economic aspects of flexibility.

Flexibility for Whom?

The model of internal flexibility which we have described in Chapter 2, and the institutional and legal changes which we have identified in Chapter 3, point to the same end - to make the workforce more flexible so that it can better meet the needs of industry and commerce. That the workforce may itself have different and distinct requirements for flexibility from industry and commerce is not an issue which has been much discussed. Indeed, if this is the case, then these distinctive flexibilities are not well articulated, and we can only impute them from the thrust of collective bargaining and from social survey work. Greater autonomy over working time is probably among the most important here - not just in terms of attendance patterns and start and finish times, nor yet just in terms of atypical shift schedules, but also including working time profiles over the course of a lifetime, involving such flexibilities as the right to move between part and full time work and back without detriment, partial early retirement and flexibility over retirement date. The balance between productive output and education, training and retraining is another area in which it is likely that workers would have their own demands, in terms of greater access to, and choice over, training, time off for education, sabbaticals etc. Greater autonomy and responsibility on the job without being subject to hierarchical control systems is another field in which workers are likely to have flexibility needs.

The issue here is not to impute what such needs and priorities might be, but to identify how such needs can most effectively be articulated, and to assess how far they are compatible with the flexibilties sought by the employers.

Strategic Choice between Flexibilities

We have argued that employers are seeking to increase flexibility in several directions at the same time - most clearly numerical flexibility and functional flexibility. For many reasons it seems likely that the more firms advance in one direction (eg increasing the numerical flexibililty of the workforce through using more part timers), the less are they able to advance in the other (eg additional training costs and increased labour turnover preclude greater functional flexibility). This is why segmentation occurs, as different flexibilities are sought from different groups. It is not at all clear that the short term pressures to adjust to recent acute recession and market uncertainty would push firms towards the same balance between flexibilities as would the longer term pressures flowing from technological change, for example.

Thus, to a significant extent employers have a choice over what balance they decide to achieve between core and peripheral employment. It is not a free choice, of course; it is conditioned by a host of factors in product markets, labour markets, work organisation and legislated regulation, but it remains a choice.

The issues are how far do employers explicitly recognise this choice, and what factors most strongly influence the outcome? In particular, how far are they driven by short term cost cutting rationales, and how far do the labour formations which result represent the most appropriate long term structure?

Transitional Costs

The adjustment to change necessarily implies a cost burden, but where it falls is largely a matter of choice, and this raises issues of economic efficiency and social justice. The model which we have described sees the employer as increasingly willing to bear the cost of adjustment for core group workers; in terms of continuity of employment and income, in terms of retraining and redeployment etc. The employer is increasingly unwilling to bear the costs of adjustment for peripheral workers, however; these are increasingly passed to the state, to other employers, or to the individuals themselves. Quite apart from issues of social equity here, there are issues of economic efficiency; what, for example, is the most cost effective means of providing transferable pensions? Is it to fall back on a state scheme for all, to encourage individual provision, or to impose free transferability between all corporate schemes? Similar questions arise over the provision of income support during layoffs, and the retraining costs of the unemployed or peripheral worker. The issue is how far is the burden of transitional costs to fall according to chance, and how far is it a legitimate area for cost-benefit analysis to identify alternative outcomes which may draw together economic efficiency and social equity.

Protective Legislation

As we have argued above, the trend towards deregulation of labour market protective measures clearly places economic efficiency above social equity (to a greater or lesser extent according to state). In attempting to achieve a new balance between these two ends it may be necessary to reconsider the manner in which protective legislation is conceived. For example, in the case of temporary employees, protective legislation could take several forms - for example, to impose comparable pay rates and conditions of employment between temporary and permanent workers; or to limit the duration of temporary contracts before such workers should transfer to permanent status; or to limit the proportion of temporary workers in the workforce; or to impose minimum conditions on agencies supplying such temporaries; or to ensure that temporaries were given priority access to permanent vacancies. The issue is how far can a balance between employers' needs and workers' interests be achieved through amending the thrust of protective legislation towards those provisions which least inhibit employers, while providing some form of protection for workers?

A second issue here concerns the operation of thresholds. Should such legislation apply to all firms equally - of different sizes, in different markets etc? Conventionally it is believed that small firms are less able to conform to the minimum standards of protective legislation, or are more inhibited by the prospect of having to, than are larger firms. The issues arising here are what are the appropriate criteria and levels for such thresholds and what are the effects of changing them?

Status

The creation of a peripheral workforce often has the effect of creating atypical patterns of employment which may demonstrate some undesirable characteristics; they may be precarious, they may be low paid, they may offer little training or career progression. In short they are likely to demonstrate disadvantage on both the internal and the external labour market. But, in so far as such workers do not share some of the norms associated with more typical groups, they may face disadvantage in other areas outside the labour market altogether. For example, how readily can a worker on a temporary contract take out a bank loan or mortgage? How far can part time workers join join social insurance schemes? How far can tele-workers join in social activities at the place of work? It is evident that most of our social and economic mores, both outside and inside the labour market, are based on the conception of a worker which no longer applies to many people. **The issues are, how far does this add up to real discrimination against such workers, what forms does this take and what initiatives are appropriate to address it?**

Implementation of Change

The social and economic consequences of labour market flexibility are likely to be affected as much by the manner of implementation as by the extent of change and the new forms of work which are thereby created. As we have already pointed out, the degree of consensus on external labour market flexibility, particularly in respect of pay determination, is limited; on internal flexibility there is greater consensus, particularly on the benefits associated waith functional flexibility, but less so on the forms of peripheral labour associated with distancing and numerical flexibility. The shift to greater flexibility can, therefore, be characterised by unilateralism or bi-lateralism on the part of employers and/or government, with the trade unions usually relegated to a position of reluctant acquiescence. This is most obviously the case in the UK, but elements of unilateralism can be observed in most European states. It is not yet clear how far such initiatives can be driven by unilateralism; nor yet how permanently can such changes be maintained. **The issue here is, to what extent do the intrinsic demands of labour market flexibility imply conflict, or are these conflicts largely about** the extrinsic aspects, such as less favourable conditions of employment for peripherals. If they are principally about the latter, and on balance, and in the internal labour market, it would seem that they are, then the prospects for consensus would seem to depend substantially on the manner of implementation - that it should be by mutual agreement and that it should focus on the intrinsic aspects of flexibility, rather than on the extrinsic ones.

ISSUES IN JOB SHARING

Joyce Epstein

London,
MARCH 1986

Preface

The European Foundation for the Improvement of Living and Working Conditions has commissioned an analysis of job sharing as part of a larger investigation into new forms of work. Job sharing is envisaged as one among many recent developments in alternative patterns of work/non-work relationships with which countries in the European Community are experimenting. Changes in economic conditions, in attitudes to work and family life, and in the very nature of the workforce -- in the form of the steadily rising participation rate of women in the labour market throughout the post-war period in most European countries -- have stimulated a new range of organisational and individual responses. Job sharing is one of them.

What is job sharing

Job sharing is the arrangement whereby two (or more) people voluntarily share a single full-time job, with the salary and employment benefits divided pro-rata.

It has to be noted from the outset, however, that behind this simple definition lies a welter of ambiguities and inconsistencies, and a number of differing practices with differing motives go by the name of 'job sharing'. The purpose of this paper is to examine the issues involved in job sharing, if not to impose clarity, then at least to be clear about the areas of confusion.

Job sharing is a term that first came into general usage in the US in the late 1960's. Workers, and in particular those with significant non-work commitments and interests, were feeling dissatisfied with the choice of either conforming to the existing rigid schedules of full-time work, or taking part-time jobs that were typically low-level, badly paid and held out poor career prospects. An organisation which started in California, called New Ways to Work, was suggesting an alternative: if two workers share the responsibility of an ordinary, existing full-time job, then the rights, benefits and prospects normally associated with full-time work should be conferred upon part-time workers. Thus they could have good jobs and free time.

Job sharing, then, was conceived primarily as a means of improving the quality of work for people unable or unwilling to work full-time. The practice had developed -- even before the term 'job sharing' came into general usage -- directly out of the dissatisfaction of trying to fit non-work needs around the demands of traditionally-structured full-time work. It "...was pioneered by people...long before labour force analysts and policy makers began to question the appropriateness of a standardised forty-hour week " (78). The job sharing idea represents a way of fitting work to the worker, rather than the other way round. As such, job sharing has been described, by personnel experts in Germany, as "the humanisation of work" (35), a way of looking at employment that relates to the whole of one's life, not just to work.

Job sharing development in Europe

Before we look at trends in Europe, we should note that the idea caught on in the US, especially among 'professional' women who wanted to find a way of combining work and family interests. Job sharing is now, some fifteen years later, firmly established in the US. As of 1982, 25 states, plus the federal government, had official policies to enable or promote job sharing. Over half the health care organisations in the US offer job-shared positions. Some 11-12% of banks and insurance companies offer job sharing. And hundreds of schools in California alone have job-shared teaching positions.

In the UK job sharing has been the subject of considerable interest and, more recently, of rapidly growing implementation, particularly in the public sector. New Ways to Work, in London (no connection to the organisation of the same name in California) was established in 1977, originally under the name of the Job Share Project, and has been instrumental in the growth of job sharing in the UK. It has succeeded in getting job sharing onto the public agenda, and in the past two years a number of major national organisations have conducted seminars to inform their members, and others, about job sharing, including the Royal Institute for Public Administration, the Institute for Personnel Management, the National Council of Voluntary Organisations, and the Industrial Society. As a result, job sharing now seems to have got a firm foothold in the UK:

The national government Cabinet Office, together with the Council of Civil Service Unions, recently (1985) announced a Programme of Action to encourage all departments of the civil service to offer job sharing. Even before this, job sharing was taking place in six departments of the civil service, though mostly on a small scale, with the exception of the Department of Health and Social Security where over 500 staff are currently job sharing, and 1000 applications for job sharing are pending.

The London metropolitan government, more than half the London boroughs, and several other metropolitan, district and county authorities, as well as education and health authorities, have policies to offer job sharing positions (or allow job sharing with no formal policy being adopted). Some local authorities in the UK now routinely advertise vacancies with an added note such as: "Job sharing applications will be welcomed with or without a partner".[1] There are at least 50 other commercial, voluntary and other public organisations that are known to have job sharing policies or practices, including the Stock Exchange, Fox's Biscuits, the Royal National Institute for the Blind, BBC Schools TV, International Voluntary Service, National Westminster Bank, Adams Foods, the British Council, and others.

However, job sharing being a new and still very marginal practice, no official statistics are collected by the Department of Employment in the UK (or by departments of employment or labour anywhere else in Europe) on job sharing.[2] Job sharers are classed as part-time workers. The Civil Service is currently in the process of collecting data on the number of job sharers (in national government offices only), but these were not yet ready at the time of writing. There are therefore no figures available at all on the exact extent of job sharing. Depending on how job sharing is defined, the number of posts actually being share in the UK could be estimated at 2,500.

---

[1] Selected at random from among the Public Appointments vacancies appearing in the Guardian newspaper, January 15, 1986. (This particular job share referred to a management position in a Housing Department, salary £19,000.)

[2] In the course of preparing this paper, contact was made with every department of employment in Europe, plus research institutes with work-time interests, equal opportunites agencies, unions and union research groups, and employer groups. No comprehensive statistics on job sharing are, as far as could be established, available.

At any given time, New Ways to Work has about 200 people on their computerised register seeking job share partners, and there are equivalent though smaller organisations in a number of other British cities including Sheffield and Manchester, and in several London boroughs, that maintain registers and promote job sharing.

In Germany there has also been interest and discussion of job sharing. Between 1980 and 1985 a great deal of debate was focussed on job sharing 'models', starting with the model devised by the Chemical Industry, through to variants put forward by CDU/CSU, the International Institute of Management, and the Randstad Organisation. Each proposed different terms and conditions for job sharing that were much discussed, especially the provision in the first (Chemical Industry) model that if one partner leaves the other is automatically sacked. This, rather severe, condition seems to have been unique to German job sharing, and might be presumed to have had a negative impact on job sharing's development in Germany. (In the UK if one partner leaves the terms may specify that the remaining partner is either offered the job full-time and/or the other half of the job is re-advertised. Perhaps more usually the terms are left vague, which leads to a different set of problems. See page 34ff for further discussion). At any rate, in Germany very recently (1985) the government adopted legislation protecting job sharers from such harsh practices and defining some of the terms and conditions for job sharing in the national statutes. These new statues were themselves the result of pressure brought to bear by 10 of the 11 'lander' in Germany who wished to clarify the conditions for job sharing. At least 3 of the lander -- Lower Saxony, Baden-Wurttemberg, and Saarlandes -- have actually implemented some job sharing posts in government offices.

Surveys in Germany have indicated that 1-5% of firms in the private sector employ job sharers (7, 36). Because of problems of terminology, it has been suggested that there is "latent" job sharing taking place (38). That is, many more firms offer job sharing than use or accept the term for it and are therefore not reflected in such surveys. The German literature and other sources specifically identify over two dozen firms and organisations that employ job sharers, including the Federal Press Office, Hoechst, Berlin Hospital, Ikea (several branches), Walther Chemical Factory, Beck am Rathauseck, North German and West German radio, Otto-Versand, Siemens and others.

In Ireland there is interest in job sharing but implementation appears to be at what can only be described as an embryonic stage. The Irish Civil Service introduced a job sharing policy in 1984 and, as of October 1985, 225 civil servants were sharing a job (although 405 had applied to do so). The Department of Public Service in Ireland has been promoting job sharing vigorously in the past year, putting out leaflets and posters advertising the scheme, as well as offering to find partners within the civil service for those having difficulty, through a central list.

The literature identifies several other organisations in Ireland with job sharing, including Aer Rianta, Radio Telefis Eireann, the Industrial Development Authority, Gardner Merchant Ltd. and AnCo. Irish teachers' groups are also interested.

As for the rest of Europe, there are known instances of firms employing job sharers in France, the Netherlands, Belgium and Denmark, but they seem (in the absence of hard information) to be isolated cases. The phenomenon is certainly not much in evidence outside of the UK, Germany and Ireland. One French study (87) in 1985 identified 50 job sharers in five private firms, although the study made no claims that this was exhaustive. The authors state that there may be more job sharing in France than is apparent, again because of a terminology issue: employers think of it as part-time, but it has all the attributes of job sharing. The authors state, as well, that because of the questionable way that job sharing fits, or rather does not fit, French labour laws, employers may be reluctant to report or publicise instances of job sharing.

There are no statistics anywhere on the degree to which job sharing is taking place in Europe. Sharing has been, as we shall see, predominantly an individual work arrangement negotiated between the sharers and the employer, so its extent is difficult to define. There are strong suggestions (see p.19ff) that more people want to share than are currently sharing. There is certainly a general conviction in the literature that job sharing interest is growing, eg:

> "...'partage de post' ou 'job sharing' applique d'abord aux Etats Unis...puis en Angleterre...suscite aujourd'hui un interet de plus en plus grand dans d'autres pay europeens" (84)

But it is not possible to document this trend, if there is one, in the absence of comprehensive worksite surveys. It should also be noted that there are those who feel job sharing is not taking off, and certainly many who feel it should not take off. The paper will deal with attitudes to job sharing further down.

* * * * * * * * * *

The very widespread development of job sharing in the US has meant that more job sharing research has been able to take place there than in any other country. Therefore what follows in this paper necessarily relies heavily on American research, but draws also on research in the UK, Germany, France, Belgium and Ireland.

Let us now take a closer look at the motivational issues which underlie the job sharing concept.

Why job sharing

It is important to note that job sharing, wherever it is taking place, in the US and Europe, has in almost every case been introduced originally at the initiative of workers - not organised workers, but rather individual workers who have preceived in job sharing the solution to their various needs and problems. Typically, existing employees approach the manager or personnel director with a request to job share. It is very often they -- the employees rather than the employers -- who have worked out a preliminary plan for a method of sharing the tasks, whether the job will be split into two more or less independent modules or 'truly' shared, who will do what, how intercommunication and 'hand-over' will take place, and so on. The impetus and motivation, in other words, arises from the employees, who then 'sell' the idea to the boss. The organisation may then evolve a formal policy about it, and the initiative shifts somewhat back to the organisation.

But organisations are essentially responding to the needs of individuals. It is this individual, ad-hoc nature of the phenomenon that not only has made job sharing difficult to document, but has also led to the adoption of rather differing practices all called 'job sharing', and has created confusion and uncertainty over rights and conditions. These will be dealt with later.

Job sharing has become strongly identified with the child care needs of working mothers, and in fact the desire to make time for family interests is the motivation for the overwhelming majority of sharers.

But the constituency for job sharing is not just housewives. The whole nature of work and work needs is changing. An OECD study (104) identified a variety of population groups that form the (potential) constituency for sharing, and in one US survey (64) nearly one-third of the people job sharing were doing so because they neither need nor want full-time jobs, not because they had to look after children. This survey showed that for 18% of job sharers, non-work time is spent on leisure activities, and 11% of sharers spend their non-work time in further education or training. A small UK study of sharers (59) too revealed a variety of reasons, all showing the decreasing centrality of a paid job to these workers -- "Wanted...to have a useful amount of leisure time" (male, age 35); "having more spare time, can pursue painting" (male, age 32); "work...unrewarding and unstimulating" (male, age 25); "Leisure...to pursue photography" (female, age 27).

British and French studies of sharers have reported that, although child care was the main non-work activity, not all non-work time was devoted to it; job sharers use their free time for leisure as well, and in a later section of this paper, the changed outlook of job sharers toward their whole quality of life will be discussed.

In some cases, job sharing has been introduced to ease the pressure of particularly high-stress jobs. In the US there are now numerous examples of two doctors sharing one internship, a position which has classically placed extreme demands on the post-holder's time and energy. Research has also documented the enormous toll that job stress takes in industry. One study, which notes that 30 million days are lost annually due to stress-related illness in the UK, urges employers to adopt a more imaginative approach to work time, to relieve stress (19).

Job demands do not have to be as extreme as those imposed on interns or chief executives in order to seek relief and a better balance between work and family life. A German study of technical and administrative job sharers in a factory (35) showed that the major worker objective was to gain greater control over time. The split does not have to be half-and-half; job sharers can divide up a post in any way that suits them -- eg it could involve a 3/4 - 1/4 sharing agreement, it could involve alternate weeks, split weeks, a.m./p.m. share -- but more important than that, follow-up interviews with sharers show that within the agreed overall framework, sharers swap times amongst themselves as the need arises.

Job sharing has also been used as a way of easing into retirement for older workers who find the strain of a full-time job too great, or simply to get used to the idea of retirement. This practice has been largely confined to the US where it is used to treat what the Americans call 'burn-out'; implementation in Europe has until now been severely hampered by penalties imposed on pension rights.

Job sharing can be motivated by health problems of workers of any age, not only retirement age. It has been strongly recommended by, for example, the chairman of a working party in the UK that studied job opportunities for those with multiple sclerosis (20). Job sharing was seen as a way of providing equal opportunities for a variety of disabled people who find a full-time job too tiring. But there have been few known instances of job sharing taking place to meet the needs of the disabled. Attitudes of employers toward disabled workers has always been a serious problem. Not untypical is one Irish company that offers job sharing, but that specifically rules out job sharing to help out with "...problems of ill health" (47). The public sector may be taking a lead in this. One English city council is currently considering a policy of job sharing to actively promote equal opportunities for the disabled, and a survey of job sharers in UK central government showed that "poor health" was cited by some as their reason for switching to sharing (88).

Why not part-time

The deficiencies of part-time work have been well documented and it is not intended to devote a great deal of space covering that ground again here. But it is perhaps appropriate to review briefly the status of part-time work, so that the need felt by workers for an alternative -- job sharing -- can be more clearly understood.

A recent review of part-time work in 15 countries (80) identifies the specific problems for part-time workers in each country, in terms of rights to equal pay, dismissal protection, social security and representation. But even where such rights are ostensibly 'guaranteed', in practice they may be found to be absent. For example a UK study documented cases of discrimination against part-timers in respect of basic hourly rates of pay (85).

In addition to these basic deficiencies, part-timers are usually ineligible for other employment benefits such as extra training. An interesting 'catch 22' situation described in one English city council vividly illustrates the problem: part-time staff in the library were ruled ineligible for council-sponsored further training, on the grounds that the training was not relevant to their current, low-level jobs, because the increased assets were not seen by the council to be usable in part-time posts. Part-timers were thus ineligible to apply for more responsible posts because they were not trained and therefore continued to remain at a disadvantage for extra training. There was no way out. Or rather up.

But not only are the terms and conditions of part-time workers disadvantageous by comparison to their full-time colleagues, a major additional problem is that part-time jobs themselves are confined to those at the lower end of the labour market. The higher level, good quality jobs are simply not made available by employers on a part-time basis. Again, the concentration of part-time jobs at the lower end of the market has been well documented. For example, a study of part-time jobs in France, Germany and the UK found them to be concentrated among low-skilled occupations (6). The UK study cited earlier identified company policies in banks, retail shops and public sector organisations which specifically excluded part-time employees from the higher graded positions. A Europe-wide study concluded that "...of all the forms of discrimination liable to be encountered by part-time workers, those relating to promotion and career are the most difficult to tackle" (50).

It needs to be noted that these disadvantageous conditions of part-time work amount to discrimination against women, because the overwhelming majority of part-timers throughout Europe are female. Concern over the need to improve the conditions of part-timers has been growing slowly, but a greater sense of urgency may soon develop: several recent studies have identified the increasing importance of part-time work for men. In the UK, for example, during the 1970's the number of part-time jobs done by men increased by 23%, during a period when total male employment actually dropped by 9% (89).

Nature of job sharers and jobs shared

Job sharers

The majority of job sharers are women. Surveys have found the size of this majority varies -- from 70% to 100% -- in different times and places. The US seems to have more male job sharers, but the information from other countries is much sparser and therefore less reliable.

Whether male or female, job sharers are usually married and have a working spouse. Without a second income, many people could not consider job sharing. Average age of job sharers is about 35 years. Most, but not all, have young children. In one survey, it was found that 11% of sharers were married to each other.

Men who are job sharing feel (or fear) they are attracting the image of a 'drop-out'. Giving up half a job is not considered masculine. Although interviews with some women sharers reveal concern that they may not be taken seriously, professionally, there are evidently much stronger sanctions against sharing felt by men than by women. Hostile attitudes toward men sharing seem to be the reason for failure of a scheme in the Netherlands; the sharers' co-workers at a car plant felt it was not appropriate for men to share, and refused to support or co-operate with the experiment.[1] One American male sharer acknowledged: "...it's hard putting yourself outside social expectations, social role models, though I don't think I'm particularly hung up on it now" (67).

---

[1] This experiment has been referred to briefly in the literature (*International Management*, August 1982) but no detailed information is available.

Most analysts close to job sharing in the US and UK agree with the German personnel consultant who predicts rising interest among men as "...increasingly management staff, mostly young people renounce higher career goals and no longer regard their jobs as the sole centre of their interest in life. In this connection job sharing will...open up new perspectives" (36). Others (see page 37) feel job sharing will never appeal to men on a significant scale.

Jobs shared

The job sharing literature is rich with anecdotal material on job sharing posts, everything from frozen food sales rep to sheriff. The few surveys that have been done show that job sharing is concentrated in the white collar services sector, with very little sharing taking place in the manufacturing industries. A survey of German firms suggests little future for job sharing in industrial production: only 10% of firms thought it could be used in manufacturing, while 47% of firms thought job sharing could be introduced in administration. (36)

The surveys indicate that in fact half or more of the job sharing takes place in administrative posts. The rest are mostly in teaching; social, health and community services; or similar professional and technical posts.

Impact of job sharing

We come here to the main question: does job sharing work ? This section summarises the findings of research studies (1, 18, 28, 36, 59, 60, 63, 64, 72, 73, 74, 75, 77, 87, 88, 92) that have examined the success or failure of introducing job sharing, by looking at the effects primarily on the sharers' colleagues, assistants, and supervisors. Most of the studies are small-scale, but the results are consistent so they are of considerable interest and value.

The results are overwhelmingly positive. The research literature is dominated by accounts of the advantages and satisfactions found in job sharing both for employees and employers who have tried it.

For employees, various surveys of job sharers have shown that

- they are convinced sharing has created better part-time work opportunities for themselves in higher level jobs, permitting them to find jobs reflecting their skills;

- they enjoy their work more; they have more energy and patience for the job, feel relief of tension and stress; they are less fatigued; have higher morale; return to work after their "off" time feeling refreshed.

- they derive comfort and social support from knowing that their partner has the same stake in the job that they do; it leads to relief of stress to know that their partner is worrying about the same things;

- the job tasks themselves become more interesting and exciting; sharers use partners to "bounce" ideas off, and for mutual support and stimulation, in a way that never happened with ordinary work colleagues;

- time is more at their disposal; they use their partner in an active and positive way to manipulate their time in order to meet their non-work interests and obligations;

- life in general, both work and non-work, takes on a calmer rhythm; there is an improvement in the quality of life; they enjoy their new flexible lifestyle, as one said "I feel I am a changed woman, more balanced (60).

For employers of job sharers the results show

- greater productivity and efficiency, eg one study found that output was 33% higher per man day for job sharers than for full-timers (72); another, a survey of American firms employing job sharers, found that 60% reported increased productivity (75);

- decrease in absenteeism; one firm, eg reported a drop from 7.6% to 0.4% after job sharing was introduced (72);

- increased flexibility, peak period coverage, continuity during holidays;

- availability of a wider range of job skills; ability to tap a wider labour market; higher quality of work because of such skill diversity;

- lower turnover; ability to retain experienced, trained staff, especially after maternity leave; reduced wastage of valuable skills;

- improved workplace atmosphere and better morale;

- improved image in the community; firms employing job sharers receive favourable media attention; one such firm was named "Employer of the Year".

Published reports of job sharing research thus show the arrangement to be highly successful.

However, there are two possible problems with the job sharing research that must be noted. One is that research is usually done at an early -- pilot or experimental -- stage of the arrangement. People who are job sharing are trying extra hard to make it work. The 'right' to job share is often won only after long struggle with management (see p.33) and job sharers may feel a strong investment in making it succeed, so much so that one researcher described their attitude as positively "evangelical" (59). How the effects would change, should job sharing acquire an every-day status, is not known.

The other problem is the researchers. A considerable number of the research projects are carried out by (or reported by) people who are themselves job sharers. They are distinctly sympathetic to the job sharing concept and this may colour their treatment of the subject. Reports of failed job sharing arrangements are few and isolated, with little detail

provided. Unfavourable job sharing effects -- which will be dealt with
immediately following -- particularly those that amount to disadvantages
for the employer, are usually downplayed in some way:

- there was x problem at first, but it was gradually overcome
- there was x problem, but it was negligible
- there was x problem, but it was far outweighed by advantages

But most seriously of all, there may be an unwarranted emphasis in the
research on higher-level, more 'interesting' job sharing, but the report
will discuss this particular issue further down (see p.23-24).

There is, in short, a certain lack of rigour in the job sharing research
reports due, it would seem, to an interest in 'selling' the idea. The fact
that experience with job sharing has generated a group of highly committed
enthusiasts is in itself significant. As far as one can tell, no other
alternative working arrangement -- reduced hours, telework, part-time,
flexi-year, etc. -- had gathered around it such a group of devotees. That
alone says a great deal about how satisfying and successful an arrangement
job sharing in fact is. But devotion may mean flaws are not treated
carefully. In perhaps typical fashion, one report (90) lists "Advantages"
of job sharing, but only "Potential drawbacks". Here, then are the
"Potential drawbacks":

For employees, there is the fully-realised disadvantage in job sharing, as
opposed to full-time, that salary is cut in half. This has been found to
be the major reason why job sharing offers may not be taken up and, as well,
the reason why people revert to full-time after trying to job share. In
one 2-year follow-up of a job sharing project (72), almost 20% of sharers
had been found to have switched back to full-time mainly because they could
not manage on a half salary. It has been proposed (38) that people who job
share should get tax relief but this may be viewed as a fairly remote
possibility for now.

The financial disadvantage of job sharing does not of course apply to those job sharers for whom a complete absence of work, or part-time work, is the alternative. In fact, one study (72) found that former part-timers preferred job sharing because it paid more in the higher level jobs they were enabled to obtain).

But there are other financial drawbacks. In some workplaces where increments are dependent on work time accrued, job sharers receive rises only half as frequently as full-timers, though of course the cost of living increases at the same rate for job sharers as for full-timers. Most state social security systems in Europe and the US are not set up to accommodate job sharing and there is often a penalty, in terms of loss of coverage of some sort. Job sharing does not always carry with it all the workplace benefits of full-time jobs, especially pensions[1], but sometimes even pro-rata sick and holiday pay are not included in the share terms. Although job sharing might be making higher level jobs accessible to part-time workers, promotion opportunities, once a job share is obtained, appear so far to be virtually negligible. There have been few known cases of sharers being promoted as a team, and the higher level entry jobs remain just that: entry jobs. Job sharers in the researched projects are acutely aware of and concerned over this problem. But even worse, financially, than not being promoted, is not having a job at all, and there are worries that people who switch from full-time to job sharing may be risking the security of their job. Because it is so new, however, and because the research has not addressed this question, no evidence has accumulated to show job sharers are more at risk than full-timers.

There may be interpersonal problems between sharers and other workers. Jealousy or hostility from full-time colleagues has been mentioned as a factor which could lead to problems, as in the Netherlands example (se p.11).

---

[1] Recent (1986) legislation in the UK will protect some job-sharers' pension rights.

But it is difficult to assess how serious a problem this is because of the tendency to gloss over difficulties by those sympathetic to job sharing (and the tendency to magnify them by those opposed). Most studies have reported that hostility has not materialised (eg 18): "Regarding relationship with other employees, there was only mild 'humorous' resentment in one case" (out of ten).

There may be more serious problems in the nature of sharing itself. Job sharing self-evidently requires a partner. Jobs open to sharing usually require that people find their own partner (the example on page 3 notwithstanding). One survey showed that two-thirds of sharers knew their partner before, so what happens if a would-be sharer knows no one to share with? There are reports in the research that inability to find a partner, or a compatible partner, is a major problem.

The question of compatibility is much discussed in the research interviews with sharers, unfortunately with no very clear outcome. See the following two opposing conclusions:

> "The vital prerequisite in any job sharing arrangement is that both sharers should be... genuinely compatible" (91)
>
> "...the partner relationship...does not hold the...key to success" (64)

The belief that personal affinity between sharers is important to its success has led many employers to stipulate that sharers must find/choose each other, and that partnerships must not be imposed by employers. However, some employers, eg the metropolitan government in London, feel that relying on established personal relationships means that job sharing operates as a sort of 'closed shop' with entree to the good jobs limited to those who know the right person. They fear that job sharing can run counter to their Equal Opportunities policy, because personal compatibility may reflect discriminatory views about people's race, sex and age. This particular employer is thus no longer allowing job sharers whose partners leave to have any say in the selection of their new partners.

As we have already seen, one of the advantages found for job sharing is the 'special' working relationship that develops between sharers. Whether this advantage would disappear in employer-created teams is not known. In the US employers have long used job sharing specifically as a means of promoting equal racial opportunities, especially in teaching, by bringing in young ethnic minority graduates to job share with existing tenured (white) teachers. Studies of job sharing in the schools yield the usual positive results, and in particular the mix of experience and ability levels[1] in teaching pairs, with each sharer taking his/her 'strong' subjects, showed that the quality of teaching improved, although no mention is made of the quality of the relationship.

Whether job sharers are friends or not, there is at least a need to co-operate professionally, both with each other and with colleagues, supervisors and assistants, in co-ordinating the job tasks, and there are frequent references in the research literature to difficulties based on failures of communication. Job sharing introduced into an organisation has sometimes been found to have negative impact because information does not flow efficiently and effectively. But, again, in research interviews with job sharers there is almost always a "happy ending" to these difficulties. Perhaps this should be accepted at face value; sharers may in fact absorb and resolve difficulties because on balance they feel the advantages of sharing far outweigh the problems. Communication problems are usually solved by the sharers' taking it upon themselves to sort things out in their own free time, which amounts to unpaid work. There are a few reports that sharers may feel underpaid because they cannot manage to keep to the reduced hours of work.

---

[1] Surveys in the US show that job sharers, particularly in teaching, frequently do not get paid at the same rate. This is often used as a device to reduce education authority costs: experienced (expensive) teachers who wish to job share are paired with new graduates who are paid at a lower rate.

In the US, where job sharing has been going much longer, research has shown that such problems of sharing -- communication, compatibility, co-ordination -- are really learning problems: second job share pairings have been found to work better than first efforts as a result of what has been learned.

Disadvantages for employers focus mainly on increased cost, but results are mixed and inconclusive. No comprehensive cost/benefit research has been done. Research usually reports small increases in administrative and training costs and sometimes increased employer contribution to social insurance (usually no increase in capital or equipment costs), offset by higher productivity and efficiency, lower absenteeism, and greater continuity and improved scheduling. One employer -- an education authority -- responding to a research question about costs of job sharing, said "That's not the point. We allow job sharing because the teachers like it. And since they like it, they're happier and they teach better." (73)

That statement would seem to apply to job sharing in general: despite the existence of problems, job sharing has been found to be highly advantageous for the majority of people -- workers and employers -- who have tried it. The best 'proof' that it is a successful arrangement is the recurring number of cases in the literature where job sharing is introduced initially on a very small scale and is then allowed to expand.

Potential demand for job sharing

After enumerating the many and varied ways in which part-timers are exploited, a recent European review of part-time labour noted that such treatment "...apparently does nothing to slow down the demand for part-time jobs" (6). If job sharing is viewed as a more attractive alternative to part-time, then the potential for job sharing could be the 13 million Europeans now working part-time. Only one survey specifically to assess part-timers' interest in job sharing could be found, (90) and it revealed great interest in job sharing among those currently working part-time. It is significant that about half the part-timers in this study had previously (in their full-time incarnations) held higher level, supervisory positions, and were acutely aware they were being exploited and their talents wasted.

But the evidence suggests that most people currently working as job sharers come from the full-time labour force, not the part-time force. And we know from surveys of full-time workers (38), half of married women would rather be working part-time.

Thus there is 'latent' demand for job sharing among full-time workers. Given the choice, how many full-timers would job share ?

One survey in Germany (46) showed that 31% of female workers and 25% of male workers were "interested". "Interested" is a long way from actually sharing, though. Perhaps a better gauge are surveys undertaken by public sector employers in the US announcing their intention to offer job sharing and asking employees how many of them would wish to apply. In these somewhat more realistic circumstances, responses show between 6% and 12% of the workforce is interested in job sharing (72). A UK survey in Scotland (unpublished) was somewhat more specialised - it focussed on female solicitors and found that 29% might elect to job share after a maternity break.

It might seem logical to look at the number of people actually job sharing to assess demand. But the number of people job sharing cannot be used as evidence of demand, partly because we do not know how many people are job sharing, but mainly because workers wishing to job share are frequently prevented from doing so by management policy. In a regional authority in Scotland, to name just one example, 38 employees have applied to job share during the past 4 years, but all have been turned down on the grounds that the council did not have a job sharing policy; these failures no doubt deterred others from applying. This example is particularly interesting, though, because very recently (in January 1986) two of the rejected applicants took their case to an Industrial Tribunal. The Tribunal ruled that the council's position amounted to employment discrimination against women, because "...it was inevitable that the proportion of women who could comply with a requirement to work full-time would be substantially smaller than the proportion of men". (Glasgow Herald, 31.1.86).

But in the absence of a job sharing policy, it may not even occur to workers to ask to job share. In relation to any new practice or concept, we may not reliably know if there is demand until the opportunity is actually made available. Surveys of employers (eg 44) show that they believe there is no demand for job sharing. As we shall see in a later section, employers themselves do not like the idea of job sharing (if they have not tried it), and their belief that their employees do not want it may reflect a certain amount of wishful thinking. At one large enterprise in Germany, the author of the present study was told they do not offer job sharing and they confidently asserted there is no demand for job sharing and never will be. At this same enterprise, though, there is a work pattern with the (unfortunate) title of 'housewives' half-shift' which looks and sounds very like job sharing, where two workers split one full shift. While it is not entirely clear why the firm does not regard this as job sharing, it would appear to be because the firm believes that if each worker's hours are fixed (as they are in this case) rather than left flexible between the two, it does not qualify as job sharing. Be that as it may, the firm had so many applicants for each half-post available in 'housewives' half-shift' that there is now a waiting list, but the firm continues in the fantasy that there is no demand for job sharing.

But even take-up figures within workplaces having acknowledged job share policies are unreliable guides. In many instances demand for job share posts exceeds supply; management usually places a ceiling on the proportion of posts that can be shared. But, in other cases, there are virtually no 'takers'. A good example is to be found in the education field. One of the most widespread and successful applications of job sharing in the US has been in teaching jobs. But an offer by the Belgian authorities to allow job sharing in the schools in 1982 was hardly taken up at all. Research at the University of Liege is soon to begin on why teachers did not come forward to job share in Belgium.

There is as yet insufficient systematic research on the circumstances under which job sharing policy offers will be taken up. Sometimes what happens is that, faced with demand initiated by employees, senior management will institute a job sharing policy but it is still left to middle level supervisors to approve individual job share applications, and their approval is not forthcoming. Sometimes just the opposite occurs: faced with demand from some employees, management offers job sharing, and employees (particularly working mothers) then feel pressured to "volunteer". However this latter circumstance is complicated by other management motives as well which will be discussed on page 26ff.

Thus we return to surveys of attitudes, to detect demand for job sharing. Although what people say they would like may have only remote relation to what they actually would do, a unique set of surveys in Germany, (43) conducted in 1981 and 1983, is especially interesting: it showed rapidly increasing proportions of people favourable to the idea of job sharing. Conducted on a random sample of 1000 adults in Germany and West Berlin, the surveys show that 38% liked the idea in 1981, rising to 55% by 1983. Amongst women, the 1983 figure was 62%; for men 47%. The younger the respondent, the more favourable to job sharing. There was little consistent difference across occupational level or schooling, but strong political differences: among SPD supporters, 60% were in favour of job sharing; for CDU/CSU supporters, 44%. When asked specifically would you yourself like to job share, the proportion in favour dropped, but still remained in the same relationship to other variables. Among the total population, 35% said in 1983 they themselves would like to job share; for women this was 47%, for men 28%.

Is job sharing different from part-time

"There is very little difference in essence between job sharing and part-time work" (5).

Many would agree with that statement. Job sharing has been dismissed as 'upmarket' part-time or glorified part-time. Those who are supporters of job sharing would probably be pleased if it were indeed 'glorified'. The problem is that glory may in practice be distinctly lacking.

Job sharing is supposed to make accessible the kinds of well-protected jobs with good career propsects that traditional part-time does not. But the reality may be different. We have already seen that job sharing does not always succeed in conferring all the employment benefits of full-time work -- pensions, promotions, etc. This is a very serious challenge to the concept of job sharing. If some employers are continuing to regard sharers as two part-timers for the purposes of work benefits, calling it 'job sharing' is pointless.

Apart from fringe benefits, the question of whether job sharing is succeeding in making available the more senior, better level jobs, unavailable on a part-time basis, is a crucial test of the job share concept, but is still far from settled. Proponents of job sharing seem to feel this is the case - that job sharing is taking place mainly in the better jobs. The research that has been done reports sharers' own beliefs that they are in posts they would never have been able to get part-time (see page 13). We also have a plethora of published (and highly publicised) case histories of particularly impressive job shares that would have been inconceivable on a part-time basis. One that is constantly cited in the UK is the executive position that is shared in the Stock Exchange.

But there is a serious question as to whether this is representative. For example, of the 500 job sharing posts newly created in the Department of Health and Social Security in the UK, virtually _all_ are limited to the lowest level clerical posts. A somewhat better result was yielded in a recent (November 1985) survey of 75 shared posts in a local authority, but still only 40% were found to be in senior positions (71). A survey 5 years ago found that only one-third of job sharers held supervisory posts.

It is well established that employers take a very conservative view of job sharing -- eg they feel job shares must not involve client contact, tasks must have high predictability, etc -- and most especially there is a pervasive conviction amongst employers that "higher level jobs cannot be shared" (87). Informal conversations between the author of the present paper and a number of governmental managers whose departments have job sharing confirm that sharing is often limited to lower-level, clerical, repetitive jobs, in the public sector. This has in fact been recognised as a problem in the latest civil service announcement on job sharing, which has particularly called attention to the need to extend job sharing to more senior level jobs.

The conviction amongst management that higher level jobs cannot be shared runs counter to the intended ethos of job sharing, but seems very firmly entrenched indeed. In one workplace in France, for example, (60) where management refused to extend its job sharing policy to higher-level jobs despite demand for it from women junior managers, even private secretaries were not allowed to job share. Management maintained that the only true, permissible partnership for a private secretary was between the secretary and her boss.

It is hard to reconcile attitudes like this with the belief held by job share proponents that sharing is generally taking place in better level jobs.

Here we are severely hampered by the absence of systematic research comparing job-shared and ordinary part-time posts. We simply do not know how powerful a tool job sharing could be in raising the quality of part-time work, or whether job sharing is in practice consistently different from part-time work. A group of researchers in Belgium (84) feel that the further removed from America, the more diluted the job sharing concept has become. Although the original US concept saw it as clearly differentiated from part-time, the European version (which the Belgians blame on "la reforme anglaise") looks less and less different from part-time.

In the absence of research, the field is open to critics from both sides -- those who feel, like the Belgian researchers, that job sharing is no better than part-time and is not succeeding in making available good quality jobs; and those who feel that job sharing is *too* elite: a middle-class phenomenon solely for the benefit of a few female high-fliers, which is how some unions see job sharing. It is probable that in some professional (ie "elite") fields, job sharing is successful in creating access to jobs not available part-time. But it is also certainly the case that job sharing is being applied to low-level, monotonous jobs.

It should be pointed out that even in monotonous, dead-end jobs, sharing may be conferring advantages over part-time working. Interviews with job sharers in a factory in France showed that the presence of a partner made possible a degree of time flexibility and control that is usually not possible in ordinary part-time, and that the workers in this factory highly valued such flexibility. In research at the same site, interviews suggested another possible advantage of job sharing, compared to part-time, even in low level jobs. Job sharers said they liked the "security of sharing a full-time job" (60). Other sources as well have suggested that job sharing is a way of providing greater job security than part-time, and not only at the factory level. For example in the UK the NUT (a teachers' union) prepared an advisory note for its members saying that job sharing may be a way for part-time teachers to "consolidate" their positions. But it has to be noted that so far there has been no evidence available to either support or refute the claim of greater security for job sharing a full-time position than holding an ordinary part-time position.

Clearly, though, despite the possibility of advantages in security and flexibility, the existence of job sharing in low level jobs with poor employment benefits has served to blur the concept of job sharing as distinct from part-time. There are already moves to up-grade part-time work, and many observers feel this is a preferable strategy to job sharing. There is at present an EEC draft directive which would confer all the employment rights and benefits of full-time work on part-timers. Even the main organisation in the UK for promoting and developing job sharing, New Ways to Work, acknowledges that "...if those who worked less than full-time had the same benefits and access to reasonable jobs, there might not be the need to create such a pattern of employment as job sharing" (69). But part-time work is very far now from equalling the rights and opportunities of full-time work, and the EEC directive is far from being enacted. Job sharing may be a quicker way in. Or, at least, another way in.

Though there are areas of doubt as to the distinction between part-time and job sharing, job sharers themselves seem to be able to distinguish between the two. Over and over the literature reports studies that it "feels" different. This should not be dismissed; it concerns the elusive quality-of-work factor that can make the difference between good working conditions and bad working conditions. It may be described by sharers as a "sense of legitimacy" on the job market (64), of "achievement" (1), or a "feeling of continuity and belonging" (77) but however it is described, the research has frequently found some sort of positive feeling among job sharers that contributes to the quality of their working lives in a way that ordinary part-time does not.

Job sharing, worksharing and flexibility

This paper has focussed on job sharing as a quality-of-life measure. Job sharing was originally conceived primarily to meet the needs of workers, and it has largely been introduced in workplaces at the initiative of workers who voluntarily sought to share their job in order to make time for non-work activities and interests.

However, long before the job sharing idea of the 1960's, the practice of having two people share one job existed. It began in the 1930's when various programmes were put in place to combat the Depression. Worksharing, as it was (and is) usually known, was introduced to avoid redundancies. It was initiated by management as a temporary measure, it involved government subsidies and usually also placed various operating restrictions on the firm during the interim period, eg firms could not hire new workers.

The economic pressures which began in the 1970's have revived the worksharing idea.[1] In 1977 the European Commission proposed that worksharing be introduced to redistribute the total volume of work in the economy, in response to rising unemployment. Worksharing can include a number of measures, besides converting a full-time job into two part-time jobs. It can also mean lowering the retirement age, restricting the use of overtime, reducing working hours, and so on.

In several European countries, such as Britain and the Netherlands, governments have introduced worksharing in the form of the division of one full-time job into two part-time jobs. In the UK, for example, the government pays employers £840 for every job so converted, provided the 'extra' part-time job created is filled by a registered unemployed person.[2]

Proponents of job sharing take great pains to distinguish job sharing from worksharing. Their task is made enormously more difficult by the fact that writers in the field often use the terms interchangeably.

---

[1] In some countries it was never abandoned. Germany has had a worksharing programme since the 1930's.

[2] There are other eligibility rules, but being unemployed is the main focus.

The basic difference lies in the voluntary/compulsory dimension: job sharing is seen as a wholly voluntary agreement between two workers to share a job in order to suit their own needs. Worksharing is introduced by management, and is a measure to reduce work time on a percentage basis for all, as an alternative to unemployment of a corresponding percentage of the work force. As such it has a strong compulsory element. Both the EEC and the OECD recommend worksharing, but have emphasised that worksharing should be offered on a 'voluntary basis'. But as one researcher said, "Exactly what 'voluntary' means, given the state of the labour market, is rather unclear. None of the instances (of worksharing) which we have examined have had a voluntary component, beyond that of 'take it or leave it' " (12).

Worksharing is now being promoted in the public and the private sector as a means of reducing unemployment, particularly youth unemployment, whether or not conditions conform to governmental schemes. Job sharing has rarely made claims for impacting unemployment. The two 'strains' -- the 'quality-of-lifers' and those whose aim is to lower the unemployment figures, do not sit well together. One supporter of worksharing (or as he calls it, job sharing) as a means of cutting unemployment pokes fun at the quality-of-life image of New Ways to Work: "...the office...nestles among the antique boutiques of Islington...bowls of macrobiotic cress on the windowsills and posters advertising old CND rallies on the wall...an aura of simmering nut cutlets about the whole idea" (31).

But there is not necessarily a distinct difference between job sharing and worksharing, and to some extent the edges are being blurred. Job sharing was originally conceived in an era of economic expansion. It is now taking place in an entirely different context: the economic outlook is not so good, and employers are perceiving that greater efficiency can be the result of relying on flexible working arrangements. This is coinciding with the aspirations of some workers who need/want work patterns compatible with other activities. So that in many cases voluntary job sharing demanded by staff is appearing in worksites where employers welcome the opportunity to have existing employees 'double up' and share a single job. Not only does it avoid the necesssity of having to make redundancies, it also gives the employer greater workforce flexibility and increases the productivity per job post.

Thus job sharing is now being presented, in literature aimed at the commercial sector, as a means of maximising flexibility by maintaining some workers on the periphery of the organisation, and of "...minimising commitment to the worker" (4). This is an interesting new twist to the job sharing concept. It represents the exact opposite of the motives of job sharers, themselves, who share in order to reduce their hours but at the same time get beneficial terms and conditions and be well integrated into the mainstream workforce. It makes their statements about sense of "belonging" and "legitimacy" on the workforce (see page 26) seem foolish and naive.

This is the crux of the criticism that has been levelled at job sharing by some analysts. If job sharing for the 'right' reasons has the effect of increasing productivity in a post, it will inevitably be subject to manipulation and abuse by those who 'merely' want to improve company profits. So far job sharing has been taken up mainly by the public sector. If taken up by the private sector, it may become an altogether different phenomenon, although it should be noted that even the public sector is not exempt from wanting to reduce overheads. The author of the present paper was told by one manager in the public sector that when two employees approached him with a request to job share, he readily agreed because it coincided with his department's "cuts" policy. The UK Civil Service job sharing policy stresses that "...job sharing should not be used as a means to reduce overall complements" but the temptation is evidently strong, and there is a suspicion amongst some job share "purists" that government/political motives in offering job sharing are unrelated to worker quality-of-life.

Union attitudes

This situation can be summed up by saying that unions in Europe are generally opposed to job sharing but there are signs that union attitudes are changing, at least in the UK.

Unions object to job sharing on essentially four grounds:

1. Job sharing will slow or halt the hard-won trend toward the shorter working week.

Since it is a relatively easy burden, on each worker, for two workers to fill a 40-hour job, there would be less pressure to reduce the work week, should job sharing become widespread.

Job sharing is not widespread, so we do not know yet what the effect would be. Some labour analysts do not regard the two moves -- toward reduction of the work week and introduction of job sharing -- as mutually exclusive. And there are signs of a change in union attitudes. One union research group feels "...Job sharing is _not_ an alternative to a shorter working week for all without loss of pay. These are both demands which can be fought for at the same time and are complementary to each other" (94).

2. Job sharing is a threat to full-time jobs.

Or, as one union put it, job sharing is a threat to "real" jobs, because anything less than full-time work has not really had legitimacy with unions. Union activity has been geared toward the protection of full-time jobs.

But does job sharing threaten full-time jobs ? Here the situation may be complicated by the job sharing/worksharing confusion. Worksharing may be seen to represent a clear threat to the existence of full-time work; a full-time job is compulsorily converted into two part-time jobs. Job sharing, on the other hand, may be seen as a voluntary agreement between two workers who want to share an existing full-time job. The status of the job, in theory, does not change. Indeed that is the purpose of job sharing -- to have access to legitimate full-time jobs. But as we have seen theory may be far removed from practice and employers, at least, may regard job sharing as a way of weakening the full-time structure of work.

3. Job sharing creates conditions for the abuse of workers.

Job sharing can result in loss of benefits and reduced protection for the worker, compared to full-time work. There are risks to pension, overtime pay and to other benefits and, if hours worked per worker falls below a certain threshold, in most countries there is loss of social security and other employment protection.

It is precisely for this reason that proponents of job sharing are urging unions to take a more positive role -- to assist their members in negotiating job share agreements in order to avoid such conditions of abuse.

4. Job sharing will weaken union power and influence in the workplace.

It is an accepted view that union strength is undermined by fragmentation of the workforce. Job sharers, with only a part-time presence, are seen as more difficult to organise and, even if unionised, "there will be difficulties in them playing a part in trade union activities at the plant" (40).

But the question of union influence and power has another side to it as well. Job sharing can lead to a new locus of decision-making among the workforce, one which could marginalise the unions more seriously if they elect _not_ to promote job sharing, than if they do. A case study in France (60) illustrates this well.

At this site, women workers essentially mobilised themselves to press for, and ultimately win, the right to job share. The union, opposed as it was to the idea, abstained during this campaign. When job sharing finally came, new regular meetings were instituted to plan and co-ordinate the sharers' schedules -- meetings between the sharers and their supervisors. These meetings became an important focus at the workplace for discussion of work issues involving sharers and, later, drew in other women in the firm, non-sharers who wished to share but whose applications were being blocked by management. Introducing job sharing had the effect of creating a new special interest group, who began to think of themselves as a separate force.

The author of that study asserts that the union, mostly men, could conceive only of the needs of an abstract worker class, when they spoke of how job sharing exploits workers. They placed general interests before individual -- ie female -- interests. The result was that management was seen by (female) workers to be more sensitive to their needs than was the union, and the union became even more marginalised in their work lives. The author of the study reports that it was the evident mobilisation of an interest group that opened the union eyes to the potential for intervention, and the union eventually came round to supporting various specific demands of job sharers, after sharing had started.

This in fact represents what may be seen as a newly-developing pattern in the UK. Unions begin by ignoring or actively opposing job sharing, but as one union document said, are put in the positon of having to consider job sharing "because requests for information and guidance about job sharing are being received in increasing numbers...from members" (67).

Individual union members, almost always women, are spearheading change. There is now an increasing number of unions that have either passed pro-job sharing resolutions or have issued official guidelines or otherwise become involved in defining members' interests in job sharing. The list of unions so involved includes, in the UK, NALGO, EEPTU, CSU, NUT, APEX, NATFHE, and in Ireland, FWI. The TUC, in the UK, drew up guidelines in 1984 in draft form but these have not been agreed.

Management attitudes

The situation here can best be summarised by a CBI survey in 1985. In-depth interviews with senior executives found widespread opposition to the idea of job sharing. "However in the few cases where job sharing has been used...managers were generally extremely enthusiastic about its potential" (17).

The "potential" the CBI had in mind may have more to do with company profitability than worker quality-of-life. However, in the public sector, too, the introduction of job sharing is blocked "...by raising almost every conceivable objection " (31) but once implemented, it is found that "...the anticipated problems simply did not arise" (73).

The "anticipated problems" -- blurred lines of responsibility, communication failures, poorer output, decreased worker commitment, etc -- so clearly envisaged in advance by management are less readily apparent to workers. A study of managers and staff in the same public sector workplace (a library), neither of which group had any actual experience of job sharing, found that managers could name more problems than advantages, but just the reverse was true for staff (90).

It is this attitudinal resistance among management, which one analyst ascribes to culture and tradition, that has often been found to keep job sharing out. Even where a high level policy decision has been made to offer job sharing to meet worker interests, the evaluation literature documents a number of instances where middle management has been slow to comply and line supervisors have been reluctant to approve individual applications.

Another major area of difficulty with management attitude, already mentioned, is the pervasive conviction that job sharing, if it can work at all, must be confined to lower level jobs. Interviews with Belgian bank managers for example showed that they could not conceive of managerial jobs being shared (84). A form of job sharing has existed in banks for many years in the UK, on a very large scale (one bank alone employs thousands of job sharers) but the conditions so stretch the concept of 'job sharing' that it is not certain that it can be called job sharing.[1] Sharing is confined to the lowest level clerical jobs; sharers are not entitled to the 'perks' other employees are (eg low-cost home loans); and since most of the arrangements are alternate-week schedules, sharers rarely communicate and never even see each other except at the annual Christmas party. Although the concept of sharing is well established in banks, most bank managers cannot conceive of good jobs being shared.

Some organisations with a job sharing policy are beginning to recognise, because of such attitudinal resistance, the need to do more than merely announce a policy, but rather to encourage it. For example, one state civil service found, two years after they announced a goal of converting 2% of all jobs to job sharing, the "major factor impeding forward progress has been the existence of a pervasive adverse attitude...it is difficult to convince managers and supervisors that it is to their advantage " (72). The authority then launched an information campaign to change minds, the effects of which were unfortunately not known at the time the report which referred to it was written.

Is it legal

UK:

"Job sharing arguably presents a serious challenge to the whole legal concept of the contract of employment" (59)

Ireland:

"...it is important to address the predicament that workers find themselves in in relation to employment legislation in Ireland and how this impinges on job sharers" (28)

---

[1] Job sharing in UK banks is not reflected in the estimate on page 3.

France:

> "Considering the ambigious context of the relevant legislation, heads of companies prefer an anonymous protection rather than publicity (about their job sharing) which might leave them open to accusations of the perhaps imperfect way in which their job sharing scheme conforms to labour law" (87)

Germany:

> "Job sharing is not at all compatible with German employment law " (101)
>
> "German employment law can be applied to job sharing" (32)

This selection of views illustrates a major area of difficulty in job sharing. To some extent job sharers everywhere are operating in a twilight world of confused, inconsistent and untested legal rights. Individual job share contracts are devised on an improvised basis by employers and employees together, in an area where few have any experience, and terms and conditions may be left vague or badly worded.

Even where terms are spelled out clearly, there are problems. A major example is the German "obligation to cover" clause, in the first job share model to be introduced there, with its attendant requirement that one partner's absence means the automatic sacking of the other. This was an important cause of strong union opposition, since it implies a permanent work availability, with sharers always on stand-by. This absolute obligation to cover for each other's absences, whether for sickness or for any other reason, was in fact found never to have been applied in practice, but more important, a court case three years after the model was introduced established that "partner-dependent dismissal" was illegal anyway in German law. Regent legislation has specifically entered this protection for job sharers in German labour law.

In the UK, the question of whether employment protection legislation, with its emphasis on continuity and minimum weekly hours, does or does not protect job sharers has been the subject of uncertainty. It was the contention of one firm that an employee who worked alternate weeks was not in continuous employment and thus fell outside protective legislation. An

Employment Appeals Tribunal ruled that although the employee was indeed regularly away from work during the "off-week", she was " 'absent...in circumstances such that by arrangement or custom' she was regarded as continuing in employment" (IR-RR no.225). More recently the House of Lords ruled that alternate week working could not be averaged to give the necessary minimum continuous hours.

In France, job sharers sometimes sign a 3-way contrct (the two sharers plus the employer) even though French law recognises contracts only between two people. The 3-party contract is said to have "symbolic value" (60) though absolutely no judicial validity in case of litigation.

Difficult legal matters remain unsettled for many sharers -- the rights to benefits and promotion, the right to revert to full-time work in the organisation, what happens when one partner leaves, security of tenure, flexibility of job content, and so on. Research is currently underway in the UK to examine whether job share contracts can be squeezed into slightly re-modelled regular contracts, as is the case now, or whether a new legal framework is required.

All flexible work patterns carry with them disadvantageous treatment in legal terms, because the law was set up to protect 'normal' workers. It is an especially difficult situation with job sharers, though, because the desire to be seen to be succeeding has inhibited discussion and resolution of the problems. People who are permitted to job share are so grateful that even patently unfair and possibly illegal conditions are willingly accepted in return for the right to share. The obligation to be on call all the time, to cover for a partner, was seen by sharers "...as a justifiable and fair price to pay to be allowed such freedom to organise one's time" (87).

Legislation to protect job sharers is possible. It has been introduced on a very wide scale in the US, but it is a matter of public will. When enough people want it, it will happen. Even "...if a multiplicity of regulations, requirements or even laws stand in the way of job sharing, one must...consider whether that is really appropriate or whether...put forward in order to spare the sacred cow of traditional working hours " (25).

Conclusion

Job sharing may be seen as a true 'grass-roots' movement, with little support and sometimes active opposition from unions and management alike. Although conceived in large part to provide equality of opportunity for working women, job sharing has also been the object of scorn from certain feminist groups in Europe, who see job sharing as merely creating another women's ghetto in the labour market, and reinforcing the role of women in the home. For example the Ligestillingsradet (The Danish equal opportunities agency) does not feel that arrangements like job sharing "...are doing much for equality...as it is not realistic to believe that to any extent men will take that opportunity".[1] So job sharing even has the feminist groups against it.

Despite conceptual and practical problems, however, wherever job sharing has managed to make an appearance it turns out to be a remarkably positive work/life solution for those involved. And that is the point to stress in conclusion -- it is a solution. It cannot meet the needs of everyone, or even of everyone who wants to work shorter hours, but it is one option that should at least be studied, to see if it should be made available for those who want it, because it can be highly successful and is evidently strongly desired by some -- "evidently", because they have had to overcome such odds to achieve it.

---

[1] Personal communicaton with the author, 3 December 1985

Job sharing may be an attractive alternative when the other options are bad part-time work or, since part-time is unavailable in many positions, no work at all. Job sharing as an alternative to full-time is perhaps a different matter. Job sharing may have associated disadvantages compared to full-time work -- fewer benefits, greater risk to job security, poorer advancement prospects -- but these are by no means inevitable and established with certainty and, in any case, must be weighed against the problems, in some cases the utter impossibility, of full-time work for people with significant non-work obligations.

The research studies that have been done of job sharing have been so unambiguous in terms of job sharing's ability to impact on people's quality of life that it would seem extremely perverse to ignore or minimise it. Apart from job sharers' practical time problems being eased by the presence of a partner, "...more fundamentally these workers recognize having learned, after two years of job sharing, <u>that it is possible to live another way</u>" (60) (emphasis added). Far more appropriate than dismissing it as a practice with (current) numerical insignificance, policy makers should seriously examine how job sharing can reasonably be fitted into trends to diversify working patterns, for those whose non-work needs cannot be met in other ways.

Time and space limitations of the present analysis have meant that the issues involved in job sharing -- employer attitudes, trade union positions, legal problems, etc -- have only been briefly outlined in summary form. But apart from the requirement for brevity, fuller treatment of job sharing issues is severely limited by the absence of comprehensive research in the area. Three problems stand out in particular:

1. There needs to be European research to establish the extent of job sharing. We simply do not know enough about what is happening. In the course of preparing the present analysis, one correpondent from France noted that the job sharing phenomenon in France may be "...unknown because not studied

and not because without reality".[1] Equally, correspondents from Denmark, Greece, the Netherlands and Belgium reported that, yes, we know there is job sharing here but we do not know how much. And some added, by implication, we do not care how much. It is worth finding out more about job sharing if for no other reason than that it is arising out of worker need and is, curiously, surviving even in the face of such hostility from management, unions and feminists.

2. There needs to be comparative research to establish the nature of job sharing as opposed to ordinary part-time. Job sharing was conceived in order to achieve work benefits and status that are not available part-time. We do not know to what degree job sharing has succeeded in creating good high level opportunities for part-time workers, or to what degree it has succeeded in conferring upon part-time workers (of any level) better terms and conditions. These are important, interesting and achievable research questions that have so far not been tackled in a systematic way. The intention is not, it should be stressed, to promote job sharing at the expense of part-time (or any other arrangement) but simply to be clear about what job sharing can contribute to working life.

3. Finally, there needs to be research to establish the nature of the place that job sharing has in relation to traditional (full-time) work, and to people's working lives. Do people move in and out of job sharing ? Is job sharing a permanent work style ? Are job sharing positions precarious ? What about job sharers themselves -- ie the positions might be secure, but not the post holders. Does job sharing minimise employer commitment to the employee ? How do contractual terms fit in to this picture ? It is nearly ten years since job sharing was first introduced to Europe and, with several thousands of sharers, it ought to be possible to begin finding the answers to such questions.

* * * * * * * * * *

---

[1] Letter from Seminaire d'Economie du Travail, Paris, 8 January 1986

Job sharing, although it is perhaps the easiest of all developments to slot into the existing overall pattern of work, can be viewed as a highly radical development. It is the only one of the many new work patterns discussed that shifts the locus of decision-making, as to working hours, from the employer to the employee. The job requires x time, but it is to some degree the individual worker-pairs who decide how to fill that time. It is perhaps this slight shift in power that both excites and theatens, but as a matter of interest should be looked at more carefully.

Bibliography

1. Angier, M. "Job sharing in schools", Sheffield Papers in Education Management, Sheffield City Polytechnic, 1984

2. "Arbeitsplatz-Teilung: Ein Modell der Chemie", *Arbeit und Sozialpolitik*, Jg. 35, 1981

3. Atkinson, J. "Job sharing", IMS Report no. 77, 1983

4. Atkinson, J. "The changing corporation", in D. Clutterbuck (ed), "New patterns of work", Gower, 1985

5. Banking Insurance & Finance Union, "A discussion paper on job sharing", October 1983

6. Bekemans, L. (ed) "New patterns in employment, no. 1. The organisation of working time", European Centre for Work and Society, Maastricht, 1982

7. Born, C. and Vollmer, C. "Familienfreundliche Gestaltung des Arbeitslebens", Schriftenreihe des Bundesministers fur Jugend, Familie und Gesundheit, Band 135, Verlag W. Kohlhammer, 1983

8. Bouillaguet-Bernard, P., et al "Changes in women's participation in the labour force", (2nd phase) Commission of the European Communities 1985

9. Boyle, A. "Job sharing - A study of the costs, benefits and employment rights of job sharers", New Ways to Work, November 1980

10. British Institute of Management, "Managing new patterns of work", 1985

11. Bundesminister fur Arbeit und Sozialordnung, "Mass Arbeit", 1984

12. Casey, B. "Worksharing for young people: a study of recent experiences in the UK, Germany and the Netherlands", *Social Europe*, May 1983, pp.53-55

13. CDU/CSU "Familienpolitik im Wandel", 1985

14. Clark, G. "Working patterns: part-time work, job sharing and self-employment", Manpower Services Commission, January 1982

15. Clutterbuck, D. "Job sharing is winning wider support", *International Management*, vol. 37, no. 10, October 1982

16. Clutterbuck, D. (ed) "New patterns of work", Gower, 1985

17. Confederation of British Industry "Managing change: the organisation of work", 1985

18. Conlan, A. "Job sharing: Improving the quality of working life", MBA dissertation, University College, Dublin, 1984

19. Cooper, C. "Executive families under stress", Prentice-Hall, 1981

20. Davoud, N. "Part-time employment: time for recognition, organisation and legal reform", Multiple Sclerosis Society of Great Britain and Northern Ireland, March 1980

21. Crowley, R.W. and Huth, E. "An international comparison of work sharing programs", Relations Industrielles", vol. 38, no. 3, 1983

22. Delcroix, C. "European women in paid employment", Women of Europe Supplement no. 20, 1985

23. "Delegates like idea of job sharing", Irish Times, 8.4.83

24. Department of the Public Service, Dublin, Circular 3/84: Pilot job-sharing scheme, 1984

25. Derschka, P. and Gottschall, D. "Leisure as a standard", Manager Magazine, October 1981, p.148

26. "EEC Commission proposals on work sharing", European Industrial Relations Review, no. 51, March 1978

27. "Employers and trade unions: no to job-sharing", Social & Labour Review, no. 4, December 1981

28. Equal Opportunities Commission, "Job sharing: Improving the quality and availability of part-time work", 1981

29. "Equal opportunities in the Civil Service: explanatory leaflet giving advice to staff on how to cope with changes in domestic responsibilities", General Notice GEN 85/14

30. Goodair, C. "Job-sharing in industry - efficiency and cost effectiveness. A report on a one day conference held at the Industrial Society", 26 January 1982

31. Goodhart, Sir P. "Stand on your own four feet", The Bow Group, 1982

32. Goos, W. "Job Sharing - ein Arbeitsvertragsmodell in der Sozialpolitischen Diskussion", Gewerkschaftsreport Jg. 15, 1981, nr. 3

33. Gorges, R. "Job-sharing: Moglichkeiten fur Arbeitsteilung u. Arbeitszeitorganisation", ECON, Dusseldorf, 1984

34. Heeley, L. "Tackling the problem that will not go away", Local Government Chronicle, 11 January 1985

35. Heymann, H. and Seiwert, L. "Flexible Arbeitsseiten und Job Sharing", Personal, Jg. 34, 1982

36. Heymann, H. and Seiwert, L. "Erfahrungen mit job sharing", Management Zeitschrift, May 1983, pp.185-88

37. Hoff, A. "Job-sharing als arbeitsmarktpolitisches Instrument: Wirkungspotential und arbeitsrechtliche Gestaltung", International Institute of Management, 1981

38. Horburger, H. "Job-sharing - probleme und moglichkeiten", EEC, 1985 (unpublished draft)

39. Income Data Services, "Job-sharing: a new approach to working time", International Report, August 1981, no. 151

40. Income Data Services, "Part-time workers", Study no. 267, June 1982

41. Income Data Services, "The job splitting scheme", Study no. 289, 1983

42. Income Data Services, "Part-timers, temps and job sharers", Employment Law Handbook 31, 1985

43. Institut fur Demoskopie Allensbach, "Immer Mehr Finden Job-sharing Gut", 1983, nr. 6

44. Institute of Manpower Studies, "Jobsharing", IMS Manpower Commentary no. 18, 1982

45. Institute of Manpower Studies, "New forms of work organisation", IMS Manpower Commentary no. 30, 1985

46. "Interesse an Job-sharing - aber auch Bedenken", Suddeutsche Zeitung, 19.11.81

47. "Ireland - Job sharing at Aer Rianta", European Industrial Relations Review, no. 110, 1983

48. Irish Tax Officials Union, I.T.O.U. 37/84, "Job sharing and career breaks"

49. "It's women who have the part-time jobs", Europe 85, Sept/Oct, p.20

50. Jallade, J-P. "Towards a policy of part-time employment", European Centre for Work and Society, Maastricht, 1984

51. "Job-sharing: Abseits der Norm", Wirtschaftswoche, Jg. 35, 1981, no. 47

52. "Job-sharing: Mehr Theoriediskussion als Anwendung in der Praxis", Handlsblatt, 4.4.83

53. "Job-sharing nach dem herkommlichen System", Handelsblatt, 1.3.83

54. "Job-sharing - the Scottish perspective", Conference Report, 20 November 1982, Glasgow

55. "Job-sharing wenig beliebt", Frankfurter Rundschau, 1 August 1985

56. Kading, K. "Work sharing and the reduction and reorganisation of working time at firm level", Social Europe, no. 3/84, December 1984, p.63 ff

57. Lackowski, A. "Teilzeitarbeit - Ein Weg zur Flexibilisierung der Arbeitzeit", in "Arbeitszeitverkurzung Schriften zur Unternehmensfuhrung", Gabler Verlag, Fallstudie 43

58. LACSAB (Local Authorities Conditions of Service Advisory Board), "Job sharing", Employer Guide no. 6

59. Leighton, P. and Buckland, P. "Job-sharing - Defining the issues", The Polytechnic of North London, Dept. of Law, Research Paper no. 2, 1985

60. Loos, J. "Les enjeux de l'amenagement du temps de travail - Sept monographies d'entreprises", Centre de Recherche Travail & Societe, Paris, 1983

61. Lutz, W. "Job sharing - die alternative der zukunft", Office Management, vol. 31, no. 11, November 1983

62. Management and Personnel Office, "Equal opportunities for women in the Civil Service", HMSO, 1983

63. McCarthy, M and Rosenberg, G. "Work sharing: case studies", W.E. Upjohn Institute for Employment Research, 1981

64. Meier, G. "Job sharing - a new pattern for quality of work and life", W.E. Upjohn Institute for Employment Research, 1979

65. Moorman, B. "Upgrading part-time work - why unions should support voluntary job sharing", New Ways to Work (U.S.), 1982

66. National Council for Voluntary Organisations and New Ways to Work, "Job sharing and voluntary organisations", May 1983

67. National Union of Teachers, "Job sharing for teaching staff"

68. "Neues Modell fur Job-Sharing", Frankfurter Rundschau, 12.3.82

69. New Ways to Work, "Job sharing and trade unions", 1981

70. New Ways to Work, "Job sharing vs job splitting", 1983

71. New Ways to Work, Newsletter, August 1985; and February 1986

72. New Ways to Work (U.S.), "Job sharing in the public sector", 1979

73. New Ways to Work (U.S.), "Job sharing in the schools", 1980

74. New Ways to Work (U.S.), "Job sharing - analyzing the cost", 1981

75. New Ways to Work (U.S.), "Job sharing - general information", 1982

76. New Ways to Work (U.S.), "Opinion survey of union officials on reduced work time options", 1983

77. New Ways to Work (U.S.), "Job sharing in health care", 1984

78. Olmsted, B and Smith, S. "The job sharing handbook", Penguin Books, 1983

79. Ott, E. "Job sharing - Anspruche und Wirkungen", AFA - Informationen, Sept/Okt 1981

80. "Part-time work in 15 countries", European Industrial Relations Review, no. 137, June 1985

81. Rathkey, P. "British trade unions: an overview", Work Times, vol. 2, no. 4, July 1984

82. "Reappraisal of job-sharing shows variety of motives", Personnel Management, June 1983, vol. 15, no. 6

83. "R.F.A.: le 'job sharing controverse' ", Intersocial, no. 73, Aug-Sept 1981, pp.27-28

84. Robert, J and Bawin-Legros, B. "Le partage des posts: une réelle alternative ?",Recherches Sociologiques, no. 1, 1985

85. Robinson, O. and Wallace, J. "Part time employment and sex discrimination legislation in Great Britain", Dept. of Employment Research Paper no. 43, 1984

86. Schroeder, E. "West Germans jump on the job-sharing bandwagon", Financial Times, 15 July 1981, p.15

87. SERETE, "Le partage de l'emploi dans l'industrie francaise", Paris, April 1985

88. Shaw, D. "Job sharing in DHSS", Job Satisfaction Team, September 1984

89. "Short time", The Economist, 22 June 1985, p. 29

90. Sorby, B and Pascoe, M. "Job sharing - The great divide ?", School of Librarianship, Leeds Polytechnic, Leeds

91. Syrett, M. "How to make job sharing work", Personnel Management, October 1982

92. Syrett, M. "Employing job sharers part-time and temporary staff", Institute of Personnel Management, 1983

93. Teriet, B. "Alternative work patterns", in L. Bekermans (ed) "The organisation of working time", ECWS 1982

94. Trade Union and Community Resource and Information Centre, "Job sharing", Leeds TUCRIC, special supplement, 1983

95. Trade Union and Community Resource and Information Centre, "Job sharing Part 2", Leeds TUCRIC, special supplement, 1984

96. Trades Union Congress, "Job sharing", December 14, 1982

97. Trade Union Research Unit, "Job sharing - the pros and cons from a union point of view", no. 30, 1983

98. "Une alternative aux quarante heures: le job sharing", <u>Intersocial</u>", no. 75, Novembre 1981, pp.3-12

99. "Vers une plus grande flexiblite du temps de travail", <u>Intersocial</u>, no. 79, March 1982

100. Volk, H. "Ein Umfrage ergibt: Handwerk fur "job-sharing" aufgeschlossen", <u>Deutsches Handwerksblatt</u>, Jg. 33, 1981

101. Wagner, P. "Job-sharing: Fragestellungen aus Theorie und Praxis", <u>Die Betriebswirtschaft</u>, Jg. 42, 1982

102. Walton, P. "Job sharing", in D. Clutterbuck (ed) "New patterns of work", Gower, 1985

103. Wilce, H. "Job sharing gets a pilot scheme in London", Times Educational Supplement, 2.2.83, p.5

104. Organisation for Economic Co-operation and Development, (<u>OECD</u>), "Labour supply, growth constraints and worksharing", 1982

TELEWORK

Attitudes of the Social Partners
and the Labour Force and the
Potential for Decentralized
Electronic Work in Europe

Empirica
Kaiserstrasse 29-31
D-5300 Bonn 1

Telework - Attitudes of the Social Partners, the Labour Force and Potential for Decentralized Electronic Work in Europe

1. Introduction

New information technologies allow for decentralization or relocation of office work independent of time and space. Many office functions have become internal to computers; computers are increasingly linked by communication networks. Thus it becomes less and less necessary for office workers to be located in the same room, or in the same building.

Some futurists have predicted that the availability of low-cost computing power and telecommunications will increase the number of people working at home. The dawn of the information age will find millions of people "telecommuting" from their "electronic cottages", that is, using computers and telecommunications to do office work remotely. At present, there are only a few thousand people for whom working from the home from socalled satellite or neighbourhood offices is a fulltime substitute for working in traditonal office environments, but this number is growing and many more might be so employed by the mid-1990s.

This development goes along with profoundly changing company structures, tasks and skills requirements, and organizational forms of office work. Only very recently, however, are these changes the subject of research activities endeavouring to design options for reorganization of office work and for social innovation.

Moreover, the social partners are often in disagreement with regard to desirable new forms of work organization in connection with decentralized electronic work. To allow for the development of innovative and socially acceptable forms of telework, it is essential to put this discussion on more solid grounds.

The prime objective of the research project is to analyze the potential for telework (in kind and in volume), to clarify the positions of the social partners and to point out socially innovative and acceptable options for the use of advanced information and communication systems.

2. Definition and Organizational Concepts of Telework

In discussing telework politicians or scientists usually debate the most decentralized form "electronic home work" which has received most attention in the mass media because it is expected to have profound implications on the execution of work as well as on our daily lives.

2.1 Origin and Definition of Telework

The origin of telework can be traced back to 1969 when Alan Kiron coined the term "dominetics" in an article published in The Washington Post. Some years later, around 1971 Frank Schiff began talking about "flexiplace".[1] It was Jack M. Nilles and his colleagues who 1974 created the label of "telecommuting".[2] This expression has to be seen against the general background of the oil crisis in 1973/74 when people all over the world started to think about possibilities of energy conservation. Especially in the substitution of "transportation" through "telecommuting" which was made possible by the advances in telecommunications and computer technology a large potential for saving energy was seen.[3]

In the meantime various terms have been invented which are used to circumscribe the phenomenon of telework, or at least selected facets -particularly electronic'home-work'. The following list contains the terms most frequently applied in literature and among experts:

- Work-at-Home
- The Electronic Cottage
- Telecommuting
- Flexiplace
- Remote Work
- Telework
- Telesubstitution

---

1) Olson, M.H.: Introduction. In: Office Workstations in the Home. Washington 1985, p. 1
2) Nilles, J.M./Carlson, F.R./Gray, P./Hanneman, G.J.: The Tele-Communications-Transportation Trade Off., New York, London, Sydney, Toronto 1976; Nilles, J.M.: Teleworking: Working Closer to Home. In: Technology Review, April 1982, P. 56-62
3. See e.g. Kraemer, K.L.: Telecommunications/transportation substitution and energy conservation. In: Telecommunications Policy, March 1982, p. 39-59 and June 1982, p. 87-99 (together with J.L. King)

- Independent Work Location
- Geographically Independent Work
- Teletravail
- Telearbeit
- Fernarbeit
- Elektronische Heimarbeit
- Teleheimarbeit
- Informationstechnisch gestützte Heimarbeit

It is against this background that the following definition of telework is presented to put the ongoing debate on common ground According to this definition telework is characterized by 3 basic elements:

1. **Location**
   The location of the work site is determined by the needs of the teleworkers and is relocateable as desired or needed. This implies that the geographical site at which work is completed is independent of the location of the employer and/or contractor.

2. **Use of Electronic Equipment**
   Telework relies primarily or to large extent on the use of electronic equipment (PC, storage typewriter etc.).

3. **Communication Link to Employer/Contractor**

   3.1 Distance Working - Narrow Conception
   A communication link exists between/among the teleworker and the employer/contractor which is used for electronic communication and transmission of work results.

   3.2 Distance Working - Broad Conception
   The teleworker works at a distance (spatially separate) from his employer and/or contractor whereby work results are stored on a disc, cassette etc. There is no electronic communication link used for data transmission. The work results are delivered by traditional media, such as mail, courier or else.

2.2 Organizational Concepts of Telework

Diebold Group Inc. and M.H. Olson first identified and described feasible and alternative remote work arrangements where the locational and temporal flexibility of work organization are differentiating criteria from traditional forms of work.[1] This concept closely relates to the decentralization concept developed by J.M. Nilles et al.[2] There, the various organizational forms of telework are

- Satellite Work Centres
- Neighbourhood Work Centres
- Flexible Work Arrangements
- Work at Home.

Their work can be seen as the first extensive and successful attempt to cover all the various organizational forms that could occur in the framework of telework. Their category system proved to be sensible and was later adopted by experts all over the world.

Remote information technology based work options according to Diebold and Olson are as follows:

Satellite Work Centres are relatively self-contained organizational divisions in one firm physically relocated and separated from the parent firms. The emphasis in on locating these centres within a convenient commuting distance of the greatest number of employees utilizing the site. The number of employees working in a satellite work centre is determined by:
- "economies of scale", of equipment and services,
- the maintenance of a sufficient hierarchical structure for adequate management on site and
- sufficient social interaction among employees.

In order to benefit from economies of scale it may be optimal to relocate an entire function such as accounting or data processing. The supervision of work is generally by management staff on site.

Neighbourhood Work Centres: Neighbourhood work centres are offices equipped and financially supported by different companies or organizations. In these offices, employees of the founding organizations share space and equipment in a location close to

---

1) For the following see: Olson, M.H.: New Information Technology and Organizational Culture. In: MIS Quarterly Special Issue 1982; Olson, M.H.: Remote Office Work. Changing Work Patterns in Space and Time. In: Communications of the ACM, March 1983. Vol. 26, No. 3, P. 182-187; Diebold Groups Inc.: Office Work in the Home: Scenarios and Prospects for the 80's. New York 1981
2) See Nilles, J.M. et al., op cit, 1976

their homes. While the number of employees is sufficient to provide necessary social interaction, hierarchical structures are generally lacking and supervision of work is carried out remotely.

One of the principal motivations behind this concept is to reduce employees' time and expense of commuting. In addition, they enable firms to make use of lower office rent outside central cities. These centres, however, are often difficult to implement - particularly on a large scale - as they require extensive cooperation among different organizations.

Flexible Work Arrangements provide employees with flexibility in the scheduling and location of work. This option recognizes the need for occasional alternative work arrangements, especially for professional and managerial employees and provides mechanisms to accomodate staff/family as well as work responsibilities. Furthermore it enables, for instance, DP professionals to accomplish critical work at "non-peak" computer hours or just for convenience. Within this context work forms like "job sharing" and "flexitime" are relevant, too.

Work at Home also labelled "electronic homework" is the most decentralized form of remote work where employees work at home on a regular basis. Under this option, an employee's work week may range anywhere from a few hours to full-time. While homework depends virtually completely on remote supervision and does not provide a field for work related social interaction, it does offer employees maximum flexibility in scheduling working time. In this way, employees may work when and where is most convenient to them.

For many people with primary child care responsibility, work at home offers an employment option.

Generally work at home can be utilized as an option on an individual basis to accomodate a particular situation or need, either temporarily or permanently.

Electronic Service Offices: These are independent firms which either carry out a wide range of data-processing and computer-related services (word-processing, data-processing, book-keeping, administration of stock or highly specialized work such as secretarial offices which only offer text processing). These firms offer their services primarily to small and medium-sized firms for whom the purchase of a computer appears too expensive. Larger companies may also make use of such services during times when they are experiencing internal bottlenecks or peaks.

3. Empirical Basis

In the main, the project is based upon representative surveys among decision makers in manufacturing and service industries - subsequently referred to as DMS - in the major European countries (Federal Republic of Germany, France, United Kingdom, Italy). Moreover, survey data on attitudes towards decentralized electronic work which are available at empirica (EPS) will be evaluated in the framework of this project[1].

Figure 1 illustrates the structure of the Employed People Survey (EPS):

Figure 1:
Structure of the Employed People Survey (EPS)

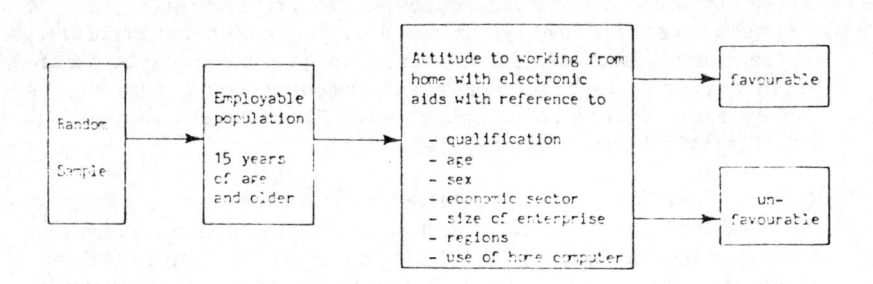

```
┌─────────┐    ┌────────────┐    ┌──────────────────────┐
│         │    │            │    │ Attitude to working  │    ┌───────────┐
│         │    │ Employable │    │ from home with       │───▶│favourable │
│ Random  │───▶│ population │───▶│ electronic aids with │    └───────────┘
│         │    │            │    │ reference to         │
│ Sample  │    │ 15 years   │    │  - qualification     │
│         │    │ of age     │    │  - age               │
│         │    │ and older  │    │  - sex               │    ┌───────────┐
│         │    │            │    │  - economic sector   │───▶│   un-     │
│         │    │            │    │  - size of enterprise│    │favourable │
│         │    │            │    │  - regions           │    └───────────┘
│         │    │            │    │  - use of home computer│
└─────────┘    └────────────┘    └──────────────────────┘
```

The Decision Maker Survey (DMS) will provide the following information:

- interest in information technology based decentralized forms of work by industries, company size, regional characteristics, age and sex of decision makers;
- tasks which are market relevant for decentralization by type;
- reasons against making use of decentralized electronic work.

Figure 2 illustrates the structure of the Decision Maker Survey (DMS):

---

1) Representative survey in the four major EEC countries. Part of this survey was used in the framework of the FAST programme.

Figure 2:
Structure of the Decision Maker Survey (DMS)[*]

```
                    ┌─────────────────────────┐
                    │    RANDOM SAMPLE        │
                    └───────────┬─────────────┘
                                ↓
    ┌───────────────────────────────────────────────────────────────┐
    │     Attitudes of decision makers in companies towards         │
    │  information technology based decentralized forms of work     │
    │                         according to                          │
    │  a) industries - b) company size - c) region - d) position,   │
    │                  age and sex of decision maker                │
    └──────────────┬────────────────────────────┬───────────────────┘
                   ↓                            ↓
```

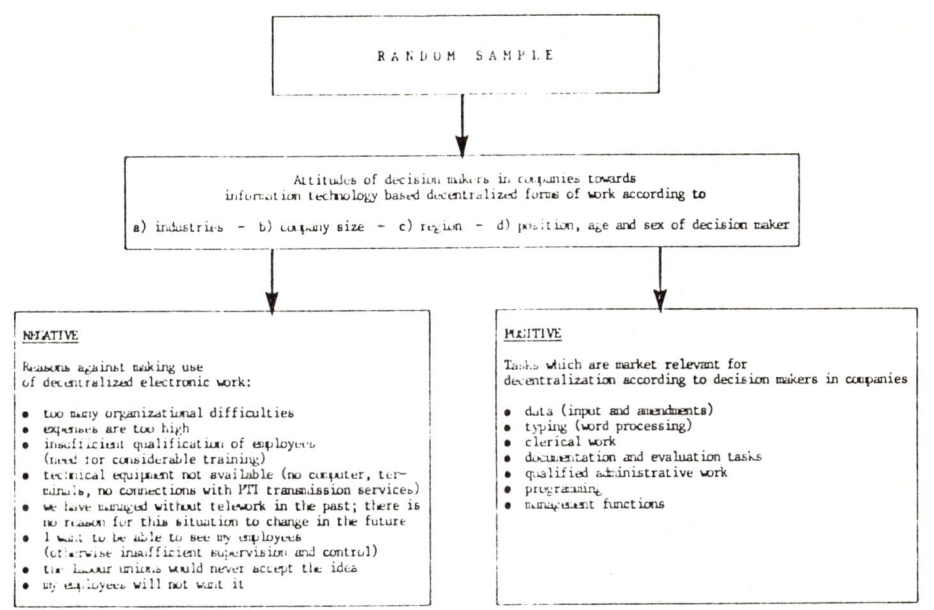

NEGATIVE	POSITIVE
Reasons against making use of decentralized electronic work:	Tasks which are market relevant for decentralization according to decision makers in companies
• too many organizational difficulties	• data (input and amendments)
• expenses are too high	• typing (word processing)
• insufficient qualification of employees (need for considerable training)	• clerical work
• technical equipment not available (no computer, terminals, no connections with PTT transmission services)	• documentation and evaluation tasks
• we have managed without telework in the past; there is no reason for this situation to change in the future	• qualified administrative work
• I want to be able to see my employees (otherwise insufficient supervision and control)	• programming
• the labour unions would never accept the idea	• management functions
• my employees will not want it	

[*] The survey covers the following countries: Federal Republic of Germany, United Kingdom, Italy, France; the survey includes about 1000 decision makers in companies in each country.

4. Evaluation of Positions of the Social Partners

The political discussion about decentralized forms of electronic work is both emotional and highly polarized. The positions of unions, political parties, employer organizations etc. are often characterized by fears or aspirations which prevent the formulation of positive and socially acceptable forms of application of new information and communication technology.

In the ongoing research project, the various positions of the social partners towards decentralized electronic work in the Federal Republic of Germany, France, the United Kingdom and Italy and to some extent in Sweden and the USA will be analyzed. The following aspects will be investigated in depth:
- general position,
- organizational forms,
- work content, qualification requirements, skills, target groups,
- legal aspects,

- main advantages/disadvantages,
- position towards the future diffusion.

The analysis of the positions of the social partners draws mainly on the available literature, expert consultations, working documents and papers. Moreover, in-depth interviews with selected representatives of unions and employer organizations will be carried out.

The results of the evaluation of positions of the social partners are then confronted with the results of the above mentioned quantitative surveys.

It is expected that on this basis, it will be possible to put the discussion on decentralized forms of electronic work on more solid grounds.

5. Workshops

In June 1986 empirica will hold workshops with representatives and employers in
- banking,
- insurance and
- software development

entitled "The Potential of Decentralized Electronic Work in Banking, Insurance and Software Development", because first results of our DMS reveal that the biggest potential for decentralized electronic work could be in these industries.

Following short presentations where representatives of these branches will present their general expectations towards decentralized electronic work applications, existing schemes will be reviewed. Finally the potential, likely diffusion and instruments of stimulation of decentralized electronic work for these industries will be discussed.[1]

---

1) For details, see P. 249

The Potential of Decentralized Electronic Work in Banking,
Insurance and Software Development

empirica
Kaiserstr. 29-31
D-5300 Bonn 1
Tel.: (0228) 21 00 70/79

Workshop Programme

9.30 - 11.00 h

General Expectations of Representatives and Employers in
- Banking
- Insurance and
- Software Development

Towards Decentralized Information and Communication Technology Based Applications
(Presentations by Decision Makers in Companies)

11.00 - 12.30 h

Decentralized Information and Communication Technology Based Applications - A Review of Existing Projects/Schemes in
- Banking (e.g. Electronic Home Banking)
- Insurance (e.g. Data Entry)
- Software Development (e.g. Various Forms of Telework)

(Presentations by Company Representatives and Employers)

12.30 - 13.30 h Break

13.30 - 15.30 h

Discussion in Workshops
The Potential and Likely Diffusion of Decentralized Electronic Work in
- Banking (Workshop 1)
- Insurance (Workshop 2)
- Software Development (Workshop 3)

15.30 - 16.00 h Coffee Break

16.00 - 18.00 h Plenary Session

Potential, Likely Diffusion and Factors Likely to Stimulate/Inhibit the Diffusion of Decentralized Electronic Work

TELEWORK
Women and Environment

Jean Tansey
Rosalyn Moran

Irish Foundation for Human Development
1 James Street
Dublin 8

APRIL 1986

TELETRAVAIL, WOMEN AND ENVIRONMENT

INTRODUCTION

For the purposes of the study, telework is being construed as one of many possible types of flexible or atypical work arrangements. Greater flexibility in working arrangements is seen as an important element in considering work/living scenarios for the future. Within this context, telework offers the potential for radical reorganisation of work place and work time and for re-evaluation of work and domestic roles of men and women. Our living and working environments can facilitate or hinder this process.

The present research project which will be carried out within a European context combines two perspectives in the exploration of telework:

- the women's studies perspective which will focus on the potential of telework to release the creative energy of women in the workforce in the context of their changing roles and status in society

- the environment/architectural psychology perspective where the implications of telework for environmental design and management will be explored. Particular attention will be given to the potential of different environments to support teletravail.

At present we propose to look at four types of telework and if possible look at two examples of each, selected from the EEC member states (see Appendix 1 for working definitions of telework).

METHODOLOGY

A multimethod apporach is being used and a flexible methodological framework adopted. The research will be based on case studies and will be largely "qualitative" in approach. Flexibility of approach is necessary as the research project depends upon a number of external considerations, e.g., existence of appropriate telework examples, availability of key personnel, and practical and financial considerations.

An important initial requirement of the project is the identification and selection of key individuals and agencies in Europe. A number of these have been selected and contract arrangements will be established where appropriate.

The areas of interest are being explored in the following manner:

1. Survey of extant literature

2. Case studies will be carried out in selected European countries amongst certain groups, e.g., teleworkers, traditional workers, etc. It is envisaged that discussions will be held with these groups. These discussions will be carried out in the context of the different types of telework identified in the literature and will focus on the women and environment themes. A questionnaire is being designed and used as a back-up

3. A network of experts is being established with whom specialist interviews will be conducted

4. Interviews and discussions will be held with specialist groups, e.g., women's organisations, women's trade union groups, architects, town planners, etc.

5. Sub-contracting arrangements will be entered into with personnel in selected European countries. Those sub-contracted will be expected to:

(i) liaise with the project leaders regarding the cultural adaptation of research instuments

(ii) set up and administer fieldwork in the relevant countries.

ISSUES TO BE EXPLORED

The following specific issues will be explored in relation to telework:

- the potential for women's employment at different stages of the lifecycle

- the implications for domestic roles of women and men

- the implications of telework for environmental planning and design, e.g., land use planning, commuting, etc.

- the implications of telework for the architectural design of joint work/living spaces in the home

- the psychological and health implications of teletravail.

In addition, a range of recommendations will be made in respect of teletravail with particular regard to the following:

- the relative roles and status of men and women in the workforce

- physical environmental context in which the social and human development advantages of teletravail can be exploited

- architectural design of joint living/work spaces.

APPENDIX 1

WORKING DEFINITIONS OF FOUR TYPES OF TELEWORK

The four types of telework being considered at present are tentatively defined as follows:

1. **Telework at Home**

    The worker is located at home; IT is used by the worker who may work for an employer or contract his/her labour.

2. **Neighbourhood Work Centre**

    Workers are located in a centre, close to their homes, which has IT facilities. Workers can be self-employed or employed by employers who are located at a distance.

3. **Satellite Offices/Branch Office**

    A satellite or branch office is located at a distance from the head or main office and is usually organisationally autonomous. The work carried out in satellite offices frequently involves the use of IT and electronic communication with head office or fellow satellites is the norm. Workers in satellite offices are usually drawn from the surrounding area and work for the same company.

4. **Shared Facilities**

    These are centres which are highly serviced with electronic facilities. Clients rent space, facilities or services (e.g., data processing, tele-conferencing, office suites, meeting rooms, etc.) for varying lengths of time. The centres are frequently located in urban areas. Those who use "shared facilities" are usually employees of different companies or self-employed professionals.

LES CONSEQUENCES DES FORMES NOUVELLES D'EMPLOI SUR LA VIE FAMILIALE ET L'ORGANISATION SOCIALE

Françoise Piotet

PARIS
MARS 1986

Esquisser une problématique sur les conséquences qu'ont dès à présent ou que sont susceptibles d'avoir les formes nouvelles d'emploi sur la vie familiale et l'organisation sociale est un projet dont l'ambition peut être jugée hors d'atteinte pour plusieurs raisons.

I - LE CONTEXTE : TRANSITION ET CRISE

Nouvelles formes d'emplois, vie familiale et organisation sociale constituent trois pôles marqués, chacun pour leur part par des changements qui, dans certains cas, constituent peut-être des mutations radicales.
Si sur certains points tels les questions démographiques, le travail féminin, le développement des emplois tertiaires, mais bien d'autres encore, on voit se dessiner des évolutions dont les ancrages ont déjà une assise suffisante pour constituer un indicateur d'une certaine permanence, sur d'autres au contraire, des tendances trop contradictoires rendent particulièrement aléatoires les interprétations possibles et, à fortiori, les projections. L'ensemble de ces changements se produisent en effet dans un contexte général de mutations profondes dont les effets se font sentir sur l'ensemble des éléments constitutifs de la société. La période que nous vivons est jugée par les observateurs les plus avertis comme une période de transition, qualifiée par ceux qui la vivent, c'est-à-dire nous tous, comme une période de crise, avec tout ce que ce mot porte en lui-même : difficulté de donner du sens, difficulté d'interpréter et de démêler dans la pléthore des faits signifiants ceux qui portent en eux le germe d'un futur plus stabilisé. Certaines utopies de la fin de la décennie soixante, nées au milieu d'une croissance économique remarquable ont vité été balayées par le chômage. Le travail est redevenu valeur lorsqu'il est devenu rare. Les technologies nouvelles qui devaient libérer l'homme du travail sont à nouveau perçues souvent comme un mal en partie nécessaire, mais aussi créatrices de chômage et leur coût aussi bien que la résistance des hommes rend leur pénétration beaucoup plus lente que ne le prévoyaient les prospectivistes du milieu de la décennie. Les femmes se sont insérées sur le marché du travail, mais l'égalité de traitement avec les hommes, à laquelle elles aspirent est encore souvent à l'état d'esquisse.

Par contre, depuis le début des années 70, la famille a sans doute profondément évolué du fait même de l'évolution du statut du mariage. La législation sociale, le droit du travail, "les acquis sociaux" sont aujourd'hui perçus comme des freins partiels à l'adaptation du système productif. Dans l'ensemble des pays européens, la "déréglementation" est vue par beaucoup comme un des moyens de la flexibilité des entreprises, voire "le moyen" de sortie de la crise. Cette ambition d'une certaine conception de la souplesse et de l'adaptabilité des entreprises, s'appuie aussi sur un déclin relatif de la force des syndicats qui ont naturellement des difficultés à mobiliser des solidarités dans une période où la crainte très forte du chômage conduit chacun à un repli sur soi avec l'espoir secret que cela permettra au moins pour soi, d'éviter le chômage.

Le chômage pour sa part, par son importance et sa durée, et par les catégories de population qu'il touche, en particulier les jeunes, risque d'affecter très durablement, au-delà même des drames immédiats qu'il provoque, les attitudes et comportements, aussi bien à l'égard du travail que de la famille ou de l'organisation sociale.

Paradoxalement et dans le même temps, y compris dans les pays de la Communauté où la prise en charge par l'Etat d'un certain nombre de fonctions collectives est la plus forte, on voit se développer un mouvement associatif important dont le champ couvre largement l'ensemble des domaines de la vie civile et en particulier tout ce qui a trait à la qualité de la vie.

Ce contexte à peine esquissé, mais suffisamment connu pour qu'il ne soit pas nécessaire de s'y attarder, au-delà de ses grands traits communs, varie à l'évidence d'un pays à l'autre car l'interprétation culturelle d'une période de transition et de crise est tout à fait fondamentale. Ces variations culturelles seront à prendre en compte dans les recherches qui devront être conduites sur les formes nouvelles d'emplois sur la vie familiale et l'organisation sociale.

II - PROBLEMES DE METHODES : AMPLEUR DES CONCEPTS - ANALYSE DES CAUSALITES

Ce bref rappel de "l'environnement" de notre sujet souligne les difficultés de méthodes auxquelles il faudra être attentif tant pour la délimitation des projets de recherches, que pour l'interprétation des données. En effet, comme cela a été évoqué, les trois pôles de notre sujet sont actuellement soumis à de fortes turbulences qui perturbent soit radicalement, soit superficiellement leurs tendances propres et leurs inerties. Le champ même de chacun de ces pôles est relativement délicat à délimiter. Lorsqu'on parle de nouvelles formes d'emplois, on parle à l'évidence de formes très hétérogènes qui concernent aussi bien l'emploi salarié que l'emploi indépendant. Par ailleurs, certaines de ces formes, telles par exemple le travail à temps partiel ou le travail temporaire sont fort anciennes, alors que d'autres sont issues des progrès de la technologie et que certaines enfin sont peut-être simplement conjoncturelles. Le concept de famille s'élargit et se modifie. L'accroissement des couples non mariés ou des divorces modifie la répartition ou l'équilibre des rôles et des statuts au sein des couples. Que faut-il enfin entendre par organisation sociale ? Le concept peut être compris de manière très extensive et il englobe alors l'ensemble du champ social, ou au contraire, de manière plus restrictive tel qu'il est compris par exemple lorsque le terme "social" est opposé au terme "économique". Il s'agit alors de la législation sociale, des relations professionnelles, mais aussi de tout ce qui contribue à la qualité de la vie : logement, transports, urbanisme, etc...

S'il est nécessaire de bien préciser les concepts qui seront utilisés, il est tout aussi important de bien délimiter le champ assigné à notre problématique.

Il s'agit d'examiner les conséquences sur la vie familiale et l'organisation sociale des formes nouvelles d'emploi, tout en s'interrogeant sur le développement éventuel à court ou moyen terme de ces emplois.

Malgré sa formulation, le sujet implique qu'il ne soit pas traité de manière "mécanique", il vaudrait mieux dire "mécaniciste" pour au moins deux raisons :

- La première tient à ce qui a été évoqué précédemment.

    Si chacun des champs qu'il nous est demandé d'observer entretient avec les autres des relations étroites, chacun a aussi sa zone d'autonomie propre et les changements qui se produisent en leur sein ne doivent pas systématiquement être imputés à des actions externes (il serait ainsi hasardeux d'imputer le développement de la divorcialité au seul travail posté par exemple). Ce qui rend toutefois la tâche particulièrement difficile tient aux très importants changements que connaissent chacun des pôles. Il est toujours beaucoup plus aisé d'atteindre une cible fixe qu'une cible mouvante !

- La deuxième raison tient à ce que l'on pourrait nommer l'effet de système pris dans le sens le plus large du terme. Les formes nouvelles d'emploi ne se développent pas dans un environnement totalement perméable qui absorberait sans réagir les contraintes qui lui sont imposées. Là encore, l'analyse est très complexe. La crainte du chômage conduit à des comportements d'acceptation des formes nouvelles d'emploi beaucoup plus forts qu'en période de plein emploi. A titre d'exemple, et pour prendre le cas de la France mais qui, en l'occurence n'est pas un cas isolé, la majorité des Etats Majors syndicaux refusent l'annualisation de la durée du travail. Par contre, dans les entreprises, les partenaires sociaux n'hésitent pas à signer un nombre considérable d'accords dérogatoires.

On assiste à l'acceptation de certains changements face aux contraintes de l'environnement, mais aussi sans doute à des résistances fortes sur certains points (tels par exemple le travail de fin de semaine) qui entravent le développement prévisible de certaines formes d'emplois.

Il s'agira donc d'expliciter aussi clairement que possible, aussi bien les conséquences immédiates et futures de ces nouvelles formes d'emploi sur la vie familiale et l'organisation sociale, mais aussi les limites provoquées à ce développement par les exigences individuelles et collectives de la main-d'oeuvre.

III - LES NOUVELLES FORMES D'EMPLOI : DE QUOI PARLE-T-ON ?

La liste indicative des emplois qui est proposée à l'examen montre qu'il s'agit en fait d'observer tous les emplois qui ne correspondent pas au modèle dominant et devenu traditionnel, d'un emploi qui présente des caractéristiques spécifiques quant à son statut et son mode d'exercice.

3.1. Définition de l'emploi dit normal

Quant au statut, il s'agit d'un contrat de travail à durée indéterminée et dans le cas spécifique de la fonction publique, d'un emploi garanti sur l'ensemble de la vie active de l'individu.

Quant au mode d'exercice, il s'agit d'un emploi salarié qui s'exerce dans un lieu de travail extérieur au domicile, pendant une durée de temps et un rythme collectif régis par la législation ou les conventions collectives très homogènes.

Ce modèle, dont on trouve des traces assez anciennes dans l'histoire de nos sociétés, s'est généralisé avec la révolution industrielle pour devenir un véritable modèle dominant autour duquel se sont progressivement organisés les rythmes familiaux, mais aussi l'ensemble de l'organisation sociale.

C'est par rapport à ce modèle qu'il s'agit donc d'identifier toutes les formes déviantes dont certaines sont elles-mêmes assez anciennes, dont d'autres constituent la résurgence de formes d'emplois "pré-industriels" adaptées peut-être à nouveau aux évolutions d'une société qui deviendrait "post-industrielle", auxquelles il faut ajouter les innovations spécifiques à notre temps, innovations dues en grande partie aux technologies nouvelles.

La "déviance" par rapport à l'emploi traditionnel peut porter sur l'ensemble des éléments constitutifs de cet emploi "traditionnel" ou sur certains de ces éléments :

- Elle peut porter sur la nature du contrat de travail, par exemple contrat à durée déterminée par opposition à durée indéterminée, ou bien encore travail intérimaire.
Elle peut porter sur la durée et le rythme de travail, temps partiel, travail de week-end, travail à la demande, etc... Elle peut enfin porter sur le lieu d'exercice de l'activité, travail à domicile, travail à distance, etc...

Le premier travail à effectuer devrait donc consister à tenter d'identifier l'ensemble de ces formes nouvelles d'emploi par référence à l'emploi salarié traditionnel.

3.2. Une offre très différenciée

Ces formes nouvelles d'emploi , qu'il vaudrait peut-être mieux qualifier temporairement d'emplois "atypiques" puisque certaines formes, qualifiées de nouvelles sont en fait relativement anciennes, n'ont pas toutes et de loin, la même importance.

Parce qu'elles sont mal identifiées, un nombre non négligeable de ces formes d'emploi échappent aux recensements des systèmes statistiques nationaux. Hormis le travail à temps partiel, le travail intérimaire et les contrats à durée déterminée pour lesquels on a des connaissances statistiques assez fiables et sur une période assez longue pour en mesurer les tendances, les autres formes d'emplois aussi bien en volume qu'en évolution, sont largement méconnues.

Les innovations technologiques considérables de ces dernières années ont conduit de nombreux observateurs à formuler des hypothèses concernant le développement de certaines formes d'emploi liées à ces technologies, qui ont trop souvent été prises pour des réalités.

Parce que potentiellement, l'informatique permet une délocalisation du travail, on en déduit que cette délocalisation non seulement serait certaine, mais encore suivrait et serait proportionnelle au taux de pénétration de ces technologies. Or, malgré l'absence de données fiables, on connait assez bien par exemple, les expériences du télé-travail. Les évaluations de ces expériences aux Etats-Unis par exemple en soulignent aujourd'hui les limites et incitent à une très grande prudence à l'égard de leur développement futur, au moins à court terme. Le nombre des salariés concernés par ces emplois est encore très réduit et n'a sans doute pas encore atteint un seuil significatif pour devenir observable.

Par contre, on assiste aujourd'hui, semble-t-il, au développement d'un travail artisanal à domicile lié à l'externalisation d'un certain nombre de productions spécifiques. Les entreprises mettent à la disposition ou aident par exemple certains de leurs ouvriers qualifiés, à acheter un équipement performant pour la fabrication d'un produit et passent avec eux des contrats de sous-traitance. Cette forme nouvelle d'emploi dont il est aujourd'hui encore impossible d'évaluer le volume est dans certaines branches et dans certains pays, une forme très traditionnelle d'emploi. L'emploi dans l'industrie textile de la région de Prato au sud de Florence est identique à ce qui vient d'être décrit et a pourtant un très très long passé.

Ces quelques indicateurs d'un développement du travail à domicile ne sauraient nous permettre d'en déduire une tendance au développement important de ce type d'emplois dans les années à venir. Hormis les régions ou les quelques branches de forte tradition de travail à domicile, il apparaît nécessaire, au-delà du simple constat chiffré d'analyser les raisons qui conduisent les entreprises à ce type de pratique. S'il s'agit de raisons strictement conjoncturelles, il n'est pas évident que cette forme d'emplois dure et se développe. Par contre, si ces choix sont véritablement stratégiques, ces formes d'emplois devraient sans doute connaitre un développement relativement important dans les années à venir.

Le travail de fin de semaine tend à se développer et, semble-t-il, de manière sans doute durable car il repose sur une volonté de rentabilisation des équipements, mais aussi sur une demande accrue de l'accès à certains services et en particulier la distribution. Mais ce travail de fin de semaine peut prendre des formes très diverses. Il peut être une rotation du travail en équipes sur sept jours, auquel cas, les salariés concernés ne travaillent que de manière épisodique et régulièrement répétitive pendant le week-end : les conséquences sur la vie familiale et l'organisation sociale ne sont alors pas de même nature que s'il s'agit de salariés travaillant exclusivement le week-end. Mais là encore, combien sont concernés ?

Les formes d'emplois "atypiques" les plus connues, telles le travail à temps partiel ou le travail intérimaire connaissent dans l'ensemble une certaine stabilisation en volume. Ces formes d'emplois augmentent fortement aujourd'hui dans les pays qui y ont eu jusqu'à présent le moins recours. Dans ces pays là, elles se stabiliseront probablement au niveau atteint par les autres pays. Par contre, il semble que la forme même de ces emplois se modifie. Traditionnellement, le travail à temps partiel a été conçu comme un travail à mi-temps, réparti régulièrement sur la semaine de travail.

Progressivement, ce temps partiel qui recouvre un minimum d'heures reconnues par la législation ou un accord, prend des formes très diverses : temps plein sur la moitié de la semaine ; Temps partiel décalé en fonction des contraintes de service et dans certains cas, temps partiel sur l'année.

Les données statistiques disponibles sur le travail temporaire semblent indiquer une stabilisation en volume de ces formes d'emplois, dont le développement semble avoir été freiné en partie par une législation plus restrictive à son recours, mais aussi par l'extension de l'utilisation de contrats à durée déterminée qui sont venus semble-t-il, concurrencer le marché du travail intérimaire.

Enfin, divers articles mentionnent l'apparition de pratiques d'entreprises qui, pour des tâches spécifiques et pour une durée déterminée, feraient appel à un travailleur indépendant pour accomplir cette tâche. Ce type d'emploi s'apparente au travail de baby-sitter ou du pompier, il implique de la part des personnes le pratiquant, une très grande disponibilité. Il est toutefois très difficile de savoir combien sont concernés et pour quel type d'emplois.

Les entreprises ne sont pas les seules responsables de la création d'emplois "atypiques". Les pouvoirs publics dans leurs actions de lutte contre le chômage favorisent ou soutiennent aussi la création d'emplois que l'on peut aussi qualifier d'atypiques tels par exemple, les contrats de travaux d'utilité collective réservés en France aux jeunes chômeurs, contrats réservés à certaines catégories d'employeurs : collectivités locales, associations, entreprises ou fonction publique. Ces emplois visent à la fois une population et des employeurs spécifiques, mais aussi des travaux particuliers. Le chômage étant devenu, pour longtemps semble-t-il, une constante de l'univers du travail, il est permis de penser que ces formes particulières d'emplois, non seulement seront maintenues, mais connaitront aussi un développement important.

3.3. Des effectifs très variables par catégories d'emplois atypiques

Les données statistiques nationales ou européennes ne permettent guère d'appréhender l'importance des phénomènes qu'il nous est demandé d'observer, sauf, comme nous l'avons déjà dit, pour les formes plus traditionnelles d'emplois atypiques. Plusieurs interprétations peuvent être données aux carences de la statistique :

La première tient à la visibilité même des phénomènes observés. Chacune de ces formes particulières d'emploi représente des effectifs peut-être trop infimes pour pouvoir être saisis par les divers recensements. Si c'est le cas, il n'est peut-être pas forcément pertinent de s'intéresser à quelques phénomènes marginaux et de développer des recherches sur des problèmes mineurs alors que les connaissances sur les grandes évolutions contemporaines du travail sont très insuffisantes.

La seconde interprétation possible, probablement la plus juste, renvoie à la faible capacité descriptive des appareils statistiques nationaux. Cette faible capacité descriptive est grave dans la mesure même où elle oberre considérablement les possibilités prédictives de ces instruments. Elle tient essentiellement aux méthodologies de recueil de l'information : difficultés de recoupement des enquêtes auprès des employeurs avec les recensements de la population, ou les enquêtes auprès des ménages, mais surtout les questions posées ne permettent pas la mise à jour des faits nouveaux qui apparaissent dans la gestion de la main-d'oeuvre. Le cadre descriptif de l'emploi dans ces instruments statistiques est un cadre relativement traditionnel avec des catégories stéréotypées, très bien adaptées aux formes d'emplois traditionnelles du secteur de la production secondaire.

Si la première interprétation s'avérait juste, il serait peut-être inutile de lancer des recherches sur toutes ces formes atypiques d'emplois et il suffirait sans doute de se contenter d'étudier les conséquences sur la vie familiale et l'organisation sociale des principales formes d'emplois atypiques bien identifiées. Par contre, si la seconde interprétation est la plus fondée, ce que nous croyons, il faut alors donner la priorité à des recherches nationales comparatives dont l'objet serait dans un premier temps, d'identifier ces emplois atypiques dans toutes leurs dimensions.

Mais il faut sans doute aller plus loin et ne pas conclure trop hâtivement à la non pertinence d'une recherche sur ces formes nouvelles d'emplois s'il s'avérait que chacune d'entre elles, pris isolément, ne représenterait qu'un volume d'emplois très faible. Les hypothèses fondées sur des premières observations très empiriques indiquent leur développement et plus sûrement encore la recherche de formes alternatives à l'emploi classique. Le discours ambiant sur "la flexibilité" renforce cette hypothèse. La longue série de travaux de recherches conduits sur le travail posté décrivaient des formes relativement traditionnelles et stabilisées de rotations d'équipes même si, ici ou là, en fonction des contraintes de la production, on voyait poindre des formes plus atypiques. La crise économique, les mutations technologiques conduisent à une nouvelle approche de la rentabilisation des investissements productifs qui pénètrent aussi le secteur tertiaire. Le travail posté se développe sous des formes nouvelles et touche des secteurs jusque-là épargnés.

Diminution des coûts de main-d'oeuvre, rentabilisation des équipements, accroissement de la productivité conduisent à la recherche de formes nouvelles d'emploi : recours sous des formes diverses à une main-d'oeuvre non permanente pour des tâches ponctuelles, externalisation de certaines tâches, aménagement très diversifié du temps de travail. Ces éléments constituent un indice important de la modification profonde des formes traditionnelles d'exercice des emplois. Le sociologue français Georges FRIEDMAN, dès les années 60, voyait dans les premières formes d'automatisation et dans les premières expériences de réorganisation du travail, la marque de la fin du taylorisme comme modèle "orthodoxe" d'organisation du travail. La prolifération de ces formes nouvelles d'emploi marque peut-être aussi la fin d'une certaine orthodoxie en matière d'emploi. A ce titre, leur exploration et leur connaissance est fondamentale, même si tous les rameaux de ce nouvel arbre ne sont pas appelés à la même croissance. <u>C'est un système qui est destabilisé.</u>

Cette affirmation péremptoire mérite peut-être toutefois quelques nuances. Le discours sur la flexibilité pris dans son sens très large est un discours qui, par certains de ses aspects, est un discours plus "politique" que "réaliste". Il est incontestable que l'aménagement du temps de travail va prendre beaucoup plus d'ampleur dans les années à venir. La législation ou des accords de branches ou d'entreprises entérinent déjà ces pratiques.
Par contre, il n'est pas certain qu'il en aille de même pour les autres formes d'emploi. En effet, parallèlement à ce discours sur la flexibilité se développe aussi l'idée que la performance de l'entreprise n'est plus seulement le fait de la modernité de ses équipements ou de tout autre facteur, mais bien de la qualité et de la mobilisation de la main-d'oeuvre. Les entreprises commencent à penser que la main-d'oeuvre ne peut plus être considérée comme une simple variable d'ajustement mais bien comme l'élément essentiel autour duquel doivent être organisés les autres facteurs de production. (si cette idée non seulement se répand, mais est vraiment mise en pratique, elle sonnera vraiment le glas du Taylorisme).
Cercles de qualité, culture d'entreprise, groupes de projets, etc. essaient de concrétiser cette idée de mobilisation du personnel qui ne peut se construire qu'à partir d'un très fort sentiment d'appartenance. Or, ce sentiment ne peut se développer que si un lien durable existe pour le salarié avec son entreprise. Ce ne peut être le cas pour des salariés intérimaires, à contrat à durée déterminée ou même, comme le soulignent certains travaux américains le télé-travail ou le travail à domicile. En fait, les entreprises découvrent

que, sauf exceptions, si toutes les formes d'emplois présentent des avantages immédiats, les inconvénients à moyen terme peuvent être très élevés. On peut alors faire l'hypothèse que ces formes nouvelles ne sont que très temporaires et constituent des moyens d'ajustement conjoncturels dans une phase de profonde mutation.

IV - NECESSITE D'UNE TYPOLOGIE DES EMPLOIS ATYPIQUES

Dans la période de très fort chômage que connaissent tous les pays européens, l'offre d'emploi prévaut sur la demande, s'impose à la demande. La conjoncture favorise d'une certaine manière la marge de manoeuvre des entreprises en la matière. Elles peuvent en effet actuellement, soit imposer, soit obtenir par voie contractuelle de leurs salariés, des aménagements d'organisation du travail qui auraient sans doute été refusés en période de haute conjoncture. Mais, aussi bien pour les entreprises que pour les salariés, ces formes atypiques d'emplois ne sont pas toutes de même nature, tant s'en faut. Cette typologie doit permettre en effet de formuler les premières hypothèses sur les conséquences que ces formes nouvelles d'emplois sont susceptibles d'avoir sur la vie familiale et l'organisation sociale.

Pour élaborer cette typologie, on a retenu comme variable indépendante, mais ceci est à l'évidence sujet à discussion, le lieu d'exercice de l'emploi, la nature du contrat de travail, et le statut social pris dans son sens large, des salariés constituant, pour continuer à utiliser le vocabulaire des sociologues, les variables dépendantes ou explicatives des conséquences de ces formes atypiques d'emplois.

Le tableau 1 qui présente les grands traits de cette typologie mérite quelques commentaires. (Cf. tableau page 13).

Le premier critère de classement est effectivement le lieu d'exercice du travail selon qu'il est effectué à domicile ou au contraire, que le travail est exercé au sein d'un collectif de travail. Dans cette seconde catégorie, il faut distinguer les activités qui s'insèrent dans un collectif de travail unique ou au contraire, dans une multiplicité d'entreprises parce que ces deux types d'insertion n'ont pas les mêmes conséquences aussi bien pour l'entreprise que pour les salariés.

Certaines formes d'emplois atypiques peuvent se retrouver dans plusieurs catégories. Les nouvelles technologies, par leur souplesse d'utilisation, permettent des modalités très diverses d'utilisation. Ainsi, le télé-travail peut s'exercer soit à domicile, soit dans des antennes éloignées de l'entreprise, mais où l'on regroupe quelques salariés de l'entreprise qui effectuent à distance le travail qui leur est demandé.

Le travail à domicile pour sa part échappe par essence à tous les rythmes de travail imposé. Il s'agit d'un volume de travail qui est commandé à une personne qui l'effectue au moment qui lui convient le mieux : week-end, etc...

La nature du contrat de travail "croise" plusieurs types d'emplois atypiques indépendamment du lieu d'exercice de l'emploi. Le télé-travail à domicile peut se concevoir avec un contrat à durée indéterminée ou avec un statut de travailleur indépendant. Par contre, certaines formes d'emplois impliquent un statut spécifique : un contrat à durée déterminée ou travail indépendant.

Cette typologie sommaire semble autoriser un premier classement de l'ensemble des emplois atypiques, mais permet aussi d'esquisser une problématique des conséquences de ces formes d'emplois sur la vie familiale et l'organisation sociale, à condition que cette problématique ne soit pas conçue de manière mécanique mais qu'elle s'articule au moins sur le statut social des personnes concernées par ce type d'emplois.

TABLEAU 1 - TYPOLOGIE DES EMPLOIS ATYPIQUES

LIEU D'EXERCICE	TYPES D'EMPLOIS	NATURE DU CONTRAT DE TRAVAIL
Entreprise unique	- temps partiel (sous toutes ses formes) - travail de week-end - travail posté (12 heures) - temps plein réduit - télé travail etc...	- contrat à durée déterminée - contrat à durée indéterminée
Multiplicité d'entreprises	- travail temporaire - travail sous contrat - groupement d'emplois - "on call" work etc...	- contrat à durée déterminée - travailleur indépendant
Travail à domicile	- télé travail - travail sous contrat - "on call" work	- contrat à durée indéterminée - déterminée - travailleur indépendant

V - UNE PROBLEMATIQUE DES CONSEQUENCES

Une problématique des conséquences des formes atypiques d'emplois et de leur éventuel développement sur la vie familiale et l'organisation sociale n'est pas indépendante de leur volume et des personnes concernées par ce type d'emplois.

Plusieurs problèmes de nature différente doivent être pris en compte dans l'élaboration de cette problématique qui, pour ne pas être totalement abstraite et intellectuelle devra se fonder sur une connaissance beaucoup plus précise de la réalité que celle que nous avons actuellement.

5.1. Les populations concernées

Le premier problème, et probablement le problème fondamental, est l'identification des populations concernées par ces formes atypiques d'emplois. Les formes les plus traditionnelles de ces emplois atypiques sont occupées par des populations spécifiques : l'emploi à temps partiel dans tous les pays est un emploi féminin, c'est un emploi peu ou moyennement qualifié ; Le travail temporaire, sauf exception, concerne davantage une main-d'oeuvre mixte, mais également caractérisée par un faible niveau de qualification ; Le travail exclusif de week-end, les travaux d'utilité collective sont plutôt réservés aux jeunes. Pour ce que l'on en sait, il semble donc que les emplois atypiques offerts en règle générale, sont des emplois peu qualifiés occupés par une main-d'oeuvre qui a des difficultés pour des raisons diverses à s'insérer normalement dans le marché du travail. Par ailleurs, les informations dont on dispose sur ces emplois nous fournissent les "stocks" à un moment donné. Il faudrait suivre les cohortes qui passent par ces emplois pour savoir si ils correspondent à un moment spécifique de la vie active des salariés, ou au contraire, s'ils sont des emplois permanents sur l'ensemble d'une vie professionnelle.

Le travail temporaire semble être un moyen d'accès à l'emploi permanent pour des jeunes disposant soit d'un diplôme technique spécifique, et pour les moins jeunes sans aucune qualification. Il en va de même pour les contrats à durée déterminée. L'emploi indépendant qui semble se développer touche, semble-t-il, des populations beaucoup plus diversifiées et au niveau de qualification beaucoup plus élevé. L'emploi indépendant se développe dans des secteurs qui ont recours à des emplois qui se sont exercés de manière artisanale, tels les transports routiers et le bâtiment. Cette description rapide indique bien que les conséquences de ces formes atypiques d'emplois sur la vie familiale et l'organisation sociale ne sauraient être les mêmes selon les populations concernées, et surtout selon que ces populations exercent ce type d'emplois de manière durable ou non.

5.2. L'effet de système

Le deuxième aspect à prendre en compte dans une problématique des conséquences est celui du système que forment entre eux, les trois éléments que nous devons observer. L'hypothèse centrale sous-jacente à la question qu'il nous est demandé d'explorer est que les déséquilibres (le terme étant pris ici dans son sens neutre) qui peuvent se produire dans l'un de ses éléments, ont des effets sur les autres et inversement. La question est de savoir si les réciprocités et les forces de ces différents éléments sont identiques.

D'une certaine manière, le discours qui se développe aujourd'hui sur la nécessaire flexibilité des entreprises, comprise avant tout comme une flexibilité de l'emploi essaie de fonder sa rationalité sur la réciprocité de ces éléments. Les tenants des théories de la flexibilité la justifie par la nécessité pour les entreprises de s'adapter aux contraintes du marché, mais aussi comme une réponse à une forte demande de la population active.
A titre d'exemple, sont cités les horaires variables qui, contrairement à la position initiale de nombreuses organisations syndicales qui s'y sont opposées, correspondaient à une demande de la population active aussi bien qu'à un besoin des entreprises, (mais il ne s'agit pas vraiment là d'emplois atypiques). Justifient aussi cette analyse les grandes difficultés rencontrées par les entreprises lorsqu'elles souhaitent modifier le système de rotation du travail posté ou même le diminuer, essayant par là de démontrer que ce sont les salariés qui sont demandeurs de ce type d'organisation. En fait, de nombreuses études soulignent que si le temps de travail est un temps contraint, le temps familial et le temps de la vie sociale le sont aussi. Ces temps s'ajustent au temps de travail, mais une fois l'équilibre trouvé, toute perturbation importante est vécue avec beaucoup de réticence par les personnes concernées.

Dans l'analyse des conséquences des formes atypiques d'emplois, il est donc tout à fait important de construire une typologie de ces formes en les observant du côté des salariés qui les occupent et en fonction de leur durée et de leur rythme. La vie familiale par exemple, finit par s'organiser et trouver une certaine régularité, même si les parents travaillent en équipe ou à temps partiel... Par contre, les moments de rupture dans les rythmes traditionnels de travail, même s'ils sont atypiques sont en général très mal vécus s'ils impliquent des ajustements brutaux. Ces rigidités, ces temps sociaux contraints externes à la vie de travail expliquent peut-être que ces emplois atypiques soient occupés par des populations spécifiques qui n'ont pas les moyens de gérer aisément les aléas que font peser sur la vie familiale et sociale ce type d'emplois.

Comme le démontre magistralement Herbert SIMON, les entreprises ont dans le domaine de l'organisation, de faibles capacités de véritable innovation. Lorsqu'elles envisagent le développement d'emplois atypiques, implicitement ou explicitement, elles se réfèrent à des expériences réussies ici ou là, et qui parfois sont très anciennes. Ainsi, dans l'industrie textile italienne, le travail à domicile qui a une histoire très ancienne semble ne poser aucun problème majeur, ni pour la vie familiale, ni pour l'organisation sociale, qui se sont ordonnées depuis longtemps à cette réalité.
Un autre exemple de même nature pourrait être trouvé dans les activités de décolletage de la vallée de la Maurienne.
En fait, ces expériences ne sont que très partiellement probantes à cause de leur durée même. Dans ces deux cas, le système social et familial et le système de travail ont trouvé un mode de régulation adéquat, précisément à cause de l'ancienneté de l'expérience, et donc de "la culture", ce terme étant ici pris dans son sens anthropologique, qu'ils ont permis de développer. Ce qui serait perturbant serait là le retour à une forme d'emploi traditionnel.

5.3. L'existence de passerelles entre emploi traditionnel et emploi atypique

Dans cette problématique, il est tout aussi important de prendre en compte les passerelles qui existent entre ces formes atypiques d'emplois et les emplois plus traditionnels en fonction des événements susceptibles d'intervenir sans la vie des personnes concernées. Le travail à mi-temps est-il un travail à vie ou correspond-il à une souplesse accordée par exemple aux jeunes mères de famille qui souhaitent à un moment donné plus de liberté ? Est-il une contrainte vécue par les salariés comme une astreinte ou au contraire comme une liberté supplémentaire ? La même question pourrait être posée pour le travail temporaire, les contrats à durée déterminée, certaines formes d'emplois à domicile, voire même le travail indépendant.

Une telle problématique dans les recherches qui devraient être développées, permettrait d'éviter les visions par trop manichéennes ou déterministes souvent associées à ces formes atypiques d'emplois. Si il s'avérait que celles-ci touchent exclusivement certaines catégories de la population, qu'elles constituent des contraintes imposées et aléatoires, <u>ce qui est par ailleurs probable</u>, elles renforceraient la thèse des chercheurs qui depuis de nombreuses années déjà, dénoncent une dualisation croissante du marché du travail . Mais il faut aussi peut-être éviter de "jeter le bébé avec l'eau du bain". Sous un certain nombre de conditions dont les exemples nous sont soumis par les formes d'emplois atypiques traditionnelles, elles peuvent être source d'équilibre et de liberté. Reste à identifier clairement ces conditions.

VI - L'ORGANISATION SOCIALE ET LA VIE FAMILIALE

Les formes atypiques d'emplois ont des conséquences spécifiques sur chacun de ces deux domaines. Toutefois, les relations qui existent entre ces deux domaines et l'univers du travail sont telles qu'il apparaît indispensable d'analyser comment ces relations sont susceptibles d'atténuer ou d'accentuer les effets positifs et négatifs des formes particulières d'emplois sur chacun d'entre eux.

6.1. Un équilibre rigide

L'industrialisation a eu entre autre pour caractéristique de soumettre l'organisation sociale et la vie familiale à ses contraintes propres. Cela ne s'est pas fait sans résistances fortes, voire même des révoltes qui ont conduit à des aménagements du système du travail. Le syndicalisme est d'ailleurs né de ces réactions.

Après une période d'intense mutation, une sorte d'équilibre relativement stable s'est progressivement construit entre ces trois domaines, cet équilibre n'excluant pas des rigidités et des zones fortes de dysfonctionnement atténuées ou rendues moins visibles par la période de croissance exceptionnelle qu'ont connue les sociétés industrielles développées, que certains économistes ont qualifié de "trente glorieuses". La croissance remarquable des niveaux de vie, l'élévation des niveaux de formation, l'aspiration à l'égalité sexuelle entre autres, ont conduit à l'émergence d'une revendication nouvelle concernant la qualité de la vie, d'abord hors travail mais aussi dans le travail. Pour reprendre un slogan syndical qui sous des formes diverses a connu un important succès en Europe autour des années 70, "on ne voulait plus perdre sa vie à la gagner".

Cet investissement dans le "hors travail" a été accompagné ou a eu pour conséquence une véritable crise du travail. A partir de la deuxième moitié des années 60 jusqu'au premier choc pétrolier, les travaux de recherche se sont multipliés sur cette "crise" du travail qui cessait d'être une "valeur", on a même parlé à l'époque d'une véritable "allergie" au travail des jeunes et peut-être aussi des adultes !

Les entreprises ont de diverses manières réagi à cette crise. Le mouvement pour l'amélioration de la qualité de la vie au travail a connu dans tous les pays industriels un essor important. Sans modifier radicalement l'organisation du travail, les entreprises ont essayé de répondre aux demandes des salariés à plus d'autonomie, de responsabilités, et elles ont fait des efforts importants pour diminuer l'ensemble des nuisances existant sur les lieux de travail.

Sans entrer dans le détail de ce mouvement, des réalisations auxquelles il a conduit, et des analyses qui en ont été faites, il apparaît aujourd'hui comme un renversement de tendance radicale par rapport à la période qui l'a précédé. En poussant le trait, on pourrait dire qu'il a été une revanche de l'environnement, de l'organisation sociale et de la famille sur le travail. C'était au travail et à son organisation de se plier aux contraintes de la vie familiale et de l'organisation sociale.

Pour illustrer ce phénomène, on peut prendre l'exemple des horaires flexibles dont la mise en place a été révélatrice à la fois de l'équilibre trouvé par le système et des dysfonctions qu'il avait engendrées.

La raison principale avancée par les entreprises à la mise en place de ce système reposait sur la volonté de diminuer l'absentéisme et en particulier de l'absentéisme féminin. Une analyse de cet absentéisme a fait apparaître qu'il était dû à des rigidités existant dans l'organisation sociale et l'environnement de l'entreprise : difficulté de garde des enfants pendant les congés scolaires ou les maladies, difficultés d'accès à certains services dont le rythme de travail était identique à celui des entreprises. L'offre d'un horaire variable a en règle générale, été accueilli très favorablement par les salariés. Par contre, dans un premier temps, et malgré cet accueil, il a soulevé l'hostilité des organisations syndicales qui y ont vu une atteinte directe à l'exercice du droit syndical. L'horaire variable était le début d'un démantèlement du collectif de travail. De manière plus pragmatique, il rendait plus difficile l'information et le contact avec les salariés par les militants syndicaux. Cette protestation syndicale n'a pas survécu à l'absence de soutien des salariés concernés.

La crise économique et en particulier le chômage, renverse à nouveau les tendances qui s'étaient faites jour à la fin de la période de croissance, sans pour autant qu'il y ait un retour à la situation précédente. En fait, plusieurs éléments se conjuguent aujourd'hui, porteurs peut-être d'un équilibre nouveau entre ces différents sous-systèmes.

Le travail redevient une valeur, non seulement parce qu'il est redevenu rare, mais aussi parce qu'il change de nature. Même si elles ne mettent pas encore en oeuvre de manière massive cette nouvelle philosophie, les entreprises ont semble-t-il, pris conscience que la main-d'oeuvre ne pouvait plus être considérée comme la variable "d'ajustement", mais qu'elle était au coeur de performance productive. Les nouvelles technologies ne peuvent produire leurs effets bénéfiques que si elles sont mises en oeuvre par une main d'oeuvre qualifiée et motivée. Pour reprendre l'heureuse expression d'un très récent rapport du Commissariat Général du Plan en France "on passe avec les nouvelles technologies, d'une civilisation de la peine à une civilisation de la panne". L'enjeu devient alors la correction rapide de "la panne", ce qui ne peut se faire que grâce à l'intelligence et non la force musculaire.

Dans le même temps, l'organisation sociale tente à son tour de devenir moins rigide. Une complémentarité entre les différents horaires de travail se développe peu à peu, qui conduit inéluctablement au développement de formes nouvelles d'emploi. Développement du travail en deux équipes, mais aussi travail du week-end et annualisation des horaires de travail. Même les services publics envisagent aujourd'hui une plus grande flexibilité de leur fonctionnement.

Ce système plus souple de travail, ces formes nouvelles d'emploi impliquent cependant des adaptations de l'organisation sociale dans son ensemble et de la vie familiale en particulier.

La crise économique fonde aujourd'hui la demande de souplesse et cette demande s'appuie sur une forte pression collective. Les avantages "acquis" sur le travail par la sphère du "non travail" pendant la période de forte croissance sont présentés comme autant de rigidités qui font obstacle à l'adaptabilité. On assiste de fait à un retournement complet de la problématique développée à la fin des années 1960. "Gagner sa vie" est à nouveau un enjeu majeur. Le risque est de voir cet enjeu "tenu" à n'importe quel prix, c'est-à-dire en ignorant totalement les contraintes propres des univers externes à l'entreprise, chaque entreprise se fondant sur ses seules contraintes pour s'organiser. Le système très uniforme d'organisation que nous avons connu dans les précédentes années risque d'être remplacé, si le retour de balancier va trop loin, par un système extraordinairement diversifié, en particulier d'aménagement du temps de travail pouvant conduire à l'instauration d'un système anomique. Paradoxalement, ce système anomique pourrait conduire aux mêmes résultats que le système qu'il est amené à remplacer. Si la régulation de l'aménagement du temps de travail et de formes particulières d'emploi dépendent du seul niveau de l'entreprise, voire de l'établissement, on peut aboutir à autant de systèmes spécifiques que d'entreprises. A nouveau, l'univers du travail exigera de l'environnement social et de la vie familiale une soumission totale à ses contraintes. Poussé à son extrême, un tel système peut altérer gravement toutes les formes de vie sociale.

Sans prétendre à l'exhaustivité et sans hiérarchiser les questions évoquées, un certain nombre de points doivent donc être soulevés.

6.2. L'insertion dans des espaces de travail

Autour des années 70, économistes et sociologues du travail, face au début de l'introduction des nouvelles technologies, mais aussi du développement de formes d'emplois diversifiées (travail temporaire, contrats à durée déterminée, temps partiel) ont développé une double thèse dont certains éléments se recoupaient partiellement : celle de la dualisation du marché du travail et de la "polarisation des qualifications". Les recherches actuelles conduisent à une remise en cause de ces analyses, en particulier sur celles qui concernent la qualification. Plutôt que de déqualification, les chercheurs observent le développement de nouvelles formes de qualification qui se dissocieraient de plus en plus d'un certain déterminisme technique pour acquérir un contenu plus social. Les chercheurs européens utilisent d'ailleurs plus volontiers aujourd'hui les notions de "professionnalité" "d'espace professionnel" ou de "professionnalisation" que la notion de qualification. Marc MAURICE va jusqu'à écrire : "la qualification du travail tend à être davantage conceptualisée aujourd'hui en référence aux "rapports sociaux" dans lesquels elle s'inscrit et qu'elle peut aussi bien contribuer à développer. Par rapport à la notion classique de qualification ("SKILL") qui se définit davantage en termes de "niveaux" correspondant à une "classification" hiérarchisée des "postes" de travail, celle de professionnalité renvoie davantage aux processus de socialisation professionnelle par lesquels le travailleur acquiert et développe l'ensemble des savoirs et des savoir-faire (qui constituent sa capacité productive) au sein des "espaces de travail" qu'il tend à maîtriser au cours de sa carrière, en coopération ou en compétition avec d'autres. Dans ce cas, la formation scolaire initiale ne détermine qu'un potentiel que l'entreprise s'efforcera de développer par une gestion de la mobilité interne et des carrières ; en ce sens, les diplômes détermineront moins qu'avant la nature d'une "qualification" spécifique. Ils seront plutôt associés à un processus de socialisation par mobilités successives intra-entreprises ou inter-entreprises.

Si cette analyse de la qualification est juste, elle pose bien des questions à l'égard du développement des formes atypiques d'emplois. En ce qui les concerne, la question est alors de savoir comment ces formes nouvelles d'emplois s'inscrivent dans ces "espaces de travail" qui permettent le développement de savoir et de savoir-faire. La typologie de ces formes d'emplois montrent que tous n'offrent pas les mêmes possibilités en la matière. Mais là encore, tout dépend des catégories concernées, des possibilités de mobilité qu'elles offrent, mais aussi de l'organisation sociale qu'elles suscitent.

6.3. Les droits individuels et collectifs

Exemplaire à cet égard est l'évolution du travail temporaire en France. Pendant de nombreuses années, cette forme d'emploi a été considérée comme une des formes les plus élaborées d'exploitation de la main-d'oeuvre. Réservés aux emplois les moins qualifiés, au mieux, ces emplois permettraient une insertion progressive au sein d'un système d'emplois plus stables, à moins qu'ils ne permettent une marginalisation voulue à l'égard du travail, conçue comme un mal inévitable. Dans la majorité des cas, ils servaient à gérer les aléas de fonctionnement de l'entreprise et étaient subis plus que souhaités par la main-d'oeuvre qui y avait recours. Une législation plus restrictive du recours à ce type d'emplois, mais aussi un développement de l'organisation des salariés ont conduit à la négociation et à la signature d'un accord garantissant des droits collectifs et individuels (exercice du droit syndical et accès à la formation) aux salariés des entreprises de travail temporaire. Les résultats sont aujourd'hui significatifs puisque le niveau de qualification des travailleurs temporaires s'est très sensiblement élevé.

Ces possibilités d'organisation ne sont pas identiques pour toutes les formes d'emplois atypiques et on voit bien les différences qui peuvent exister par exemple entre le travail temporaire et les contrats à durée déterminée qui offrent beaucoup moins de capacité d'organisation des salariés bénéficiant de ce type de contrat.

Ces remarques sont encore plus fondées concernant le travail à domicile qui peut définitivement éloigner le travailleur des processus de qualification professionnelle, mais aussi limitent considérablement les contrôles ayant trait à l'exercice du travail sur la santé du travailleur.

Ces formes nouvelles d'emplois peuvent incontestablement contribuer à une expérience professionnelle élargie ; elles contribuent à développer la capacité d'adaptation des salariés. Encore faut-il que le système de travail dominant le reconnaisse. Le travail à temps partiel cantonné aux emplois les moins qualifiés et qu'on ne souhaite pas faire évoluer risque de priver les salariés de possibilités de mobilité ultérieure, même si, sur le court terme, il répond à une contrainte économique ou à une demande d'une main-d'oeuvre qui a temporairement besoin de plus de temps disponible pour gérer des contraintes de la vie hors travail.

Pour que les conséquences sur les travailleurs de ces formes nouvelles d'emplois ne soient pas négatives, il faut qu'un certain nombre de conditions puissent être remplies qui ont trait aux droits individuels et collectifs. Ceci implique aussi un changement des comportements des organisations professionnelles qui doivent à leur tour inventer de nouvelles pratiques pour s'adapter aux évolutions du travail.

Conséquences sur la formation, sur la qualification, sur la mobilité et sur l'exercice des droits collectifs, ces formes nouvelles d'emplois affectent bien d'autres aspects de l'organisation sociale ayant des conséquences directes ou indirectes sur la vie familiale.

6.4. Les contraintes sur l'aménagement des espaces

L'industrialisation s'est partout accompagnée d'un important développement urbain. Ce développement a eu pour tous avantages et inconvénients. En règle générale, pour le sujet qui nous concerne, il s'est traduit par un allongement des temps de trajet domicile-travail, et par une politique du logement conçu comme un lieu réservé exclusivement à la vie familiale.

Les transports urbains se sont adaptés aux horaires normaux de travail. En règle générale, cela s'est traduit par une surcharge des réseaux aux heures de pointe correspondant aux heures de début et de fin de travail, identiques pour l'ensemble de la population. Les entreprises ayant massivement recours au travail posté ont souvent dû créer leur propre système de transport. Les horaires variables ont permis aux salariés, outre les avantages déjà cités, d'utiliser ces transports à des heures moins chargées, diminuant ainsi la fatigue quotidienne due à ces transports. Dans tous les cas, les statistiques dont on dispose font apparaître un temps de trajet quotidien entre le domicile et le lieu de travail qui peut être considérable. Ce temps incompressible rend beaucoup moins attrayant le travail à temps partiel. Le développement des emplois atypiques rend prioritaire une amélioration des transports et, dans ce domaine, beaucoup reste à faire.

Amélioration des transports, mais aussi du logement. Certains pays ont mis en oeuvre des politiques spécifiques concernant la qualité des logements des travailleurs postés et en particulier, la qualité d'insonorisation de ces logements. Il n'en reste pas moins que l'ensemble des rythmes familiaux sont perturbés par ce type d'emplois. Sur ce sujet au moins, les recherches abondent qui permettent de bien cerner l'ensemble des problèmes qui y ont trait, et une partie des solutions qui peuvent y être apportées.

6.5. La mutualisation des risques
Au-delà de ces problèmes spécifiques et relativement bien identifiés, les formes atypiques d'emplois apparaissent encore mal acceptées par l'organisation sociale en général, et font reposer sur le seul travailleur et éventuellement sa famille, l'ensemble des risques qui sont dans d'autres circonstances pris en charge par la collectivité. Les problèmes varient d'un pays à l'autre, ils y ont une acuité plus ou moins forte, dans tous les cas, ils se posent.

Un salarié permanent d'une entreprise a accès à diverses formes de crédit. Il a accès à un certain nombre de facilités offertes directement ou indirectement par le biais des prélèvements obligatoires aux salariés de ces entreprises. Outre l'accès à la formation permanente déjà mentionnée, il existe en effet, selon des formes diverses et avec une importance qui varie en fonction de la taille des entreprises, des possibilités de prêts complémentaires pour l'accession à la propriété, des services collectifs d'achats pour les biens de consommation courants. Des centres collectifs de vacances et de loisirs sont mis à sa disposition pour lui-même et sa famille. Ces avantages indirects dont la liste n'est pas exhaustive sont exclus pour certaines formes d'emplois atypiques.

Cette exclusion n'est pas sans conséquence sur la vie familiale. Elle n'est pas sans conséquence non plus sur les catégories de population qui ont recours à ces emplois. S'il est démontré que certains de ces emplois sont occupés par des catégories spécifiques de la population, il faut peut-être rechercher dans les conséquences indirectes qui viennent d'être mentionnées, les raisons de cette ségrégation. Les jeunes qui n'arrivent à trouver que des contrats à durée déterminée ou temporaire ne peuvent aisément s'insérer dans une organisation sociale qui ne tolère que difficilement toutes les formes d'incertitude que fait peser ce type d'emploi sur ceux qui les occupent. Ceci est d'autant plus vrai que le statut de ces emplois offerts est peu qualifié. Ces emplois atypiques présentent donc pour certains un risque de marginalisation professionnelle d'autant plus grand qu'il se cumulerait avec un risque de marginalisation sociale.

6.6. Le développement possible d'une économie souterraine

Le développement de ces emplois atypiques, quelle que soit leur forme, conduit enfin aujourd'hui sans doute à un développement non négligeable de ce que les économistes nomment l'économie souterraine.

Les résultats des travaux de recherches sur le travail posté et en particulier sur les nuisances induites par certaines formes de rotation ont conduit les entreprises spontanément ou sous la pression des pouvoirs publics et des organisations syndicales, à modifier les rythmes des rotations. En règle générale, ces modifications se sont heurtées à une forte résistance des salariés concernés, non seulement parce que ces changements modifiaient les équilibres du temps hors travail et ceux de la vie familiale, mais aussi parce que cela conduisait à une remise en cause d'une activité secondaire, non seulement lucrative, mais aussi souvent vécue comme constituant un travail autonome et épanouissant.

Le travail à temps partiel, en se modifiant, peut conduire également à un tel développement. Un accord vient d'être signé en France dans une entreprise qui propose non plus un mi-temps sur la semaine, mais sur l'année. Six mois d'activités pleines correspondant aux activités saisonnières de l'entreprise et six mois de temps libre. Peut-on raisonnablement espérer que ces six mois se traduiront par six mois de vacances pour des salariés qui ne touche- tont un salaire que pour six mois de l'année ? Mais le travail à temps par- tiel lui-même n'échappe pas à ce type de conséquences, surtout lorsque le temps de trajet ne vient pas altérer les avantages de ce type d'emplois.

Travail temporaire, contrats à durée déterminée, travail exclusif de fin de semaine, mais aussi travail à domicile, vont favoriser le développement d'un travail "au noir" qui peut lui aussi prendre des formes très diverses.

L'organisation sociale supporte mal cette économie souterraine qui échappe à tout contrôle et en particulier, au prélèvement fiscal auquel elle de- vrait donner lieu. Cette forme de travail a été réputée caractériser cer- tains pays du sud de l'Europe et en particulier l'Italie. Des rapports récents indiquent qu'elle connaît un important développement en France, mais aussi en Angleterre et en Allemagne. Si certaines mesures peuvent éventuellement en limiter les effets nocifs, il serait hasardeux de vou- loir la contrôler totalement sans soulever des résistances très fortes de tous ceux pour qui cette forme de travail est aussi un moyen d'épanouisse- ment.

6.7. Les conséquences sur la vie familiale

Les principaux effets de ces formes nouvelles d'emplois sur l'organisa- tion sociale suggèrent un certain nombre de conséquences qu'elles sont susceptibles d'avoir sur la vie familiale.

Les travaux déjà conduits pour la Fondation sur le travail posté et les très nombreuses observations faites dans les différents pays européens in- diquent que la donnée majeure, le point central à prendre en compte est le fait que les temps de la vie familiale sont des temps tout aussi contraints que ceux du travail. Le rythme de vie des enfants, le temps des loisirs, de la vie intime sont subordonnés à des rythmes biologiques et sociaux qui ne sont pas modifiables sans danger pour eux. Toutes les formes particulières d'emplois qui portent sur des aménagements spécifiques du temps de travail ne doivent pas ignorer ces contraintes. Il serait très dangereux de les ré- server à des populations spécifiques (jeunes célibataires ou salariés plus âgés par exemple). Mais il apparait aussi important de veiller à ne pas perturber fréquemment les rythmes choisis. La régularité des rythmes de travail, même s'ils sont atypiques, permet une organisation de la vie familiale qui supporte mal les changements fréquents.

Il est frappant à cet égard de constater à quel point spontanément les salariés, lorsque des horaires variables leur sont proposés, adoptent pour eux-mêmes, au sein de cette souplesse, des horaires fixes. Le même exemple nous est fourni concernant les difficultés de modification de notation des équipes postées.

La vie familiale évolue elle aussi. Les contraintes ne sont pas les mêmes selon l'âge des enfants. Les équilibres entre vie familiale et vie de travail doivent donner lieu à des ajustements qui devraient pouvoir être régulés par le contrat collectif, voire même la législation.

Le travail à domicile implique pour sa part, quelle que soit l'activité exercée, un aménagement de l'espace interne de la maison qui rende possible cette activité. Les logements urbains se prêtent peu à cette activité. L'universitaire qui dispose chez lui d'un bureau peut sans doute sans difficultés, utiliser un micro-ordinateur. Il n'est pas évident que la secrétaire puisse diposer aisément de la place suffisante chez elle pour l'installation d'une machine à traitement de texte .

Au-delà de l'ensemble des contraintes que l'on pourrait qualifier de physiques que risquent de faire peser sur la vie familiale ces formes particulières d'emploi , il en est d'autres plus subtiles qui sont sans doute d'ordre culturel et psychologique. La révolution industrielle a séparé univers du travail et vie familiale, et cette coupure a été en elle-même une véritable révolution sur la vie familiale et la socialisation des enfants. D'un univers fusionnel on est passé à deux univers qui s'ignorent au point aujourd'hui que les enfants ne connaissent que très peu de choses de la profession de leurs parents. Cette rupture a forcément eu des conséquences durables sur le façonnement des mentalités collectives et des psychologies individuelles. Quelles conséquences aurait alors un nouveau développement du travail à domicile ? La réponse, sur ce point, des recherches des psychologues est tout à fait fondamentale.

Certaines formes d'emplois atypiques occupés principalement par des jeunes, contrats à durée déterminée, travail du week-end, posent des problèmes spécifiques à cette catégorie de population pour la conquête de son indépendance et la création d'un foyer. Les revenus instables associés à ces emplois précaires, la difficulté de développer un véritable projet professionnel contribuent à marginaliser ce groupe, ce qui n'est pas sans risque pour l'avenir.

*
* *

Lorsque l'on traite du fonctionnement d'un système humain, les problématiques centrées sur une analyse des conséquences se sont très souvent avérées être des problématiques dangereuses, car fortement réductrices de la réalité. Sans se référer spécifiquement aux grandes théories explicatives du changement, l'exemple contemporain des recherches sur "les conséquences" des nouvelles technologies sur l'emploi ou la qualification devrait inciter à la plus extrême prudence. Trop de recherches ont prêté aux technologies des qualités ou des vertus qu'elles ne possèdent pas en propre, contribuant ainsi à créer une mythologie, des frayeurs ou des espoirs qui se sont perdus dans les sables mouvants de la réalité sociale.

Il en va de même pour l'analyse des formes d'emplois atypiques. Par rapport à la référence de l'emploi dit "normal", ces formes d'emplois atypiques se sont construites à partir d'une "déviance" portant sur l'un ou plusieurs des trois éléments constitutifs de ce contrat "normal" à savoir : le statut du contrat à durée indéterminée, le lieu d'exercice du travail et la durée et le rythme de travail. Une observation statistique rétrospective semble indiquer une stagnation des emplois atypiques par leur statut ou par leur lieu d'exercice, alors que les emplois atypiques associés à une durée et à un rythme de travail particuliers semblent connaitre une très forte expansion.

Trois facteurs se conjuguent aujourd'hui qui renforcent cette tendance : demande d'adaptabilité de la part des entreprises qui souhaitent pouvoir utiliser plus longtemps ou mieux, leurs équipements, revendication des organisations syndicales qui voient dans la réduction et l'aménagement du temps de travail un moyen de réduction du chômage. Souhait enfin de la population salariée pour qui le temps plus que l'espace est vécu comme la contrainte majeure.

Mais cette évolution des rythmes de travail, cette "dérégulation" du temps rejaillit très fortement sur l'organisation sociale et la vie familiale. La souplesse dans un domaine induit celle des autres. Comment organiser une société qui, potentiellement, peut travailler 24 heures sur 24 ? Comment éviter que cette société ne devienne totalement anomique ? Comment préserver l'exercice plein et entier de la citoyenneté ? Comment enfin préserver les rythmes de vie familiaux dont les contraintes sont strictes ?

On peut vouloir en particulier au nom de la défense et du développement de l'emploi, ignorer totalement les contraintes qui pèsent sur la vie familiale et l'organisation sociale et s'attacher exclusivement à l'univers du travail en le libérant de toutes les contraintes apparentes ou réelles qui semblent entraver son dynamisme et son expansion. On risque alors de constater bien des effets pervers de cette déréglementation sur le système social pris dans son sens large. Pour avoir trop souvent été peu attentif ou même avoir méconnu le système de travail dans lequel on introduisait de nouvelles technologies, celles-ci n'ont souvent pas permis d'atteindre les résultats qu'on en escomptait quant à l'efficience globale du système et dans certains cas, elles se sont même révélées contre productives.
Il en va de même pour le sujet qui nous intéresse ici. La manière et la méthode choisies pour l'instauration ou le développement de ces emplois atypiques sont sans doute plus importantes que la nature même de ces emplois. Le changement imposé comme une contrainte est vécu en général comme une astreinte intolérable tant par les individus que par la société. Le changement négocié peut être source d'efficacité et de liberté supplémentaire. La méthodologie du changement est au coeur de notre problématique. C'est sur elle que la recherche devrait porter prioritairement.

AUSWIRKUNGEN VON NEUEN ARBEITSFORMEN AUS BETRIEBS- PSYCHOLOGISCHER SICHT

Otto Renda
Hans-Jürgen Reuter

Institut für angewandte Bebriebspsychologie

BERLIN,
MÄRZ 1986

Vorwort

Im folgenden Report werden mögliche betriebspsychologische Auswirkungen durch neue Arbeitsformen und -technologien beschrieben. Wenn neue Technologien oder Arbeitszeitregelungen eingeführt werden sollen, so sind zwei Dinge besonders zu beachten:

1. Die bereits bekannten und für den Menschen positiven Auswirkungen wissenschaftlicher Erkenntnisse müssen beachtet und - wann immer möglich - umgesetzt werden.

2. Potentielle Gefahren für die Mitarbeiter sollen vor-gedacht, beschrieben und damit - wenn möglich - abgewendet werden.

Im Bericht werden Chancen und Grenzen neuer Arbeitsformen aus der Sicht der Psychologie behandelt. Daß an einigen Stellen besonders ausführlich auf die potentiellen Gefahren eingegangen wird, soll in keiner Weise einige der neuen Arbeitsformen diskreditieren, sondern entspringt der Einstellung: _bewahre_ Dinge, die dem Menschen helfen - _vermeide_ Dinge, die ihm schaden können! In einigen Passagen werden deswegen mögliche negative Auswirkungen detailliert abgehandelt, was aber nicht eine erhöhte Auftretenswahrscheinlichkeit gegenüber positiven Auswirkungen präjudizieren soll. Nur, wir wollten bewußt auf kritische Aspekte eingehen, um Auswirkungen erkannter und benannter Fehlentwicklungen im Vorfeld zu begrenzen.

Einleitung

Im Zusammenhang mit der Einführung neuer Technologien und der Weiterentwicklung der Informations- und Kommunikationstechniken ergeben sich zahlreiche Veränderungen von Arbeitsinhalten und -abläufen, d. h. zunehmend mehr Arbeitnehmer müssen anders geartete Aufgaben übernehmen, die andere Qualifikationen erfordern bzw. alte Qualifikationen überflüssig machen. Die Technologien gehen einher mit zahlreichen, die Persönlichkeit der Arbeitnehmer tangierenden Auswirkungen (z. B. Statusverlust, Qualifikationsverlust) sowie mit Veränderungen in der organisatorischen Struktur der Betriebe (z. B. Zentralisierung, Ökonomisierung der Zeitstruktur). Neue Arbeitszeit- und Arbeitsformen und deren psychische und soziale Auswirkungen auf die davon Betroffenen sind zu bestimmen. Das Bild, das sich bis dato zu diesen Fragestellungen ergibt, ist sehr heterogen. Vieles, was gesagt wird, beruht auf Plausibilitätsannahmen, gedanklichen Hochrechnungen oder auf Studien, die mit relativ geringen methodischen Mitteln erste Erkenntnisse sammeln wollten (was in einem frühen Stadium wissenschaftlicher Erkenntnisermittlung ein durchaus legitimes Vorgehen darstellt). So beschränken sich denn viele Untersuchungen, welche psychosoziale Auswirkungen neuer Arbeitszeit- und Arbeitsformen klären wollen, dabei auf die Angabe von Indikatoren (z. B. Fluktuation, Absentismus, Arbeitsqualität und -quantität), die eine vage Beziehung zu psychologischen Konstrukten aufweisen (z. B. Arbeitszufriedenheit, Streß), deren Art der Beziehung zu diesen Konstrukten oft aber selbst relativ unklar ist. Vielfach wurden Daten durch kurze Befragungen oder Einschätzungen seitens der Vorgesetzten oder der direkt Betroffenen erhoben. Empirisch exaktere Messungen fehlen jedoch vielfach. Diese Situation sollte verändert werden. Die psychischen und sozialen Auswirkungen neuer Arbeitszeit- und Arbeitsformen sind durch methodisch gründlichere Studien zu erheben.

So zeichnet sich momentan ein Bild ab, das geprägt ist von

Widersprüchen und Unklarheiten. Sehen die einen in den neuen Technologien den Durchbruch für Humanisierungsbemühungen im Sinne von Höherqualifikation, Verringerung von Sinnentleerung, Erweiterung des Handlungs- und Entscheidungsspielraumes der Arbeitnehmer, so befürchten andere eine zunehmende Taylorisierung der Arbeit mit der Folge einer sich verstärkenden Dequalifizierung und Sinnentleerung sowie weiter zunehmender Arbeitslosigkeit. Die Diskussion um die Richtung der Auswirkungen kann hier nicht entschieden werden. Vielmehr kann nur gezeigt werden, welche Probleme bei der Einführung von Informations- und Kommunikationstechniken bestehen können. Betont werden soll hier allerdings, daß es nicht die Techniken selbst sind, die ursächlich mit den Folgen ihrer Implementierung zusammenhängen, sondern daß es Annahmen darüber sind, wie die Techniken möglichst ökonomisch und effizient einzusetzen sind. Momentan bietet sich ein Bild, das die Taylorisierung der Arbeit als Rationalisierungsstrategie im Zusammenhang mit der Computertechnologie favorisiert. Daraus resultieren viele unnötige, negative Folgen für Arbeitnehmer wie für die Unternehmen selbst. Hier hat die Forschung anzusetzen. Sie muß Wege und Modelle aufzeigen, die unterstreichen, daß andere Arbeitsformen, die weniger Zentralisierung und Spezialisierung zur Folge haben als eine Taylorisierung der Arbeit nicht weniger ökonomisch und effizient sind, und dabei bestimmte negative Auswirkungen taylorisierter Arbeit vermeiden (vgl. Jacobi u.a. 1980, Weltz, Sullies 1983).

Es bedarf dazu gezielter Analysen i.S. von Tätigkeitsanalysen, die aufdecken, welche Belastungen auftreten und wo klar wird, welche Veränderungen stattfinden müssen, um die Bedürfnisse der Unternehmen wie Arbeitnehmer befriedigende Arbeitsstrukturen zu erhalten (vgl. Vorbrücken 1984). Aus betriebspsychologischer Sicht interessant ist, wie bestimmte Arbeitsbedingungen, die mit neuen Arbeitszeit- und Arbeitsformen einhergehen (wie z. B. Heimarbeit, Arbeit auf Abruf, 3-4 Tage à 12 Std.) sich in Verbindung mit neuen Technologien psychisch und sozial auswirken.

Im folgenden soll versucht werden, auf bestehende Entwicklungen und Möglichkeiten hinzuweisen, die mit einigen der oben angesprochenen Arbeits- und Arbeitszeitformen zusammenhängen.

Eindeutige Ursache-Wirkungsverhältnisse sind hierbei noch nicht zu erwarten. So bedeutet beispielsweise die Einführung neuer Technologien nicht zwangsläufig die Notwendigkeit einer Flexibilisierung der Arbeitszeit, ebensogut kann eine Flexibilisierung der Arbeitszeit als kollektives Bedürfnis einer Gesellschaft die Entwicklung neuer Technologien nötig werden lassen. Was wir benötigen und das wurde auch schon im März dieses Jahres auf dem Foundation-Workshop in Dublin deutlich, sind multifaktorielle Designs, die in der Lage sind, die vielfältigen Beziehungen, die Interaktivität der Variablen adäquat abzubilden (was empirisch ohne Zweifel ein schwieriges Unterfangen ist).

1. Folgen und Belastungen im Zusammenhang mit neuen Technologien

Wenn man die bisher gemachten Studien in der BRD danach durcharbeitet, welche Folgen neue Computertechnologien in der Fertigung und in der Verwaltung haben und welche Auswirkungen von den Betroffenen geäußert werden, so ergibt sich ein Bild, das den Möglichkeiten, die durch neue Technologien gegeben sind, entgegensteht (vgl. Frese 1981, Jacobi u.a. 1980, Weltz, Lullies 1983). Das beruht darauf, daß die Einführung neuer Technologien überwiegend nach einem Rationalisierungsparadigma erfolgt, das auf drei Grundannahmen beruht, welche die arbeitsorganisatorische Einbettung bestimmen.

Diese sind:

1. jede weitere Stufe der Arbeitsteilung in einer Organisation führt zu einer Erhöhung der Effizienz,

2. mit dieser Arbeitsteilung seien stets positiv zu bewertende Spezialisierungsmöglichkeiten verbunden;

3. die Erfahrung mit effizienzsteigernden Maßnahmen im Produktionsbereich seien unmittelbar auf den Verwaltungsbereich übertragbar (vgl. Naschold 1979, Cakir 1984).

Die Überprüfung dieser Annahmen macht deutlich, daß die Umsetzung der Rationalisierungsstrategien Zentralisierung und Spezialisierung nicht nur zu Inhumanitätserscheinungen in der Arbeit führen, sondern darüber hinaus dysfunktionale Wirkungen für die Gesamtorganisation (z. B. mangelnde Flexibilität durch zu starke Formalisierung) zeitigen.

Zentralisierung heißt Ausgliederung technikbezogener Tätigkeit aus dem organisatorischen Kontext, räumliche und organisatorische Zusammenfassung der ausgegliederten Tätigkeit, sowie technikorientierte Arbeitsabläufe in zentralen Organisationsbereichen (z. B. zentraler Schreibdienst; vgl. Jacobi u.a. 1980, Weltz, Lullies 1983, Frese 1981, Pirker u.a. 1982). Daraus resultieren einseitige Belastungen bei wenigen Tätigkeiten, weitgehende Isolierung der Arbeit vom inhaltlichen Kontext (Sinnentleerung, hoher Entfremdungsgrad), sowie ein durch technische Sachzwänge bestimmter Arbeitsprozeß. Die Folgen einer zunehmenden Spezialisierung oder besser Entmischung sind der Verlust qualifizierter Arbeit durch z. B. Einschränkung des Handlungs- und Entscheidungsspielraumes, Häufung von unproduktiven, monotonen Arbeitselementen, Verlust an tätigkeitsbezogenen wichtigen Informationen, Erhöhung der Beanspruchung durch Maschinenbedienung, d. h. die Arbeit wird vom Arbeitenden mehr und mehr physisch wie psychisch als stärker beanspruchend empfunden, resultierend aus Eintönigkeit und Unterforderung bzw. Überforderung.

Hinzu kommt, daß mit der Abnahme energetischer Anteile und der Zunahme sensorischer und kognitiver Anteile bei der computerisierten Arbeit die Möglichkeit der Arbeitsverdichtung wächst (z. B. bei Mehrmaschinenbedienung, bei der der Anteil energetischer Arbeit relativ abgenommen hat und der sensorische und kognitive Anteil relativ zugenommen hat).

Eine Zunahme von Arbeitsvorgängen, die sich auf den Kern der Informationsverarbeitung reduzieren, findet statt. D. h. es kommt zu einer Erhöhung kognitiver Beanspruchung durch Zunahme der Verarbeitung abstrakt-formaler Informationen. Durch die Zunahme der Informationsverarbeitung ergibt sich eine neue Form von Leistungsverdichtung und neue Formen der Beanspruchung. Es gibt kaum noch einen Arbeitsbereich, in dem nicht technisch gestützte Maßnahmen zur Planung, Steuerung und Überwachung von Prozessen eingeführt werden (CAD, CNC etc.). Dabei besteht die Gefahr, daß bisher vorhandene Freiheitsgrade der Arbeit weiter abgebaut werden und damit neue Belastungen für die Menschen auftreten können. Belastungsschwerpunkte sind hierbei die Zunahme der Intensivierung der Arbeit, wachsender Autonomieverlust, zunehmende Zerstückelung der Arbeitswirklichkeit. Es sollte aber den Arbeitnehmern mehr Gele-

genheit zur Selbstverwirklichung angeboten werden - vor allem
durch Gewährleistung von Eigenrhythmik und Eigensteuerung.

Der zunehmende Versuch der Taylorisierung der Arbeit hat negative Auswirkungen auf die Arbeitszufriedenheit; er führt zu
Demotivation und Dequalifizierung und resultiert in einer er-
höhten Beanspruchung durch Leistungsverdichtung und Leistungsintensivierung, soziale Isolation und Sinnentleerung. Was die
Veränderung der Qualifikationsanforderungen anbelangt und die
mit der Technologisierung oft einhergehende Dequalifizierung,
so ergeben sich noch andere Probleme. So wirkt sich eine Veränderung der sachlichen Voraussetzungen des Arbeitsprozesses
durch Computertechnologien in doppelter Weise aus. Die neue
Technik verändert die stoffliche Gestalt des Produktionsprozesses und begünstigt die Freisetzung von Arbeitskräften. Können die freigesetzten Arbeitnehmer alle wieder beschäftigt
werden, so werden sie jedoch oft an Arbeitsplätzen beschäftigt,
die andere Anforderungen an sie stellen. Für die Betroffenen
bedeutet dies eine Anpassung an technisch-veränderte Arbeitsplätze mit veränderten Anforderungen an die psycho-physische
Leistungsfähigkeit, sowie eine Anpassungsleistung an eine
oft damit einhergehende Veränderung des sozialen Zusammen-
hangs im Betrieb (vgl. auch Franke 1980, Köppl 1981). Neben
den technologischen Faktoren, die eine Umstellung der Arbeitskräfte verlangen, wirken sich auch die mit der Organisation
der Arbeit verbundenen Änderungen der Arbeitsplätze auf die
Beanspruchung aus. Dies erfordert Umschulung und Training.
Notwendige Umschulung und Training als Vorbereitung auf den
veränderten technischen Arbeitsablauf wird jedoch nicht
selten nur in dem Maße durchgeführt, wie sie nicht zu umgehen
sind. Eine systematische Vorbereitung auf die neue Arbeit
findet noch nicht in ausreichendem Maße statt, d. h. keine
ausreichende Qualifikation, verstärkte Beanspruchung durch
Überforderung, mangelndes Kontrollerleben verbunden mit einem
Gefühl des Ausgeliefertseins (vgl. auch Gebert 1981). Bei
Veränderungen der technischen Anlage wird zwar technische
Planung systematisch betrieben, aber vorausschauende Perso-

nalbedarfsplanung, Tätigkeitsanalysen oder genaue Qualifikationsvorbereitungen der Arbeitskräfte kommen noch viel zu selten zur Anwendung. Die betriebliche Arbeitsorganisation wird als ein Faktor angesehen, der sich relativ leicht und kurzfristig auf die objektiven Bedürfnisse der Technik einrichten läßt. Die mögliche breite Disponibilität der Arbeitskräfte, die die lebenslange Bindung an eine spezifische Teilarbeit aufheben könnte, verkehrt sich in zusätzliche Belastung und Entwertung der persönlichen Qualifikation. Überbeanspruchung mit all seinen Folgen ist oft das Ergebnis falsch oder nicht ausreichend angepaßter Arbeitskräfte an einen normal beanspruchenden Arbeitsplatz.

Überlastungstendenzen treten vor allem im Bereich sensumotorischer Arbeitsformen auf. Die fehlende Habitualisierung erfordert eine laufende Kontrolle und Korrektur des Bewegungsablaufes. Mangelnde Übung birgt die nicht zu unterschätzende Gefahr in sich, ein ungenügendes Arbeitsergebnis zu erbringen, d. h. der Arbeitnehmer muß hohe zusätzliche psychische Anstrengung erbringen.

So bedeutet die ungenügende Vorbereitung auf den Arbeitsplatz zusätzliche psychische Anstrengungen, da die Kontrolle des Arbeitsablaufes wegen des geringen Kenntnisstandes der Funktionsweise mit vielen Unsicherheiten belastet ist, die der (die) Mitarbeiter(-in) durch zusätzliche Anspannung der Aufmerksamkeit kompensieren muß.

Diese Überforderung ist bedingt durch zu kurze Anlernzeiten und die oft frühzeitige Übernahme in den Leistungslohn (vgl. Jacobi u.a. 1980). Die Bindung der Lohnhöhe an die geforderte Leistung einer ungenügend eingeübten Arbeitskraft verstärkt die Arbeitsbelastung außerdem, da nun auftretende Qualifikationsmängel, Fehler oder Minderleistungen, die allein durch die mangelnde Beherrschung des Produktionsprozesses zustandekommen, als Risiko der Arbeitskraft aufgebürdet werden (z. B. Akkordarbeit, Prämienentlohnung; vgl. auch Jacobi u.a. 1980,

Pirker u.a. 1982).

Dauerhafte Überbeanspruchung führt schon nach kurzer Zeit wegen der hohen körperlichen Verschleißerscheinungen zum Absinken der Leistungskurve. Hinzu kommt, daß die erworbene Erfahrung im Arbeitsbereich immer seltener einen akkumulierbaren Vorteil darstellt. Die beschleunigte Durchsetzung der technologischen Neuerungen entwertet fortlaufend die Arbeitserfahrungen und die persönliche Qualifikation (z. B. Setzer, technischer Zeichner) und bedeutet zudem eine permanente Statusgefährdung mit der potentiellen Gefahr des Arbeitsplatzverlustes.

Was heute mehr und mehr gefordert ist, ist eine hohe Anpassungsfähigkeit an wechselnde Arbeitssituationen und maximale aktuelle psycho-physische Leistungsfähigkeit. Nötig ist die Bereitstellung betrieblicher Zeitreserven zur Weiterbildung, sozialer Kommunikation und Interaktion. Dies fördert Kompetenz und Kontrollfähigkeit, d. h. Wiederaneignung der fachlichen, sozialen Kompetenz der Arbeitnehmer. Gefordert werden muß der Abbau betrieblicher Zeitzwänge und Verhaltensfestlegungen. Die Herstellung von zeitlichen und sachlichen Handlungs- und Gestaltungsspielräumen durch entsprechende Arbeitsorganisation und Qualifikation der Arbeitnehmer innerhalb des Arbeitsprozesses sind notwendige Voraussetzungen der Rückgewinnung von Kompetenz und Kontrollfähigkeit und die daraus erwachsenden Bestimmungsgrößen (vgl. auch Naschold 1979).
Die Folge der Nichtbeachtung dieser Voraussetzungen sind langfristig Qualitätsverschlechterung und Ineffizienz, die durch leistungsintensivierende Maßnahmen nicht mehr zu beheben sind. Das Gefühl des Druckes und der Arbeitshetze durch die enge Anbindung an den Lauf der computerisierten Maschine sowie als Reaktion darauf die Anzahl psycho-physischer Beschwerden nehmen deutlich zu. Funktionelle Symptome wie Nervosität, Gereiztheit, dauernde Müdigkeit werden nicht selten von Arbeitnehmern berichtet, die solchen technologischen Veränderungen der Arbeitsstrukturen ausgesetzt sind (vgl. Frese 1978,

1981). Die Quantifizierung der Leistung wird zudem von vielen als Diskriminierung empfunden. Leistungsdruck und intensivierte Mensch-Maschine-Kommunikation verschlechtern die Arbeitsbeziehungen in der Gruppe, verringern die Möglichkeit informeller Kontakte. Dies kann zu Spannungen zwischen den Mitgliedern der Gruppe führen. Leistungserfassung, Sollvorgabe, Prämienentlohnung, dies alles sind Bedingungen, die zu einer erheblichen Erhöhung des Leistungsdruckes und der Beanspruchung führen können, der der Arbeitnehmer mangels Kontrollmöglichkeiten dann oft ausgeliefert ist (vgl. Jacobi 1980; Weltz, Lullies 1983). Nicht der Arbeitnehmer bestimmt den Arbeitsablauf, sondern die computerisierte Anlage. Taylorisierung der Arbeit schafft stärkere qualitative Unterforderung durch eintönige, repetitive, als langweilig eingestufte Arbeit (vgl. auch Frese 1981; Türk 1976). Geringe Transparenz des Arbeitsvollzuges wegen wenig sichtbarer Leistungs- und Kontrolleffekte und ein geringer Grad an Autonomie und Verfügbarkeit über den eigenen Arbeitsablauf sind dominierend.

Ungeachtet dessen ist mit der Informations- und Kommunikationstechnologie auch die Möglichkeit erhöhter Transparenz und Überschaubarkeit des Ablaufs einer beispielsweise Sachbearbeiteraufgabe gegeben. Solche Informationssysteme sind prinzipiell so angelegt, daß ein Arbeitnehmer den gesamten, von ihm angestoßenen Arbeitsablauf steuern, überwachen und einsehen kann. Dies bedarf der Einrichtung entsprechender Ablaufgestaltung im Sinne einer Zunahme von Mischtätigkeiten, die mehr Verantwortung und einen größeren Handlungs- und Entscheidungsspielraum und mehr zwischenmenschliche Kommunikation beinhalten. Solche Ablaufgestaltung wird die Entfremdung der Arbeit, die durch die Taylorisierung geben ist, verringern (vgl. Rauch 1978).

Zusammenfassend lassen sich folgende Problemfelder des betrieblichen Computereinsatzes festhalten. Neben physischen ergeben sich psychische Belastungen, die aus der intensiveren

Mensch-Maschine-Kommunikation resultieren, wie die Schwierigkeit den Inhalt des Systems zu verstehen, Schwierigkeiten bei Bedienungsvorgängen, Schwierigkeiten mit der allgemeinen Computer-Terminologie. Darüber hinaus ergeben sich psychische Belastungen aus der gesamten Arbeitssituation, die auf großer Standardisierung und Spezialisierung beruhen, Entfremdung durch Reduzierung des Kontaktes mit den Arbeitsergebnissen, Entfremdung durch die mangelnde Einsicht in den Gesamtzusammenhang der Arbeit, Kontaktarmut aufgrund reduzierter arbeitsbezogener interpersonaler Kommunikation sowie durch Entfaltungshemmnisse, die auf einer Beschränkung der Eigensteuerung und Eigenkontrolle der Arbeitsinhalte und des Arbeitsfortschrittes durch technische und organisatorische Programmierung beruhen. Besondere Beachtung muß der Ausweitung monotoner, repetitiver, sinnentleerter Arbeit im Zusammenhang mit der Computerisierung der Arbeit geschenkt werden (vgl. auch Rauch 1978, Frese 1978, Türk 1976). Die Reizarmut monotoner Arbeit kann neben Entfremdungserlebnissen auch zu einer persönlichen Regression führen. Den Inhalt der Arbeit können wir in mehreren Bezugssystemen näher bestimmen: energetisch, kognitiv, sensorisch. Dazu gehören jedoch auch noch Dimensionen wie der Anteil an Kommunikation und sozialer Beziehung sowie der Anteil der individuell beeinflußbaren Arbeit (d. h. Freiheitsgrade der Arbeit), die die Beanspruchung und das Wohlbefinden des Menschen wesentlich beeinflussen. Welche Konsequenzen größere oder geringere Freiheitsgrade in der Arbeit haben, hat sich in Humanisierungsprogrammen erwiesen. Besonders hervorzuheben ist, daß die Menschen bei ihrer Arbeit ihren individuellen Bedürfnissen entsprechend die Reihenfolge der Arbeitsschritte variieren, so daß die praktizierte, individuelle Variation im Ablauf von den Freiheitsgraden in der Arbeit abhängt; daß mit Zunahme der Freiheitsgrade individuelle Arbeitsstrategien erfolgreich erlernt und angewandt werden können und daß bei gleichen Belastungen Arbeiten mit höheren Freiheitsgraden geringere Beanspruchungen aufweisen, konnte vielfach gezeigt werden (vgl. Türk 1976, Frese 1981, Martin u.a. 1980).

Der Verlust von Arbeitsplätzen infolge technologischer Veränderungen ist nicht zwangsläufig. Komplexere Organisationsformen, Ausnützung neuer Möglichkeiten (z. B. Verlagerung von Sekretariatsaufgaben zum Sachbearbeiter), verringerte Arbeitszeit könnten den Rationalisierungseffekten der Informations- und Kommunikationssysteme ohne entscheidende Auswirkung auf den Arbeitsmarkt bleiben lassen. Die gravierendste organisatorische Änderung durch Einführung neuer Informations- und Kommunikationstechnologien liegt in der Möglichkeit der Lockerung von bestehenden Hierarchien. Es könnte zu einer Verlagerung des Entscheidungsprozesses nach unten und zum Abbau hierarchischer zugunsten funktionaler Autorität kommen. Hier liegt die Möglichkeit zur Erweiterung von Qualifikation und der Handlungs- und Entscheidungsspielräume der Betroffenen.

Mit der Vergrößerung der Entscheidungsbefugnis in niedrigen Managementebenen könnte auch der Grad der Arbeitsteilung zurückgehen. Dazu wäre aus organisatorischer Sicht allerdings eine Intensivierung horizontaler Integration nötig, wenn der betriebsinterne Zusammenhalt nicht gefährdet werden soll. Hier läge die Chance durch verstärkte Kommunikation und Kooperation eine Verbesserung der sozialen Integration der Arbeitnehmer in die Unternehmen zu ermöglichen bei gleichzeitiger Erhöhung der Transparenz der Arbeitsaufgabe. Eine solche Arbeitsorganisation würde auch die Möglichkeit informeller Kontakte aufrechterhalten, worin die Chance zur Entladung von Spannung liegt, die sonst schädlich auf die formelle Organisation einwirken würden (vgl. Rauch 1978; Franke 1980, Kubicek 1978).

2. Exkurs: Zusammenhang zwischen Technologien, Streß und partialisierten Handlungen

Immer wieder wird berichtet, daß nach Einführung hochwertiger Techniken, für die Arbeitnehmer eine Taylorisierung der Arbeit stattfindet, d. h. inhaltliche Gleichförmigkeit, hoher Wiederholungsgrad, Fremdkontrolle. Aus handlungstheoretischer Sicht bedeutet dies ein Dominieren partialisierter Handlungen. Partialisierte Handlungen sind isoliert, d. h. der Gesamtzusammenhang der Arbeit bzw. seine das Individuum übergreifenden Bestandteile werden nicht miterfaßt und mitbestimmt. Solche Tätigkeiten sind restringiert, d. h. der individuelle Handlungszusammenhang ist im Sinne einer Unterentwicklung umfassender und komplexer Planungsvorgänge gestört, an die Stelle der Beherrschung der Gegebenheiten und des Überblicks tritt die Perspektivlosigkeit und das Beherrschtwerden durch die Maschine, d. h. es fehlt die intellektuelle Regulation sowie die Teilnahme an überindividuellen, das Individuum betreffenden Planungsprozessen. Hier ist der Bezug zur Streßforschung gegeben, die sich bemüht hat, zu zeigen, daß gerade die Kontrolle über die Arbeitssituation streßreduzierend ist. Auch das Selbstbewußtsein ist erheblich von der Kontrollmöglichkeit beeinflußt. Die Erfahrung von Nichtkontrollbedingungen kann allgemeine Apathie, Resignation und Depressivität fördern (Syndrom der gelernten Hilflosigkeit). Voraussetzung dafür sind die generalisierte Einstellung, keine Kontrolle über die Bedingungen und die eigene Tätigkeit zu haben. Wichtig für die Entstehung der oben genannten Symptomatik der gelernten Hilflosigkeit ist die Erkenntnis der eigenen Unfähigkeit zur adäquaten Streßkontrolle. Wenn Arbeitstechniken, Arbeitsbedingungen, Interaktionsformen mit Kollegen und Vorgesetzten detailliert vorgegeben werden, dann ist die Kontrolle über die für solche Situationen typischen Streßfaktoren wie hohes Arbeitstempo, Monotonie, soziale Isolation stark eingeschränkt. Gerade die Vermeidung sozialer Isolation ist für die Auswirkungen von Streß von entscheidender Bedeutung, wie oben dargelegt wurde. Die Tatsache, daß durch sozialen Ver-

gleich am Arbeitsplatz die Erfahrung möglich ist, daß die
Kontrollosigkeit kein persönliches Unvermögen ist, hilft die
Symptomatiken zu modifizieren. Bei z. B. isolierter Heimarbeit
sind solche Bewältigungsstrategien nur schwer zugänglich. Die
Arbeit ist so zu strukturieren, daß die Arbeiter mehr Kontrolle erhalten über Arbeitsablauf, Arbeitsverteilung, Gruppenbildung in der Arbeitsgruppe. Gefordert ist also eine Erweiterung der Streßkontrolle besonders im Bereich der Arbeitsbedingungen und der sozialen Interaktion. Erhöhte Kontrolle, so die
empirische Erfahrungsbasis, kann zu Produktivitätssteigerungen führen, sowie zu einer Verringerung sozialer Konflikte
und zu weniger stark empfundener Belastung durch die Arbeit
führen. So zeigen sich dann auch bei arbeitsorganisatorischen
Strukturen, die Gruppenarbeit fördern, die die Verantwortung
der ganzen Gruppe, nicht dem einzelnen aufbürden, die ganzheitliche Tätigkeit unterstützen und damit vielfältige Arbeitshandlungen ermöglichen, daß Streßbelastungen wie Arbeitsdruck, Terminvorgaben, starke Anbindung an die Maschine
besser kompensiert werden können. (vgl. U. Jacobi u.a. 1980;
Pirker u.a. 1982).

Das innere Modell, das sich eine Person von sich und ihren
Umgebungsbedingungen macht und das sich aus den Erfahrungen
mit diesen ergibt, kann streßfördernd sein, insofern als es
objektiv vorhandene Bewältigungsstrategien ausschließt oder
Anforderungen unnötig scharf oder unrealistisch formuliert.
Isoliertes Arbeiten kann die Entwicklung solcher unrealistischer Strategien fördern, während die Zugänglichkeit von
sozialer Unterstützung neben dem Hilfeaspekt auch die Möglichkeit von Feedback und Realitätskontrolle bedeuten kann (vgl.
Frese 1978, 1981; Gebert 1981).

Die Ökologie des Arbeitsplatzes und die Arbeitsorganisation
können angemessene Bewältigungsstrategien behindern oder fördern. Bewältigungsstrategien ermöglichen Anpassung an schwierige Umwelten. Jede Anpassungsleistung beruht auf der angemessenen Verarbeitung von Informationen aus der Umwelt. Von daher

ist für den Arbeitnehmer entsprechende Kontextinformation nötig, die die Einordnung der Tätigkeit ermöglicht und damit den Sinnbezug zu seiner Arbeit herstellt. Dies führt überdies zur Reduktion von Arbeitsentfremdungserlebnissen. Diese aber gerade begünstigt eine Taylorisierung der Arbeit, wie sie sich bei der Einführung neuer Technologien durchzusetzen scheint.

3. Arbeitsentfremdung und neue Technologien

Die Arbeitsentfremdung äußert sich in der Tatsache, daß dem Arbeitsvollzug keine Befriedigungswerte entspringen.

Es bedeutet Macht- und Bedeutungslosigkeit, d. h. Fremdkontrolle durch die Maschine sowie Normlosigkeit. Im Arbeitsfeld können keine Lebensziele erreicht werden. Arbeit wird ein Instrument für die Freizeit. Isolierung und Selbstentfremdung bestimmen die Arbeitserfahrungen des Menschen unter tayloristischer Rationalisierungsbemühung.

Zur Arbeitsentfremdung kommt es vor allem bei sehr monotonen und repetitiven Tätigkeiten, bei denen der Arbeitnehmer den Sinn des Gesamtgefüges, in den er eingegliedert ist, immer weniger zu erfassen vermag. Die Erfüllung der Aufgaben entbehrt für den Arbeitenden der Sinnhaftigkeit, so daß sie keinen Befriedigungswert zu vermitteln vermag. Dies ist besonders da der Fall, wo die Arbeit infolge ihrer weitgehenden Vereinfachung und Eintönigkeit keine Anforderungen mehr stellt.

Modifizierend wirken sich auf das Entfremdungserleben, die an die Arbeit herangetragenen Erwartungen, die Begabungsstufe, die Art, in welcher Versagungen verarbeitet werden, aus.

Der Sinnbezug der Arbeit ist bei Arbeitsentfremdung verlorengegangen; die Arbeit erscheint nicht mehr als Befriedigungsquelle, sondern lediglich als Mittel zur Findung von Befriedigungen in anderen Lebensbereichen. Sie hat nur noch rein instrumentellen Wert (vgl. Lattmann 1982).

4. Heimarbeit

Eine besondere Form dezentralisierter Arbeit ist die elektronische Fernarbeit bzw. Heimarbeit. Sie wird auch als Computerheimarbeit, Teleheimarbeit bezeichnet. Gemeint sind Arbeitsplätze, die außerhalb des Betriebes in Wohnungen der Beschäftigten entstehen und an denen die Arbeit an Mitteln, die die Informations- und Kommunikationstechnik bereitstellt, bestimmend für die Gesamttätigkeit ist. Die Befürworter dieser Arbeit weisen auf die energie-, verkehrs- und strukturpolitischen Vorteile der Heimarbeit hin (vgl. Dostal 1985, Körte 1986). Für Heimarbeit bietet sich prinzipiell die Auslagerung vieler Tätigkeiten an: Datenerfassung, Textverarbeitung, Programmierung, kaufmännische Sachbearbeitung, technische Angestelltentätigkeit.

Im Zusammenhang mit der Heimarbeit steht aber zu befürchten, daß vor allem Frauen als Zielgruppe solcher Arbeitsformen betroffen sein werden. So zeigt sich, daß besonders leicht formalisierbare und segmentierbare Tätigkeiten, die wenig Anreize beiten und ein relativ geringes Qualifikationsniveau erfordern, ausgegliedert werden, weil hier die geringsten organisatorischen Probleme dezentralisierter Arbeit zu erwarten sind (vgl. U. Körte 1986, Huber 1984, Vogelheim 1984, Dostal 1985).

Die Frauen wird es zuerst betreffen, weil sie aufgrund ihrer Tätigkeitsschwerpunkte, ihrer geringen beruflichen Qualifikation in der heutigen Berufswelt weniger konkurrenzfähig, weniger organisiert und weniger durchsetzungsfähig sind. Frauen werden dann als selbständige Unternehmerinnen, die in Form freier Mitarbeit den Kontakt zur Firma halten, arbeiten; je nach Arbeitsauslastung können sie mehrere Arbeitgeber haben und damit mehr Geld verdienen - neben Haushalt und Familie. Die Aufnahme einer Heimarbeitstätigkeit bedeutet eine enorme Doppelbelastung durch Beruf und Familie, da am Heimarbeitsplatz familienvorsorgende Tätigkeiten wahrgenommen werden können.

Für Männer werden bisher kaum Heimarbeitsplätze angeboten, sieht man von höherqualifizierten Berufsgruppen wie Programmierer, Journalist, Wissenschaftler ab. Aber auch ihr Anteil ist eher gering.

Die Hoffnung vieler Frauen, Beruf, Haushalt und Kindererziehung bei der Arbeit besser in Einklang bringen zu können, kann vielfach nicht in Erfüllung gehen. Viele Frauen/Mütter wünschen sich aber eine Heimarbeitstätigkeit, weil sie glauben, sowohl ihre Pflichten als Hausfrau und Mutter erfüllen, als auch noch einen finanziellen Beitrag zur Erhaltung des bestehenden Lebensstandards leisten zu können. Diesem positiven Vorhaben stehen aber in der Praxis gravierende negative Effekte gegenüber.

Rolle 'Hausfrau': Ist die Frau den ganzen Tag zu Hause, so hat der Lebenspartner (und implizit die Frau selber auch oft) den Anspruch an einen tip-top-geführten Haushalt. Diese unausgesprochene oder ausgesprochene Erwartung verlangt aber eine Tageszeiteinteilung einer Nur-Hausfrau.

Rolle 'Mutter': Kleinkinder verlangen psychische und physische Zuwendungen, die sich nicht an der Uhrzeit orientieren. Gerade deswegen bleibt die Mutter ja zu Hause, um diesen Bedürfnissen des Kindes bzw. ihrer Mutterrolle gerecht werden zu können. Macht sich das Kind bemerkbar, wird die Mutter versuchen, darauf zu reagieren, d. h. in der intraindividuellen Wertigkeit steht die Mutter-Rolle an erster Stelle, dann erst folgt die Hausfrauen-Rolle.

Rolle 'Heimarbeiterin': Da meist erst an dritter Stelle die Rolle als Heimarbeiterin steht, werden viele Frauen im täglichen Ablauf den ersten beiden den Vorrang geben. Wenn sich das Kind be-

merkbar macht, wird nicht erst die Seite
in der Textverarbeitung zu Ende geschrieben
und dann das Kind beachtet werden, sondern
oftmals wird sich die Aufmerksamkeit und Zu-
wendung sofort auf das Kind richten (sonst
kann es ja Probleme mit dem Rollenverständ-
nis als Mutter geben). D. h. ihrer Rolle als
Arbeiterin kann sie erst dann nachkommen,
wenn die ersten beiden erfüllt sind. In der
Praxis bedeutet dies oft: Nachtarbeit. Die
bekannten Folgen dieser Arbeitseinteilung
brauchen hier nicht näher beschrieben zu
werden.

Die vermeintlichen Vorteile der Heimarbeit schlagen bei vielen Frauen in einen Dauerkonflikt zwischen den drei beschrie-
benen Rollen um. Daß zur Lösung dieses Problems neben einer Veränderung der "klassischen" Männerrolle auch eine Änderung des
Anspruchsniveaus der Frauen-Mutter-Heimarbeiterin-Rolle von
seiten der Frauen nützlich sein kann, sei hier nur am Rande
vermerkt.

Zudem zeichnen sich bei Heimarbeit folgende Gefahren ab, die
den Vorteilen einer vergrößerten Selbstbestimmung in bezug auf
Zeiteinteilung der Areit, einer größeren Möglichkeit indivi-
dueller Freizeiteinteilung und den Vorteilen eines höheren
Maßes an Arbeitszeitflexibilität entgegenstehen.

1. Errichtung von Arbeitsplätzen mit geringen Arbeitsinhalten und ohne Qualifizierungschancen. Um Koordinierungspro-
   bleme zu vermeiden, dürften vorwiegend wenig komplexe Tätigkeiten ausgelagert werden (vgl. Korte 1986). Das bedeutet auch hier Dequalifizierung, einfach, weil elektronische
   Heimarbeit eine starke Formalisierung der Arbeit voraus-
   setzt, d. h. die Arbeit selbst bietet wenig Anreize.

2. Gesundheitliche, physische und psychische Belastungen: bei

elektronischer Heimarbeit sind vor allem folgende Faktoren wirksam: monotone Arbeit, ergonomisch schlechte Geräte, verstärkte Belastung vor allem für Frauen durch ständige Doppelbelastung (Familie/Beruf) sowie erhöhter Leistungsdurck durch Lohnanreizsysteme.

Dazu kommt noch, daß nur die Arbeitsbelastung, nicht der Arbeitsausfall bezahlt würde. Arbeitsausfall ist von Heimarbeitern selst zu tragen. Merkmale dieser Arbeit sind keine gesicherten Arbeitszeiten, keine festgelegten Pausen.

3. Einkommenseinbußen: Dadurch, daß Tätigkeiten ausgegliert werden, die generell von vielen ausübbar sind, d. h. niedriges Qualifikationsniveau erfordern, verschärft sich die Konkurrenz auf dem Arbeitsmarkt. Der zu erwartende Konkurrenzdruck zwischen den zahlreichen Heimarbeitern (-innen) dürfte das Lohnniveau an den Rand des Existenzminimums drücken. Zudem wird der Konkurrenzdruck zwischen den Heimarbeitern (-innen) zu höheren Leistungen der einzelnen führen, sowohl durch Leistungsverdichtung als auch durch die Möglichkeit, die Arbeitszeit beliebig zu verlängern. Dies führt wiederum zur Reduzierung der Arbeitsplätze.

4. Eine sozial und materiell ungesicherte Existenz der Heimarbeiter: Neben der Einsparung von Lohnneben-, Arbeitsplatz-, und Maschinenkosten liegt ein wesentlicher Vorteil dieser Arbeit für die Firmen darin, daß das Beschäftigungsrisiko auf die Heimarbeiter verlagert wird.

5. Ständige Kontrolle: Die persönliche Kontrolle von Anwesenheit und Arbeitsverhalten entfällt und wird ersetzt durch eine perfekte Leistungs- und Verhaltenskontrolle durch den Computer (vgl. Kohl, Schütt 1984).

Wie wirkt sich dies alles aus?

Erfahrungen aus Kanada, Japan, USA liegen bereits vor. Was die psychischen Folgen betrifft, so ist eine Zunahme der Belastung durch Streß zu nennen, da die Bildschirmarbeit Konzentration und Schnelligkeit erfordert, d. h. das Arbeitstempo steigt um ein Viertel bis ein Drittel. Grund dafür ist der Wegfall von Wartezeiten aller Art (z. B. Fragen, Abwarten, Delegieren, Gespräche mit Kollegen). Folgen sind die typisch streßbedingten psychosomatischen Erscheinungen wie Kopfschmerzen, Magenschmerzen, Nervosität, Schlafstörungen. Psychische Folgen können seelische Erschöpfung, Ärger, Angst, Unzufriedenheit sein (vgl. Gebert 1981, Huber 1984, Vogelheim 1984).

Wesentliche Ursache für diese Folgen ist die mit der Heimarbeit einhergehende Vereinzelungstendenz (soziale Isolation) sowie die geringen Anreize der Arbeitsinhalte (-- Arbeitsmonotonie). So sind beispielsweise in den USA informationstechnisch gestützte Arbeitsplätze mit Aufgabenvielfalt im Bereich der Textverarbeitung und Sachbearbeitung nicht bekannt geworden. Die Arbeit ist zudem gekennzeichnet durch den Verlust vieler positiver Erlebnisfaktoren der Berufstätigkeit wie die Erfahrung und Anerkennung der eigenen Leistung durch andere und der Verlust der Sozialkontakte (dadurch, daß keine Integration in den Betrieb stattfindet). Die Folge davon kann Unzufriedenheit, Depression und Krankheit sein.

Was es auf Dauer heißt zuhause allein und isoliert zu arbeiten auf einen Bildschirm zurückgeworfen, ist momentan schlecht abschätzbar, bedarf also der Erforschung. Als mögliche soziale Folgen solcher Arbeitsformen ist darauf hinzuweisen, daß die Heimarbeiter ins Haus zurückgedrängt werden und daß sie jeden Überblick über die Arbeitszusammenhänge verlieren, was im Rahmen des Konzeptes des Kontrollverlustes erhebliche Beeinträchtigungen nach sich zieht (vgl. auch Kapitel 2 und 5 dieses Reports).

Probleme wie Arbeitszeitregelung, Arbeitsbeginn, Arbeitsende, Pausen, Freizeit, soziale Isolation, Einkommenseinbußen, mögliche Kinderarbeit, das sind mögliche negative Aspekte von Heimarbeit. Wieviel Dispositionsspielraum kann dem einzelnen belassen werden und wieviel ist durch externe Kontrolle sprich: sozial und arbeitsrechtliche Regelungen zu kontrollieren?

Heimarbeit scheint nur für einige wenige hochqualifizierte Tätigkeiten wie die des Programmierers, Wissenschaftlers, Journalisten eine sinnvolle Alternative. Hier ergeben sich die positiven Effekte, die mit modernen Technologien einhergehen wie der Wegfall monotoner Tätigkeit, rationelleres Arbeiten, Höherqualifikation. Dennoch ist auch bei diesen Berufsgruppen die soziale Isolation und der potentielle Verlust sozialer Unterstützung zu bedenken, wenn auch bestimmte Belastungen durch die Möglichkeit entsprechend gehaltvoller Arbeit hingenommen werden, oder teilweise kompensiert werden können.

Wenn man die bisherige Entwicklung der Heimarbeit betrachtet (siehe Erfahrungen aus Amerika, Japan, Kanada), dann ist zu hoffen, daß sich trotz allem die Heimarbeit unter Bedingungen realisiert, die positiv sind. So weist denn auch W. Dostal in seiner Studie darauf hin, daß auch in der Frühentwicklung der Heimarbeit bereits höherqualifizierte Tätigkeiten mit dieser Arbeitsform verknüpft sind und, daß es hoffen läßt, daß auch zukünftig Arbeitsformen bei Heimarbeit mit eher positiven Rahmenbedingungen (d. h. Mischtätigkeiten, hohe Qualifikation, rechtliche Absicherung usw.) realisiert werden. Es ist deshalb zu empfehlen, Modellversuche und Fördermaßnahmen vorwiegend auf solche Bereiche zu konzenrieren, in denen aus Arbeitsmarktgründen akzeptable Rahmenbedingungen entstehen werden. Dagegen stellt sich die Frage, ob Versuche im Stile traditioneller Heimarbeit für gering qualifizierte und gering bewertete Tätigkeiten gefördert werden sollten. So resümiert Dostal, daß die Teleheimarbeit in reiner Form in diesem Jahrhundert keine Realisierungschance habe. Begründet wird dies mit der unsicheren Rechtslage und der noch nicht vorhandenen gut ausgebauten Telekommunikationsnetzen. Denn Teleheimarbeit für Personengruppen sei nur dann für die Arbeitgeber interessant, wenn sie erhebliche Kosten sparen helfe. Dies ist aber unter den jetzigen Realisierungsbedingungen nicht der Fall. Kontrollkosten, Transportkosten, Anpassungskosten, Rekrutierungskosten, Koordinierungskosten, Kommunikationskosten lassen eine solche Arbeit bisher als nicht lohnend erscheinen. Solange die technischen Bedingungen nicht geschaffen sind und solange die rechtliche Lage der Heimarbeit ungeklärt ist, läßt sich wenig darüber sagen, wie kostengünstig Heimarbeit ist und ob sie überhaupt kostengünstiger ist als nicht dezentralisierte Arbeit (vgl. Dostal 1985).

Besondere Beachtung verdient die mit der Heimarbeit einhergehende soziale Isolation. Diese findet sich aber auch mehr und mehr in Betrieben, bedingt durch die mit Computertechnologien einhergehende Leistungsverdichtung, tayloristischer Arbeitsorganisation und durch die zunehmende Technologisierung der Leistungskontrolle unter zeitökonomischen Kriterien (vgl. Naschold 1979). Aus diesem Grunde werden im nächsten Abschnitt die psychosozialen Folgen sozialer Isolation kurz abgehandelt.

5. Soziale Isolation

Die mit den Computertechnologien einhergehenden Arbeitsbedingungen fördern das Erlebnis sozialer Isolation. Die Möglichkeit betrieblicher Alltagskommunikation wird stark reduziert oder ganz unmöglich (Heimarbeit). Die Anbindung an die Maschine dominiert. Betriebliche und außerbetriebliche Sorgen, Ängste, Erfahrungen, die in informellen Gesprächen ausgetauscht werden konnten, können nur noch selten miteinander ausgetauscht werden. Soziale Isolation führt zu einem Verlust an sozialer Kompetenz. Der Verlust sozialer Kompetenz bedeutet, daß betriebliche Belastung stärker als bisher individuell bewältigt werden muß. Ohne die Möglichkeit des sozialen Vergleichs wird die Ursache der Gefährdungen und Belastungen des Arbeitsalltages der eigenen Person, dem eigenen Unvermögen zugeschrieben. Soziale Isolation bedeutet weitgehend Wegfall sozialer Unterstützung, wie sie in Arbeitsgruppen möglich ist. Soziale Unterstützung beeinflußt sowohl die Kontrolle am Arbeitsplatz als auch die kognitiven Situationsinterpretationen der arbeitenden Person sowie die Möglichkeit, den Arbeitsablauf in seinem inhaltlichen Zusammenhang zu verstehen. Vor allem im Zusammenhang mit dem Phänomen Streß konnte die Wirkung sozialer Unterstützung empirisch festgestellt werden (vgl. Frese 1978, 1981). Sie wirkt zum einen dadurch, daß Streßbedingungen in der Arbeit direkt durch soziale Unterstützung verändert werden oder soziale Unterstützung zu einer Verringerung von subjektiver Hilflosigkeit und Niedergeschlagenheit führt z. B. durch Gespräche, emotionale Aufmunterung. Dies ist besonders wichtig unter Arbeitsbedingungen, wo der Arbeitsablauf weitgehend extern gesteuert wird. Zudem hat soziale Unterstützung einen Puffereffekt. Selbst wenn gleich hohe Streßeinwirkung besteht, werden die Streßauswirkungen durch die Anwesenheit anderer gemildert. Sie fördert eine bessere Bewältigung von Streßbedingungen, etwa wenn Informationen zur besseren Einordnung einer bestimmten Situation weitergegeben werden oder wenn Arbeitnehmer sich gegenseitig aufmuntern. Der Vorteil der Arbeit in Gruppen, im sozialen Verband liegt somit wesentlich darin begründet, daß bei der Berücksichtigung der sozialen Wertematrix gleichzeitig die wirkliche Welt im Zugriff ist i. S. einer sozialen Definition der Situation und somit die Interpretation der Situation für den einzelnen mit weniger Unsicherheit belastet ist und die eigene virtuelle Matrix stets korrigiert werden kann. Dies ist für eine erfolgreiche Bewältigung von Streßsituationen von hohem Nutzen. All diese Vorteile unterlaufen Arbeitsbedingungen, die das soziale Miteinander erschweren oder unmöglich machen.

6. Arbeitszeitflexibilisierung: Formen, Probleme, Auswirkungen

Im Zusammenhang mit der Diskussion zur Arbeitszeitflexibilisierung müssen diejenigen menschlichen Bedingungen der Organisation betrachtet werden, die im zeitlichen Ablauf, in der zeitlichen Ausdehnung und in der zeitlichen Verteilung der Arbeit begründet sind und die in der Planung und Organisation der Arbeit nicht vorhergesehen werden, obwohl sie sehr wohl vorhersehbar sind. Das menschliche Verhalten in Arbeitsorganisationen ist bestimmt von vereinbarten Ordnungsregeln, den geplanten zeitlichen Bestimmtheiten der Organisation - Termine, Bearbeitungs-, Durchlaufzeiten, Pausenmöglichkeiten. Dabei darf nicht vergessen werden, daß der Mensch ermüdet, also in seiner möglichen Arbeitszeit, seiner notwendigen Erholung, seinen Belastungsgrenzen voraussehbaren Regelmäßigkeiten unterliegt; daß er einen bestimmten zeitlichen Rhythmus der Leistungsbereitschaft und -fähigkeit hat, der die Zeiteinteilung der Arbeit (z. B. Schichtarbeit) sowie Arbeitsdauer und -tempo beeinflußt. Hinzu kommen soziale und außerbetriebliche Faktoren, die die Leistungsfähigkeit des Menschen, seine Ermüdungsverläufe beeinflussen (z. B. Wohn- und Familienverhältnisse).

Geht man von der Leistung pro Zeiteinheit aus, so gilt, daß diese von der Arbeitszeitdauer beeinflußt wird. Andere Einflußfaktoren sind: die Tageszeit, der Schwierigkeitsgrad der Aufgabe, die vorhandenen Betriebseinrichtungen, das Betriebsklima, die Gruppenarbeit, das Interesse an der Arbeit.

Verkürzung der Arbeitszeit bringt nicht notwendig einen entsprechenden Produktionsrückgang mit sich. Neue Technologien führen zu einer Leistungsintensivierung und Leistungsverdichtung der Arbeit, die für die Arbeitnehmer einen erheblichen Belastungszuwachs bedeutet. Unter diesem Aspekt wirken sich Verkürzungen der Arbeitszeit um so vorteilhafter auf die Leistung aus, je schwerer die Arbeit und je mehr Einfluß der Arbeiter auf ihren Ablauf hat. Bei schweren Arbeiten wird durch eine Ver-

längerung der täglichen Arbeitszeit (z. B. bei 3 - 4 Tage à
12 Std. oder bei 12 Stunden-Schichten) kaum noch eine Erhöhung
der Tagesleistung erzielt, d. h. vom Standpunkt der Arbeitspsychologie her sind bei Tätigkeiten mit mittelschwerer und schwerer Beanspruchung Arbeitszeiten von mehr als 8 Stunden unerwünscht. Bei extrem schweren Belastungen kann es angebracht
sein, die tägliche Arbeitszeit unter 8 Stunden zu legen. Dies
spricht für eine Ausdehnung der Teilzeitarbeit, aber gegen Arbeitsformen, die die Arbeit auf weniger Wochentage legen wollen,
bei gleichzeitiger Ausdehnung der täglichen Arbeitszeit.

Bei Tätigkeiten mit geringer Beanspruchung, die mit guter Leistung über 9 - 10 Stunden täglich verrichtet werden könnte,
sollte eine derartige Ausdehnung der Arbeitszeit trotzdem vermieden werden (vgl. Köppl 1981). Denn, wie sich zeigt, steigt
die Leistung nach 8 Stunden Arbeit nur noch wenig an. Nach 6
Stunden Arbeit sind oft ca. 95 % der 8 Stunden-Tagesleistung
erreicht. Dies spricht für eine Verringerung der täglichen
Arbeitszeit im Sinne von Teilzeitarbeit, aber gegen eine
Ausweitung der täglichen Arbeitszeit auf mehr als 8 Stunden,
selbst wenn die Arbeitswoche um 1 - 2 Tage reduziert wird
(vgl. Jungbluth 1968, Böckle 1979). Besonders erhöhter Zeitdruck wie er mit der Implementierung von Computertechnologien
im Arbeitsprozeß verbunden sein kann, führt allgemein nicht
zu Leistungssteigerungen, sondern eher zu Leistungsminderungen. Bei der Arbeitsorganisation ist von daher auf eine
geeignete Verteilung des Arbeitstempos auf eine nicht zu hohe
Arbeitsgeschwindigkeit (durch zu knappe Zeitvorgaben) und auf
eine nicht zu große Leistungsverdichtung zu achten. Wie
empirische Studien zeigen, ist bei zunehmendem Zeitdruck mit
einem Zuwachs an Fehlern, sowie sinkender Leistung, mit mehr
Streit, geringerer Arbeitszufriedenheit, höheren Fehlzeiten
und schnellerer Kündigung zu rechnen (vgl. Jacobi 1980, Weltz
1983, Frese u.a. 1981). Arbeit unter hohem Zeitdruck bewirkt
häufig schwere Ermüdungszustände, das Gefühl des Gehetztwerdens, den Eindruck mit seiner Arbeit nicht fertig zu werden.
Dies führt zu Leistungsminderungen, sowie zu Unfällen,
Ausschuß und Fehlzeiten.

hoher Zeitdruck, Leistungsverdichtung, das Gefühl des Gehetztwerdens, dies alles sind Empfindungen, die auch oft im Zusammenhang mit Computertechnologien genannt werden und die durch die Veränderung der Arbeitsanforderungen, nämlich durch die Verringerung der physischen Beanspruchung bei gleichzeitiger Zunahme psychischer Belastungen (auch i. S. sensorischer und kognitiver Anteile) zustande zu kommen scheint (vgl. BMFT Band 43; vgl. auch Kapitel 1 dieser Arbeit). Bei vielen Arbeiten hat der Mensch die Möglichkeit, seine jeweilige Arbeitsgeschwindigkeit dem Verlauf der Leistungsbereitschaft anzupassen. Bei vielen, vorwiegend maschinengebundenen Arbeiten ist dies nur schwer möglich. Hier bestimmt die Maschine das Tempo, d. h. daß bestimmte Leistungsreserven in guten Leistungszeiten nicht genutzt werden können, in schlechten Leistungszeiten das Gefühl des Gehetztwerdens entsteht (vgl. Köppl 1981).

Mit der Einführung der Computertechnologie beginnt eine neue Ära zeitökonomischer Organisationsprinzipien, die die Intensivierung des gesamten Produktionsprozesses zum Ziel haben, der in drei Formen das Betriebsgeschehen bestimmt.

1. "Arbeitsorganisation wird in zunehmendem Maße durch eine tayloristische Zeitökonomisierung der lebendigen Arbeit und durch eine Flexibilisierung der Personaleinsatzpolitik bestimmt. Die unternehmerische Leistungspolitik zielt dabei, unterstützt durch Anreiz- und Sanktionssysteme auf die Funktionsweise aller offenen und latenten Zeitreserven ab.

2. Die Ökonomisierung des konstanten Kapitals erfolgt durch den Übergang zur Fließfertigung und deren Weiterentwicklung zu teil-, oder vollautomatisierten Produktionssystemen ...

3. Computerunterstützte Steuerungs- und Informationssysteme unterwerfen nicht nur die Angestelltentätigkeit unter die industrielle Zeitökonomie mit der Folge der Intensivierung auch dieser Arbeitstätigkeit. Entscheidend werden vielmehr die

Bemühungen zur Optimierung des gesamten Produktionsprozesses durch Gesamtzeitbudgetierung und prozeßbegleitende Systemkontrolle mittels komplexer Betriebsdatenerfassungssysteme." (vgl. Naschold 1979, S. 7)

Ziel dieser Entwicklung ist die zeitliche Synchronisierung der eigenen Tätigkeiten und Bedürfnisse mit den Anforderungen des Betriebes, Arbeitsintensivierung im Sinne einer Leistungssteigerung hinsichtlich Zeitpunkt, Zeitspanne, Tempo und Dichte der Arbeitstätigkeit und eine Zeitvertiefung im Sinne einer simultanen Mehrfachtätigkeit im selben Arbeitsvollzug (vgl. Böckle 1979, Naschold 1979, Epping u.a. 1977, Seicht 1981, Schultz-Wild u.a. 1973).

All dies bedingt eine ansteigende und umfassende Verdichtung der Arbeit zu einem ständigen Zeitdruck, der sich eigenständig oder begleitend bei allen anderen Belastungen ausweitet (vgl. Köppl 1981). Es zeigt sich, daß das betriebliche Handeln durch ein steigendes Ausmaß an Verhaltensfestlegungen durch Sach- und Zeitgegebenheiten in Form von technisch-physischen Arbeitsbedingungen und kooperativen Sachzwängen gekennzeichnet ist. Die Zeitbindung des Arbeitstaktes, das Arbeitsgeschwindigkeitsverhalten stellen mehr und mehr wesentliche Konfliktursachen dar. Die Zeitökonomisierung des Arbeitsprozesses stellt beispielsweise widersprüchliche Anforderungen an die Arbeitnehmer: schnell, präzise und sicher soll unter Zeitdruck gearbeitet werden und das wird auch auf Kosten der eigenen Gesundheit zu realisieren versucht. Zusätzlich zu dieser Art von Streß durch Rollenambiguität kommt noch der soziale Streß der Konkurrenz hinzu (vgl. Naschold 1979; Gebert 1981, Frese 1978, Böhnisch 1978, Türk 1976).

Die Streßforschung konnte zeigen, daß Zeitknappheit und mangelnde individuelle Bewältigungskompetenz zusammentreffen und zu Risikoelementen der Gesundheitsgefährdung gehören (vgl. Frese 1981). Wozu diese Erläuterungen: Sie sollen deutlich machen, daß die Frage der Arbeitszeitflexibilisierung von falschen Prämissen ausgeht. Diskutiert wird vorrangig über die extensive Ausgestaltung der Arbeitszeit, wohingegen die Dichte der Arbeit pro Zeiteinheit oftmals vernachlässigt wird. Aber gerade die Zeitdichte ist es, die durch neue Technologien verändert wird und neue Belastungsprobleme aufwirft. Dies sollte bei der Veränderung von Arbeitszeitformen immer bedacht werden. Die Prämisse Arbeitszeitverkürzung führe zu einer Verkürzung und Verringerung der Belastungsexposition und zu einem Anwachsen der Freizeit und beide Tendenzen zusammen zu einer Reduzierung von Belastung und Verbesserung der Regeneration, ist in dieser Form nicht ohne weiteres tragbar. Denn Arbeitsbelastung erfolgt nicht nur - was die Zeitdimension betrifft - über die Form extensiver Zeitnutzung, sondern auch über deren Verdichtung. Der Nichtarbeitsbereich bietet überdies nur sehr wenig Freizeit, die als Freiheit für Regeneration und kreatives Verhalten zur Verfügung steht, da ein großes Ausmaß an gebundener Freizeit mit erheblichen Zusatzbelastungen erfolgt (z. B. Beruf Hausfrau).

Belastungsreduzierung hat somit von einer Entdichtungsstrategie auszugehen. Diese Entdichtungsstrategie muß von einem an die subjektive Wahrnehmung und Kompetenz der Arbeitnehmer gebundenen Belastungskonzept ausgehen. Ziel muß eine Belastungsverringerung durch Entdichtung sein und nicht eine Verkürzung extensiver Arbeitszeit bei gleichzeitiger Verdichtung der Arbeit pro Zeiteinheit wie z. B. bei Teilzeitarbeit oder Arbeit auf Abruf.

Wichtig ist es zu wissen, wo bei Veränderung der technologischen Voraussetzungen des Produktionsprozesses die neuen Beanspruchungen liegen. Für die höheren Stufen der Mechanisierung steht bei kontrollierender und überwachender Tätigkeit die nervliche Beanspruchung durch Daueranspannung der Aufmerksamkeit im Vordergrund. Der dabei oft auftretende relativ große passive Arbeitsanteil bietet die Möglichkeit zur Mehrstellenarbeit überzugehen, wenn die streng räumliche Bindung an die Maschine aufgehoben werden kann. Bei Mehrstellenarbeit würde

die Daueranspannung der Aufmerksamkeit reduziert, gleichzeitig aber die physisch belastenden Arbeitselemente in großem Ausmaß erweitert. Durch den permanenten Zeitdruck ergibt sich zudem eine zunehmend stärker werdende psychische Beanspruchung. Die Erforschung psychischer Beanspruchung hat bisher nur relativ wenige naturwissenschaftliche Erkenntnisse über die biologisch zugrundeliegenden Strukturen erbracht. Resultat dieses unsicheren Forschungsstandes ist eine Vielfalt sich widersprechender Theorien. Klar scheint, man kann bei der Beanspruchung nicht einfach von einer physischen Beanspruchung ausgehen, neben der eine psychische Beanspruchung besteht, sondern man muß eine wechselseitige Vernetzung bei der Beanspruchung bedenken. D. h. physische und psychische Anforderungen werden nicht getrennt erlebt, sondern als Gesamtbeanspruchung erfahren. Hinzuzufügen ist außerdem, daß die Belastungen aus der Arbeitssituation selten ausschließlich als Einzelfaktoren den arbeitenden Menschen beanspruchen, sondern daß sie stets kombiniert miteinander auftreten. Es muß also von verstärkenden Effekten der gesundheitsschädigenden Wirkungen ausgegangen werden.
Eine Regeneration innerhalb der arbeitsfreien Zeit innerhalb eines 8-Stunden-Arbeitstages ist bei dem mit Computertechnologien erreichten so hohen Niveau der Leistungsdichte nur noch schwer möglich. Es kann einerseits zu einem zunehmenden Defizit von Widerstandskraft und andererseits zu einem wachsenden Verlust an Regenerationsfähigkeit kommen.

Die Summe aller Anforderungen beansprucht zwar schwerpunktmäßig entweder die physische oder die psychische Leistungskapazität, unabhängig von der Ermüdungsursache stellt sich für die Betroffenen jedoch dasselbe Gefühl ein. Beide Beanspruchungsarten können prinzipiell solange erhöht werden, bis die Gesamtbeanspruchung die Dauerleistungsgrenze erreicht hat. Danach kann die eine Beanspruchungsart nur noch nach Abbau der jeweils anderen Beanspruchung ausgedehnt werden. Wird infolge technologischer Veränderung im Arbeitsprozeß ein höherer Grad an psychischer Beanspruchung gefordert (z. B. bei Bildschirmarbeit), so ist das bei vorhandener Auslastung der Arbeitskraft nur möglich, wenn eine Entlastung im physischen Bereich erfolgt. Bei den mit dem technologischen Wandel einhergehenden Arbeitsveränderungen können daher die für die Arbeitskraft eintretenden Anforderungsveränderungen als Umlastung beschrieben werden (vgl. Köppl 1981). Dabei ist noch zu klären, ob die Richtung mit steigendem Mechanisierungsniveau ausschließlich von der körperlichen zur psychischen Beanspruchung verschoben wird. Auch auf hohem Mechanisierungsniveau können neue körperliche Anforderungen entstehen.

Innerhalb der Forschung wird vor allem die auf die 8-Stunden-Schicht bezogene Definition der Dauerleistungsgrenze zugrunde gelegt. Sie orientiert sich damit an der maximalen Ausschöpfung der Arbeitskraft pro Tag, die ohne kurzfristige Verschließerscheinungen und ohne akute Krankheitssymptome erbracht werden kann. Mit der Einführung neuer Technologien und im Zusammenhang damit mit der Zunahme psychischer Beanspruchung, mit der Zunahme von Leistungsdruck, Leistungsverdichtung und erhöhtem Zeitdruck ist eine Neubestimmung der Dauerleistungsgrenze erforderlich. Dies ist bei der Diskussion um Formen der Arbeitszeitflexibilisierung zu beachten. Wie wirken sich unter diesen Rahmenbedingungen z. B. 10 - 12 Stunden Arbeit pro Tag, wie Arbeit auf Abruf aus? Eine Neubestimmung der Dauerleistungsgrenze zur optimalen Gestaltung der Arbeit wäre notwendig. Wenn über die Auswirkungen flexibler Arbeitszeitformen nachgedacht wird, müssen die obigen Überlegungen in Betracht gezogen werden, und es muß überprüft werden, wie sich die Beachtung dieser Annahmen auswirkt.

Zusammenfassend läßt sich folgendes festhalten:

Die Formel, die von einer direkten Beziehung Arbeitszeit - Belastung nach dem Motto je kürzer die Arbeitszeit, je geringer die Belastung ausgeht, ist infrage zu stellen. Die Intensivierung der Arbeit, der zunehmende Leistungsdruck, die Verstärkung der Fremdkontrolle, der Abbau vorhandener Qualifikationen, die zunehmende psychische Belastung all dies sind moderierende Größen, die eine solche Formel vernachlässigt. Während zum

Problem der Dauer und Länge der Arbeitszeit, d. h. der extensiven Zeitform, breite Forschungserfahrung vorliegt, sind die mehr intensiven Formen der Arbeitsverdichtung nur in Ansätzen untersucht. Auf dieser Grundlage wäre die Dauerleistungsgrenze neu zu bestimmen (vgl. Naschold 1979, Köppl 1981).

Das Belastungsmodell der Arbeitswissenschaft stößt hier auf Grenzen. Innerhalb dieses Modells ist Belastung als objektive Anforderung formuliert, Beanspruchung als deren Auswirkung auf das Subjekt in Form von Ermüdung, Gesundheit. Einzelne Belastungsfaktoren werden isoliert gemessen und sodann ihre Wirkung bestimmt, vorwiegend durch physiologische Größen, deren Relation zu psychischen Aspekten nicht eindeutig ist (vgl. Schmidtke 1973). Vernachlässigt wird auch oft die wechselseitige Beeinflussung solcher Größen wie sie beispielsweise bei Schichtarbeit bekannt sind. Ein solches Modell ist nur begrenzt anwendbar. Ein einfaches Reiz-Reaktions-Modell reicht nicht aus. Die arbeitswissenschaftliche Forschung ist angehalten, "ein Modell zu entwickeln, das die Subjektivität der Betroffenen mit ihrer Erfahrung, Kompetenz und Macht, die modifizierend auf die objektive Belastung durch offensive, defensive oder Anpassungsstrategie einwirkt, berücksichtigt." (F. Naschold 1979, S. 12).

Erst unter Zuhilfenahme eines solchen Modells werden Auswirkungen von Teilzeitarbeit, Verlängerung der täglichen Arbeitszeit bei Verringerung der Arbeitstage pro Woche, Schichtarbeit oder kapazitätsorientierte Arbeitszeit empirisch ermittelbar.

Das soll aber nicht heißen, daß Arbeitszeitflexibilisierung im Sinne einer Zeitsouveränität für den Arbeitnehmer nicht auch positive Auswirkungen hätte. Im Gegenteil, zeigt sich doch, daß Arbeitszeitregelungen ein besonderer Problemkreis im Rahmen der Humanisierung der Areit ist.

Eine Verkürzung der Arbeitszeit beispielsweise hat zwei sich gegenseitig verstärkende Entlastungswirkungen. Sie verkürzt die tägliche Arbeitszeit der Belastungsexposition; die Höhe der

Beanspruchung wird dadurch verringert und zugleich wird die Erholungszeit verlängert. Dabei darf nicht vergessen werden, daß auch eine Entdichtung der Arbeitsverausgabung notwendig ist. Generell betreffen die positiven Aspekte der Arbeitszeitflexibilisierung die Vergrößerung des Handlungs- und Entscheidungsspielraumes. Die Zeitsouveränität und die aus ihr entstehende Selbstverantwortlichkeit (größere Freiheitsgrade in bezug auf die Arbeit) für die Einteilung der Arbeitszeit ermöglichen es dem Mitarbeiter, seine eigene Zielvorstellungen, mit denen des Betriebes in Einklang zu bringen. Die bei solchen Arbeitszeitregelungen (z. B. Gleitzeit, Teilzeit) notwendige Delegation von Verantwortung zur Lösung beispielsweise der Stellvertreterfrage bedingt eine ausreichende Information unter den Mitarbeitern und birgt dadurch die Möglichkeit einer größeren Transparenz im Stellengefüge der Unternehmen mit sich (vgl. Heymann 1982; v. Rosenstiel 1975; Francke 1980; Teriet 1976, 1981, 1981a); Böckle 1979).

Aus ihr resultiert wiederum eine intensivere Teamarbeit. In einer Studie zur Gleitzeit zeigten sich beispielsweise folgende positiven motivationspsychologischen Auswirkungen (vgl. v. Rosenstiel 1976).

1. Fluktuation sinkt. Freizügigkeit wird mehr geschätzt als ein wenig mehr Geld in der Lohntüte

2. Eintagskrankheiten hören fast völlig auf

3. Arbeitsleistung steigt leicht an, Fehler infolge von Unaufmerksamkeit werden seltener

4. Der Ton der Mitarbeiter untereinander bessert sich. Man ist freundlicher und aufmerksamer, weil man sich gegenseitig stärker braucht als vorher.

Hinzu kam, daß die erhöhte Kooperation in der Gruppe, zu der mehr Autonomie bei der Arbeitszeitregelung zwingt, zugleich Ausbildungsfunktion hat. Arbeitszeitflexibilisierung erfordert kooperative Mitarbeiter, d. h. es werden an die Arbeitnehmer

Anforderungen gestellt wie Kooperation, Selbstverantwortlichkeit, Absprachefähigkeit (vgl. Teriet 1981a; Heymann 1982). Bei dem System der variablen Arbeitszeit haben die Mitarbeiter lange geübt, sich gegenseitig zu vertreten (vgl. auch Möglichkeiten des Job sharing: Heymann 1982; Teriet 1977). Darin liegt die Chance einer breiteren Qualifizierung, was durch Weiterbildungsmaßnahmen unterstützt werden sollte (vgl. auch Kapitel 1). Diese gewonnene Autonomie kann der Erhöhung der Aufstiegschancen und somit dem Wachstum der Persönlichkeit am Arbeitsplatz dienen. Hier liegen die Chancen einer Arbeitszeitflexibilisierung im Sinne einer Humanisierung der Arbeit, die mehr persönlichkeitsfördernde Merkmale enthält (vgl. Heymann 1982; v. Rosenstiel 1980, 1975; Lattmann 1982; Epping 1977; Francke 1980; Böckle 1979; Teriet 1976, 1977, 1982, 1984).

7. **KAPOVAZ** (Kapazitätsorientierte variable Arbeitszeit)

Bei dieser Form der Arbeitszeitregelung wird eine bestimmte Mindestarbeitszeit vereinbart. Die tatsächliche Länge und auch die Lage der wöchentlichen Arbeitszeit wird jedoch ständig wechselnd je nach Arbeitsanfall von Tag zu Tag oder Woche zu Woche festgelegt. Die Extremform 'Arbeit auf Abruf', bei der sich Arbeitnehmer telefonisch zum Einsatz bereithalten müssen, diese Bereitschaftszeit aber nicht bezahlt bekommen und auch keine garantierte Mindestbeschäftigungszeit aufweisen, ist noch recht selten. Je größer der eingeräumte Flexibilisierungsraum betrieblicher Regelungen ist, desto größer ist damit auch der Spielraum für die betriebliche Einflußnahme - sei es über direkten Druck, sei es über informelle Lenkung - auf die tatsächliche Arbeitszeitgestaltung. Gegenüber weniger durchsetzungsfähigen Arbeitnehmergruppen und Belegschaften bewirkt also das starke Ausgeliefertsein dieser Arbeitnehmer einen erweiterten Spielraum für Arbeitszeitgestaltung in Form von KAPOVAZ. Die Vorteile variabler Arbeitszeit für die Unternehmer liegen in der Möglichkeit der Anpassung der Arbeitszeit an den Arbeitsanfall. Dies bedingt eine Intensivierung der Arbeit, d. h. bei gleichem Entgelt leisten die Arbeitnehmer mehr. Eine Intensivierung der Arbeit geschieht auch über die Möglichkeit der Anpassung der Arbeitszeit an den individuellen Tagesrhythmus. Hierzu kommt eine Reduzierung von Fehlzeiten, Steigerung der Arbeitsproduktivität zu Arbeitsbeginn durch Streßentlastung (z. B. ist der Weg zur Arbeit nicht während der Hauptverkehrszeit zurückzulegen), sowie eine Reduzierung von Überstunden. Die angeführten Faktoren zur Leistungssteigerung der Arbeitnehmer erlauben bei gleichbleibendem Output den Personalbestand zu reduzieren. Die Nachteile für die Unternehmen liegen in der Notwendigkeit erhöhter Führungs- und Kordinierungsaufgaben, in der Unsicherheit über vorhandene Betriebsloyalität der Arbeitnehmer und in den Kosten für Zeiterlassungsmethoden (vgl. Böckle 1979). Es besteht hier auch die Gefahr, daß die variable Arbeitszeit in eine ausgebaute Zeithegemonie des Arbeitgebers führt mit der entsprechenden Nutzung zur Kapazitätsanpassung, Kosteneinsparung, Arbeitszeitverdichtung und letztlich zur Personaleinschränkung.

Für die betroffenen Arbeitnehmer bedeutet KAPOVAZ Arbeitsintensivierung und Leistungsdruck, denn es ergeben sich bei diesen Arbeitszeitformen kaum Verschnaufpausen, die Erholung von der Arbeit fällt völlig in die arbeitsfreie Zeit, was die aktiven Gestaltungsmöglichkeiten in der freien Zeit behindert. Der variable nicht beeinflußbare unvorhersehbare Einsatz, d. h. die Verfügbarkeit der Arbeitnehmer gemäß wechselnden betrieblichen Erfordernissen, bedeutet im Hinblick auf die Vereinbarkeit von Erwerbstätigkeit mit Familienpflichten, daß der Bereich Familie dem Erwerbsarbeitsbereich ebenso nachgeordnet werden muß wie bei starren Arbeitszeiten. Zusätzliche Belastung resultiert durch die unvorhersehbaren Arbeitseinsätze. Der Arbeitnehmer muß in seiner Zeitplanung vorrangig auf betriebliche Erfordernisse Rücksicht nehmen, damit ist seine Arbeitszeit für ihn nicht mehr als feste Größe planbar. Sie wird vielmehr durch den aktuellen Arbeitsanfall oder den abwesenden Kollegen variiert. Dies hat zur Folge, daß auch die Nichtarbeitszeit teilweise seiner Entscheidung entzogen wird. Im Extremfall richtet sich die Lage, die zeitliche Dauer seiner Nicht-Arbeitszeit völlig fremdbestimmt nach den betrieblichen Erfordernissen. Die gewünschte Zeitsouveränität, mit der solche Arbeitsformen angeboten werden, ist ziemlich unrealistisch (vgl. auch Teriet 1976). Das Timing des Arbeitsanfalls kann der Arbeitnehmer kaum beeinflussen, denn Art, Umfang, Ort und Fristigkeit der betrieblichen Leistungserstellung sowie Arbeitsorganisation, Lieferanten- bzw. Kundenstruktur und Personalkapazität sind für den einzelnen Arbeitnehmer weitgehend unbeeinflußbar. Bei variabler Arbeitszeit ist die Arbeitszeit nicht mehr Datum, da sie vom schwankenden Arbeitsanfall bestimmt wird, damit ist aber auch die Nicht-Arbeitszeit nicht mehr planbar und richtet sich ebenfalls nach betrieblichen Erfordernissen. Dies schränkt den Freizeitwert der arbeitsfreien Zeit stark ein. Ausgehend von der Streßforschung liegt es nahe, daß die permanente Abrufbereitschaft, die Unmöglichkeit der

Antizipation über den Arbeitsanfall, die permanente Unsicherheit über die eigene existentielle Lage auf der Basis gibt es Arbeit oder gibt es keine erhebliche Belastungsfaktoren darstellen, die solche Arbeitszeitformen eher im negativen Licht erscheinen lassen. So zeigte sich, daß die Unmöglichkeit der Antizipation des Arbeitsanfalls starke Streßsymptome hervorruft (vgl. Frese 1981, Gebert 1981). Dennoch sind auch Vorteile dieser Arbeitszeitformen zu konstatieren.

Soweit betriebliche Interessen nicht im Wege stehen, können die Dispositionsspielräume entsprechend privaten Bedürfnissen genutzt werden. Die Angleichung an den individuellen Tagesrhythmus der Leistungsbereitschaft ist u. U. möglich. Dies bedeutet eine geringere Belastung des Organismus sowie das Gefühl der Selbstbestimmung bei der Zeiteinteilung des Tages.

Zuviel Flexibilität bezüglich der Arbeitszeit ist aber von den Arbeitnehmern nicht immer gewünscht. Der durch eine solche Flexibilisierung diktierte Arbeitszeitrhythmus muß keineswegs immer mit dem vom Arbeitnehmer gewünschten übereinstimmen. Dies zeigt sich z. B. daran, daß Arbeitnehmer mit Gleitzeitmöglichkeit ihren eigenen festen Arbeitszeitrhythmus wählen. Wo dieser durch Verlängerung eines Arbeitstages unterbrochen wird, geht dies meist auf Unternehmenswünsche, nicht auf eigene Zeitwahl zurück. Hier bieten sich also Konfliktmöglichkeiten, wenn der Wunsch zu bestimmten Arbeitszeitvorgaben nicht mit den Bedürfnissen der Arbeitnehmer abgestimmt wird.

8. Nacht- und Schichtarbeit

Viele Betriebe sehen sich aufgrund überwiegend vordergründiger Wirtschaftlichkeitsberechnungen gezwungen, zum Schichtbetrieb überzugehen. Dadurch erhöht sich der Anteil der tatsächlichen an der maximal-möglichen Betriebsmittel-Nutzungsdauer, die fixen Stückkosten werden verringert. Diese Regelung ist indes unvollständig und fehlerhaft. Denn die mehrschichtige Auslastung des Maschinenparks hat eine ganze Reihe verschleierter Mehrkosten bzw. Wirtschaftlichkeitseinbußen zur Folge, die die bekannten Vorteile des Schichtbetriebes kompensieren, ja sogar überkompensieren können, nachweisbar etwa durch höhere Ausschußquoten in Nachtschichten, Anstieg des Betriebsunfallvorkommens, steigende Fehlzeiten und Fluktuationsraten, verschlechtertes Betriebsklima, mangelnde Identifikation der Arbeitenden mit der Arbeitsaufgabe und dem Betrieb - alles Indizien geringer Arbeitszufriedenheit.

Die zum Teil interdependenten unwirtschaftlichen Effekte der Schichtarbeit als mittelbare Folgeerscheinung der Automation werden komplettiert durch eine ebenfalls negative Entwicklung im persönlichen Bereich der betroffenen Arbeitnehmer.

Schichtarbeit bringt Arbeitnehmern zahlreiche Nachteile gesundheitlicher und gesellschaftlicher Art. Obenan stehen Beeinträchtigungen des Familienlebens und des Freizeitwertes, mangelnde Partizipation am kulturellen Leben sowie soziale Isolation (vgl. hierzu Kapitel 5 dieser Arbeit). Aus arbeitsmedizinischer Sicht sind nervöse Leiden, Herz-Kreislauf-Beschwerden sowie Magen-Darm-Krankheiten häufig noch intensiviert durch einen bedenklichen Pharmaka- und Genußmittelmißbrauch und ein nachts erhöhtes Unfallrisiko (Leistungstief zwischen 3 - 4 Uhr) zu nennen (vgl. Rutenfranz 1982, Rutenfranz u.a. 1984, Bergmann 1982).

Nachtarbeit führt häufig zur Einnahme von Wachmitteln in der Nachtschicht. Tags darauf wird von Nachtarbeitern oft auf Schlaftabletten zurückgegriffen, da der Schlaf entgegen dem biologischen Rhythmus, der sämtliche Organfunktionen tagsüber autonom auf Leistungsbereitschaft schaltet, nur unvollkommen am Tage gelingen kann.

Besonders auffällig aus betriebswirtschaftlicher wie aus psychologischer Sicht ist die Tatsache hoher Fluktuation in Betrieben mit Nachtschicht. Schichtbetriebe weisen generell höhere Fluktuationsraten als normalschichtige Betriebe auf. Mitentscheidend für das Ausmaß des Anstiegs externer Fluktuationsrate ist die Nachtschichtarbeit. Unternehmen, die nur Spätschichten fahren, haben geringere Fluktuationsraten. Sowohl nachteilige Arbeitsbedingungen wie auch Arbeitszeitregelungen sind zwei wesentliche Motive des Arbeitsplatzwechsels, die zur Erhöhung der externen Fluktuationsrate beitragen. Hohe Fluktuation ist gleichzusetzen mit zahlreichen unwirtschaftlichen Effekten wie Personalbeschaffungskosten, Minderung der Arbeitsergiebigkeit, erhöhte Unfallrisiken während der Einarbeitungszeit neuer Mitarbeiter.

Schichtarbeiten ohne Nachtschichten haben weit weniger Fluktuation zur Folge, ein Indiz für größere Arbeitszufriedenheit (vgl. Neuberger 1974, 1974a).

Dazu kommt, daß Schichtarbeiter, die wegen gesundheitlicher Schäden in die Normalschicht überführt werden müssen, häufig enttäuscht und unzufrieden sind, da sie auch noch Entgeltminderungen durch Wegfall von Schichtzulagen hinnehmen müssen

Die Folge solcher Umsetzungen sind auch hier neben sinkender Arbeitsergiebigkeit und steigender Betriebsunfallhäufigkeit zunehmende Fehlzeiten sowie eine Verschlechterung des Betriebsklimas (vgl. auch v. Rosenstiel 1983).

Schichtarbeiter weisen eine höhere Morbidität sowie einen höheren Anteil an Frühinvalidität auf gegenüber normalen Tagesarbeitern. Besonders betroffen ist durch die Schichtarbeit das soziale Leben der Arbeitnehmer. Schichtarbeit beeinflußt ganz

erheblich das soziale Leben und die Zufriedenheit damit. Die
Möglichkeit, am gesellschaftlichen Leben teilzunehmen, ist überwiegend in den Abendstunden und am Wochenende gegeben (Wochenend- und Abendgesellschaft). In der normalerweise arbeitsfreien
Zeit finden nicht arbeitsbezogene soziale Aktivitäten statt. Die
zeitliche Lage der arbeitsfreien Zeit derjenigen Personen, die im
Rahmen einer normalen Arbeitszeitregelung tätig sind, d. h. Tagarbeit verrichten. Für Tagarbeiter ergeben sich vom zeitlichen
Aspekt her keine Probleme an solchen Tätigkeiten teilzunehmen.
Sie behindert eher die tagsüber anstrengende Arbeit. Für Schichtarbeiter ist die Situation völlig anders. Nicht nur die Beanspruchung durch die Arbeit, sondern auch die Tatsache, daß ihre
arbeitsfreie Zeit vielfach in den Vormittagsstunden liegt, also
in einer Zeit, in der das Freizeitangebot im Vergleich zu den
Abendstunden gering ist, stellt sie vor Einschränkungen. Die
Arbeitszeit während der Spätschicht fällt andererseits gerade
in die Zeit, in der eine Konzentration der Möglichkeiten und
Angebote zu verschiedenen Aktivitäten vorliegt. Durch die nicht
normale Lage der Arbeitszeit und Freizeit wird die Möglichkeit
der Teilnahme von Schichtarbeitern an bestimmten Aktivitäten
eingeschränkt oder sogar unmöglich gemacht. Schichtarbeiter widmen sich deshalb häufiger als Tagesarbeiter Aktivitäten, die
zeitlich flexibel sind oder allein durchgeführt werden können.
Bei der Arbeit am Wochenende ergibt sich die Schwierigkeit, daß
neben der verhältnismäßig langen Arbeitszeit 2 - 3 Tage à 10 -
12 Stunden und den damit einhergehenden Belastungen (vgl. Kapitel 6) soziale Aktivitäten mit Freunden und Bekannten, die
vorwiegend am Wochenende möglich sind, schwer realisierbar
sind. Durch die Desynchronisation der eigenen Arbeitszeit mit
der Arbeitszeit von Freunden und Bekannten ergeben sich Probleme im sozialen Bereich, die einer sozialen Isolation förderlich sein können. Zusätzlich ergeben sich Belastungen aus dem
Wissen heraus, in Zeiten arbeiten zu müssen, in denen der überwiegende Teil der Bevölkerung nicht arbeitet. Gerade dieses
Wissen erschwert das Arbeiten zu ungewöhnlichen Tag- wie Nachtzeiten. Probleme ergeben sich auch für die Familie, wenn Mann
und Frau gemeinsam einer Beschäftigung nachgehen. Gemeinsame

Aktivitäten, wie sie am Wochenende möglich wären, sind unter diesen Bedingungen kaum möglich. Häufig verzichtet der eine Ehepartner dann auf bestimmte Unternehmungen, wenn der andere daran nicht teilnehmen kann und wird sich Aktivitäten, die nicht von der Schichtarbeit des Partners beeinflußt werden, zuwenden (vgl. Born 1983, BMJFG 1978). Das Familienleben wird also erheblich durch Schichtarbeit beeinträchtigt. So erfordert Schichtarbeit eine andere Organisation des Haushaltes. Die Väter können sich weniger um die Kinder kümmern, sind am Wochenende unterwegs und nicht für familiäre Aktivitäten abkömmlich. Da Schichtarbeiter höheren körperlichen und psychischen Belastungen ausgesetzt sind, brauchen sie in ihrer Freizeit mehr Erholung und können oft nicht den Bedürfnissen und Erwartungen ihrer Familie entsprechen. Wenn beide Ehepartner berufstätig sind, verringert sich das gemeinsame Zeitbudget der Familie noch mehr. Die Rollenverteilungen, Aufgabenzuweisungen und Aufgabenerfüllungen in der Familie können sich unter dem Einfluß der Schichtarbeit verändern. Zudem ist es wahrscheinlich, daß durch die größere Belastung bei der Arbeit Schichtarbeiter in ihrem Umgangsstil durch ein größeres Ruhebedürfnis bei schlechterer Schlafqualität ungeduldig, gereizt, ungerecht reagieren.

Die biologischen Kosten der Arbeit sind verschieden je nach Tageszeit der Arbeit. Der Organismus unterliegt Schwankungen z. B. Hoch am Vormittag, Leistungstiefe nachts zwischen 3 - 4. Gegen Abend schaltet der Organismus auf Erholungsprozesse um, so daß erhebliche körperliche Anstrengungen erforderlich sind, um nachts gegen die biologische Uhr zu arbeiten.

Vollständiges Anpassen an Schichtarbeit durch Organismus gibt es nicht.

Die Probleme sind zusammengefaßt

1. soziale Probleme im Kontakt mit Familienangehörigen, soziale Isolation

2. Appetitstörungen und langfristig Erkrankungen im Magen-Darm-Bereich

3. mit relativ großer Sicherheit Beeinträchtigungen des
   Schlafes

Die Probleme scheinen nach mentalen Belastungen größer zu
sein (z. B. Telearbeit), weil der Organismus nicht so gut
abschalten kann. Nach körperlicher Arbeit ergibt sich dagegen
ein wohltuender tiefer Schlaf. Weil durch Nachtarbeit die
Tagesperiodik biologischer Rhythmen aus dem Gleichgewicht
kommt und die Güte des Tagesschlafes nie die des nächtlichen
Schlafes erreicht, sind Schichtarbeiter immer erheblichen
psychischen Belastungen ausgesetzt. Diese Stressoren können
zu oben erwähnten Störungen führen, werden sie nicht abgestellt oder kontrollierbar gemacht.

Schichtarbeit sollte nur angewendet werden, wenn sie unumgänglich ist. Aus reinen Wirtschaftlichkeitsgründen ist auf Nacht-
und Schichtarbeit soweit wie möglich zu verzichten (vgl. Rutenfranz 1982). Wo Schichtarbeit betrieben wird, sollten Schichtpläne erstellt werden, die unter Heranziehung wissenschaftlicher
Erkenntnisse die Auswirkungen solcher Arbeitszeitregelungen
minimieren und ausreichend Erholungsmöglichkeiten für die Arbeitnehmer bieten (vgl. Rutenfranz 1982, 1984; Teriet 1977,
1981; Bergman u.a.).

9. Resümee

Die Auswirkungen, die sich aus der Anwendung neuer Technologien als Bestandteil umfassender Rationalisierungsmaßnahmen ergeben, sind heute für die Beschäftigten eher negativ. Das gilt vor allem für Beschäftigung, Einkommen, Arbeitsinhalte und Qualifikationen, Gesundheit, Belastung und Fremdkontrolle (vgl. Vorbrücken 1984; Brandt u.a. 1981).

Es besteht ein starkes Defizit hinsichtlich der institutionellen Voraussetzungen einer integrierten Technologie- und Humanisierungspolitik. Nötig ist das Erstellen von Analysen über technisch-wirtschaftliche Entwicklungen und deren Auswirkungen auf die Zahl und Qualität der Arbeitsplätze, systematische Bestandsaufnahme über Arbeitsbedingungen und Belastungen.

Es konnten im Rahmen dieser Arbeit viele Probleme, die neue Technologien im Produktionsbereich schaffen, nur angerissen werden. Lösungen werden nur möglich, wenn alle Betroffenen dazu beitragen: Arbeitgeber, Arbeitnehmer, Politiker, Wissenschaftler.

LITERATURVERZEICHNIS

F. Böckle: Flexible Arbeitszeiten im Produktionsbereich
Peter Lang, Frankfurt/M. 1979

W. Böhnisch: Personale Widerstände bei der Durchsetzung von Innovationen; Neue Folge Band 37
Poeschel-Verlag, Stuttgart 1979

C. Born, C. Vollmer: Familienfreundliche Gestaltung des Arbeitslebens; Schriftenreihe des Bundesministers für Jugend, Familie und Gesundheit, Band 135
Kohlhammer-Verlag, Stuttgart 1983

G. Brandt u.a. (Hrsg.): Beiträge zur Arbeitsmarkt- und Berufsforschung: Technologieentwicklung, Rationalisierung und Humanisierung,
Nürnberg 1981

Bundesminister für Forschung und Technologie: Schichtarbeit als Gesundheitsrisiko; Humanisierung der Arbeit Band 22
Campus-Verlag, Frankfurt/M. 1982

Bundesminister für Forschung und Technologie: Neue Technologien und Beschäftigung, Band 1,
Econ-Verlag, Düsseldorf 1980

Bundesminister für Forschung und Technologie: Schreibdienste in obersten Bundesbehörden, Humanisierung der Arbeit Band 16,
Campus-Verlag, Frankfurt/M. 19

Bundesminister für Forschung und Technologie: Computerunterstützte Produktion
Humanisierung der Arbeit Band 43
Campus-Verlag, Frankfurt/M. 19

Bundesminister für Forschung und Technologie: Textverarbeitung im Büro
Humanisierung der Arbeit Band 4
Campus-Verlag, Frankfurt/M. 1980

Bundesminister für Jugend, Familie und Gesundheit: Freizeitmöglichkeiten von Nacht-, Schicht-, Sonn- und Feiertagsarbeiten, Band 11
Kohlhammer-Verlag, Stuttgart 1978

A. Cakir: Ist Bildschirmarbeit gefährlich?
Zeitschrift: Humane Produktion 9/1984

W. Dostal: Telearbeit: Anmerkungen zur Arbeitsmarktrelevanz dezentraler Informationstätigkeit
Sonderdruck: Mitteilungen aus der Arbeitsmarkt- und Berufsforschung, 18. Jg. /1985, Kohlhammer-Verlag

K. Epping u.a.: Teilzeitarbeit bei Beamtinnen
Schriftenreihe des Bundesministers für Jugend, Familie und Gesundheit, Band 55
Kohlhammer-Verlag, Stuttgart 1977

J. Franke: Sozialpsychologie des Betriebes
Enke-Verlag, Stuttgart 1980

M. Frese u.a.: Industrielle Psychopathologie
Hans Huber-Verlag, Bern 1978

M. Frese: Streß im Büro
Schriften zur Arbeitspsychologie Nr. 34
Hans Huber-Verlag, Bern 1981

E. Gaugler: Praktische Erfahrungen mit Teilzeitarbeit
Zeitschrift: Personal - Mensch und Arbeit, 3, 1982

E. Gaugler: Betriebswirtschaftliche Aspekte der Arbeitszeitflexibilisierung
Zeitschrift: Personal - Mensch und Arbeit, 8, 1983

A. Gaussmann, M. Schmidt: Monotonie am Arbeitsplatz
Zeitschrift: Humane Produktion, 3, 1982

D. Gebert: Belastung und Beanspruchung in Organisationen
Poeschel-Verlag, Stuttgart 1981

H. Heymann, L. Seiwert: Job sharing - Flexible Arbeitszeit durch Arbeitsplatzteilung
expert-Verlag 1982

M. Huber: Schöne neue Welt der elektronischen Heimarbeit
Zeitschrift: Psychologie heute, 5, 1984

A. Jungbluth, E. W. Mommsen: Angewandte Arbeitswissenschaften
Verlag Mensch und Arbeit, München 1968

H. Kohl, B. Schütt: Neue Technologien und Arbeitswelt
Reihe der Hans-Böckler-Stiftung, Band 4
Bund-Verlag 1984

W. Kohl, D. Schanzenbach: Wird Schichtarbeit mit Gleitzeit humaner?
Zeitschrift: Humane Produktion, 8, 1984

B. Köppl: Intensivierung contra Humanisierung
Arbeitssituation unqualifizierter Industriearbeiter
Campus-Verlag, Frankfurt/M. 1981

W. B. Korte: Telearbeit - Status quo und Perspektiven
Office Management, 3, 1986

H. Kubicek:	Partizipatives Innovationsmanagement in: ÖVD-Online; Sonderausgabe 1978
Ch. Lattmann:	Die verhaltenswissenschaftlichen Grundlagen der Führung des Mitarbeiters, Hans Huber-Verlag, Bern 1982
E. Martin u.a.:	Monotonie in der Industrie Hans Huber-Verlag, Bern 1980
F. Naschold:	Arbeitszeit und Belastung Wissenschaftszentrum, Berlin 1979
O. Neuberger:	Theorien der Arbeitszufriedenheit Kohlhammer-Verlag 1974
O. Neuberger:	Messung der Arbeitszufriedenheit Kohlhammer-Verlag 1974a
T. Pirker:	Schreibdienste in obersten Bundesbehörden Humanisierung der Arbeit Band 16 Campus-Verlag, Frankfurt/M. 1982
W. D. Rauch:	Büro-Informations-Systeme Hermann Böhlhaus, Wien, Köln, Graz 1982
L. v. Rosenstiel:	Die motivationalen Grundlagen des Verhaltens in Organisationen Duncker und Humblot, Berlin 1975
L. v. Rosenstiel, M. Weinkamm:	Humanisierung der Arbeitswelt - eine vergessene Verpflichtung Poeschel-Verlag, Stuttgart 1980
L. v. Rosenstiel:	Betriebsklima geht jeden an Bayerisches Staatsministerium für Arbeit und Sozialordnung, München 1983

J. Rutenfranz u.a.:	Arbeit zu ungewöhnlicher Tageszeit Hrsg.: ZDF, Mainz 1984
J. Rutenfranz u.a.:	Schichtarbeit und Nachtarbeit München 1982
H. Schmidtke:	Ergonomie 1 Carl Hanser-Verlag, München 1973
G. Seicht:	Arbeitszeitverkürzung - Aktuelle Sicht, politische Forderungen, ökonomische Konsequenzen Signum-Verlag, Wien 1981
R. Schultz-Wild, F. Weltz:	Technischer Wandel und Industriebetrieb Athenäum-Verlag, Frankfurt/M. 1973
B. Teriet:	Neue Strukturen der Arbeitszeitverteilung Verlag Otto Schwarz & Co., Göttingen 1976
B. Teriet:	Flexible Arbeitszeiten erfordern kooperative Mitarbeiter Zeitschrift: Personal - Mensch und Arbeit 3, 1981
B. Teriet:	Job sharing - neue Form der Arbeitsvertragsgestaltung Zeitschrift: Personal - Mensch und Arbeit 6/1977
B. Teriet:	Zeitsouveränität - eine personalwirtschaftliche Herausforderung Zeitschrift: Personal - Mensch und Arbeit 3, 1981
B. Teriet:	Arbeitszeit und Familie Zeitschrift: Humane Produktion, 1-2/1982

K. Türk:	Grundlagen einer Pathologie der Organisation Enke-Verlag, Stuttgart 1976
E. Ulich:	Nacht- und Schichtarbeit Westdeutscher Verlag, Köln/Opladen 1978
E. Vogelheim:	Frauen am Computer rororo-Verlag, Reinbek 1984
K. H. Vorbrücken:	Neue Technologien im Produktionsbereich und ihre Auswirkungen auf Arbeitsplätze und Arbeitnehmer, Zeitschrift: Humane Produktion, 2, 1984
F. Weltz, V. Lullies:	Innovation im Büro Humanisierung der Arbeit Band 38 Campus-Verlag, Frankfurt/M. 1983

LEGAL AND CONTRACTUAL LIMITATIONS TO WORKING TIME

Roger Blanpain

Faculty of Law
University of Leuven
Belgium

LEUVEN,
FEBRUARY, 1986

Reflections on the reorganisation of working time, as well as on our study concerning the legal and contractual limitations to working time have to be situated in the framework of the overall discussion of "flexibility", in the sense of a rapid (?) adaptation of the factor "labour" to the changing conditions of the market in its broadest sense as well as in the framework of the debate on the reduction of working time. The discussion on flexibility is undoubtedly getting most of the attention.

Different kinds of flexibility can be distinguished :

- numerical flexibility :

relates to the ease with which the number of workers can be adjusted to meet fluctuations in the level of demand. The ideal numerically flexible enterprise is the one which deploys exactly the right number of workers at each stage of the fluctuations. This may mean the easing of hiring and firing; more part-time, temporary work, (atypical forms of work), contracts for a definite period, replacement, contracts on call, subcontracting and the like ... The end result is thus that at any time the number employed/working exactly match at any time the work force needed.

- functional flexibility :

is the smooth and quick redeployment of employees between activities and tasks, present and future ones, as products, services and (production) methods evolve.

- financial flexibility :

means different things :
- adaptation of pay and other employment costs to the state and supply in the external labour market; see the argument that the minimum pay of youngsters is too high to hire them; the automatic cost of living clause is looked upon by some from the same angle;
- it means equally the extent to which the pay structure reflects also individual performance, as well of the employee as of the enterprise, as well as the market rate for the skill in question.

- finally one can distinguish, although this may be overlapping partly with functional flexibility, flexibility in the <u>organisation of working time</u>, this is flexibility in the adaptation of the hours of work to be performed.

We will concentrate on reorganisation in the area of working time; <u>how many hours and when</u>.

x x x

Reorganising working time has been addressed from different points of view and covers various interests and reasons.

<u>Trade-unions</u>, stress the reduction of working time as a way of redistribution of available labour and thus one of the ways to solve the unemployment crisis. No need to recall the strike in the German Metalworking industry in 1984.

<u>Employers</u> however oppose this and insist on the contrary on the necessity of the adaptability of the enterprise to the changing demands of the market, on the urgent need to be competitive and to disconnect individual working time and the working time of the machines, of capital investment; work any time, day, night, sundays, weekend, when economically useful and indicated. Employers argue that this is the only way to secure employment and create new employment.

Some employees may want flexible arrangements part-time, temporary work, sunday work. Evaluating e.g. the Hansenne experiments, called after the Minister of Labour in my country, allowing almost everything as far as working time is concerned, provided there is an agreement between workers and their representatives, additional employees are engaged and the "experiment" is approved by the Minister himself (there are now 50 experiments), research shows that some workers doing week-end work (twice 12 hours with 36 hours pay) are happy - at least for the time being - to concentrate their work on two days and have 5 days to do other things, while others complain that family life and social contacts are jeopardised, as well as possibilities for culture and leisure are rather limited during the week.

Some governments, in order to tackle the crisis engage in certain actions with the aim of fostering the competitivity of the enterprises and employment, thus part-time, easier contracts for a definite period, (F.R. Germany), sunday work, annualisation (Belgium, France) and the like. One has also to add that new technologies allow for greater flexibility, work "à la carte" as well as work at home and may favour "explosion of the traditional" dynosaurus enterprise toward smaller units and less group related forms of work, thus allowing for more individuality.

x x x

The purpose now of our exercise is to indicate and hopefully evaluate developments in the area of work time from the legal point of view. To examine what the legal and contractual limitations to working time are in the member states of the European Communities.

We will, for reasons of time and space, not dig into history, although this would be fascinating, since some regulations, may go back as far as the 15th and 16th century. Some were taken with the aim of tackling unemployment and promoting a better division of labour, as well as social protection. Historia docet !

Suffice it to repeat that French silk weavers in Lyon worked during the second Empire not less than 17 hours a day. That the Factory act of 1850 limited the weekly working time to 60 hours for men between 13 and 18 of age and for women of all ages.

Sunday rest was unknown. A Belgian law of 1889 protecting children and females set the limits at 6 days a week and 12 hours a day. For adult men no protection was foreseen in the "name of individual freedom".

One should recall developments since the First World War, the Treaty of Versailles and the first international Labour Conference in Washington setting the 48 hour week and the 8 hour day. The demand 3 times 8 (8 hours work, 8 hours leisure and 8 Hours sleep) became widely accepted; as well as sunday rest. The 8 hour day was adopted in Germany in 1919, in France, the Netherlands in 1921 ...

The legislation which developed was essentially of a protective nature, especially for women and children and relating to the realities of mass production of workers, all starting at the same time.

Since then working time has diminished and will probably continue to diminish over the years. These is no fundamental reason why this movement should stop, depending on economic and technological progress. When I asked, last year, Irving Jones, how he saw ICI in the year 2025, as far as employment was concerned, he said : I see 350.000 people working 20 hour a week and 10.000 crazy guys like you and me, working 80 hours a week.

It is in a sense amazing that the debate over all those years has been dominated by themes which are also now familiar :
- protection of the health of the employee, also against himself;
- international competition;
- increasing productivity;
- freedom of labour;
- leisure time, family life.

Lately however great emphasis has been laid on the battle against unemployment through reorganising the working time (reduction and/or flexibility or both).

Interesting is also to watch the evolving relationship between the law and collective bargaining as ways to determine the exact amount and the when of working time. It is selfevident, the greater the diversification of products, services and techniques the less the law can do and the more collective arrangements have to be negotiated at lower levels, close to the enterprise.

Topical are at present discussions on :
- reduction of working time;
- shift work, also for economic reasons;
- sunday work;
- night work;
- annualisation of work (the flexible work week, to be organised and be calculated in such a way that over the year a given average of worked per week (see France, Belgium));
- part-time;

- temporary work;
- overtime;
- the role of representatives of employees and of the labour inspection.

x x x

Our <u>comparative</u> study then will concentrate, by way of <u>national reports</u>, on the state of the union (where are we, where are we going) regarding legal and contractual limitation to working time.

We will concentrate on :

I. <u>(legal) sources</u> : acts of parliament, collective agreements, eventually work rules (at plant level).
In order to have a "minimum" of contact with reality, we will examine collective agreements in four sectors of <u>industry</u>; two blue collar sectors (metals, textile) and to white collar sectors (banking and insurance) and agreements or arrangements (work rules included) at enterprise level, 4 enterprises from the same sectors, as indicated (metals, textile, ...)

II. Secondly we will, in order to avoid misunderstandings, engage into the <u>meaning of the notions</u> we use; as such, the notions : working time, full-time, part-time, temporary work, ...

III. We then examine the <u>content of the legal and contractual limitations</u>, as well the general rules (e.g. 8 hours a day), as the exceptions (e.g. 9 hours in a 5-day week; 12 hours in case of continuous work ...).

We consecutively pay attention to :

- <u>the duration of working time</u>, per day, week, month year;
- <u>the limitation of work during certain days or periods</u>, sunday, holidays, annual vacation, night work, motherhood, parental leave, justified leave of absence (marriage, witness before a court, and the like);
- certain categories of <u>persons</u> (youngsters, women, retired employees);

- part-time;
- temporary work;
- shift work.

IV. We then examine possible recent measures introducing flexibility in working time, as well as reduction in working time.

V. Finally we engage in a evaluation of flexibility versus social well being; looking for the balance of what is economically necessary and socially (from the human point of view) desirable. We will also look at the ways through which changes should be introduced.

Each national report will contain a short bibliography.

Following colleagues have accepted to write a national report :

Belgium : R. Blanpain
Denmark : P. Jacobsen
France : J. Rojot
FR Germany : M. Weiss
G. Britain : B. Hepple
Greece : T. Koniaris
Ireland : M. Redmond
Italy : T. Treu
The Netherlands : M. Rood
Portugal : M. Pinto
Spain : F. Rodriguez Sanudo

OUTLINE : LEGAL AND CONTRACTUAL LIMITATIONS TO WORKING TIME

CONTENT

I. SOURCES

A. Legislation (Acts of Parliament ...)
B. Collective Agreements
    a. Interindustrywide - Regional
    b. Industrywide
        2. blue collar sectors
           - metalworking industry
           - textile industry
        2. white collar sectors
           - banking
           - insurance
    c. Enterprise level
        2 enterprises (metalworking - textile industry)
        2 enterprises (banking - insurance)
C. Work rules (enterprise level)
    a. In general (1)
    b. 4 enterprises (content of work rules)

II. DEFINITIONS

A. Working time
B. Full-time. Part-time
C. Temporary work

III. CONTENT OF LIMITATIONS

A. Duration (minimum - maximum)
    1. Daily
        a. In general

---

(1) Does the law say that work rules should say anything on working time ?

                1) Legislation (Acts of Parliament ...)
                2) Collective Agreements
                3) Work rules
          b. Exceptions
                1) Conditions
                2) Overtime
                3) Rest
    2. <u>Weekly</u>
          a. In general
                1) Legislation (Acts of Parliament ...)
                2) Collective Agreements
                3) Work rules
          b. Exceptions
                1) Conditions
                2) Overtime
                3) Rest
    3. <u>Monthly</u>
          a. In general
                1) Legislation (Acts of Parliament ...)
                2) Collective Agreements
                3) Work rules
          b. Exceptions
                1) Conditions
                2) Overtime
                3) Rest
    4. <u>Annually</u>
          a. In general
                1) Legislation (Acts of Parliament ...)
                2) Collective Agreements
                3) Work rules
          b. Exceptions
                1) Conditions
                2) Overtime
                3) Rest
B. <u>Certain days – periods</u>
    1. <u>Sunday rest</u>
          a. In general
                1) Legislation (Acts of Parliament ...)
                2) Collective Agreements

    b. Exceptions
      1) Conditions
      2) Overtime
      3) Rest
  2. Holidays
    Idem
  3. Annual vacation
    a. In general
      1) Legislation (Acts of Parliament ...)
      2) Collective Agreements
    b. Exceptions
  4. Night work
    Idem
  5. Motherhood
    Idem
  6. Parental Leave
    Idem
  7. Justified Leave of Absence
C. Certain Persons
  1. Youngsters
    a. In general
    b. Exceptions
  2. Women
    Idem
  3. Retired employees
D. Part-time
  1. Form - Conditions
  2. Remuneration
E. Temporary work
  1. Duration
    a. In general
      1. Legislation (Acts of Parliament ...)
      2. Collective Agreements
    b. Exceptions
  2. Forms
F. Shift-work
  1. Duration
  2. Conditions
  3. Overtime

IV. RECENT MEASURES INTRODUCING REORGANISATION OF WORKING TIME

e.g. Belgium

A. Annual Working Time
B. Hansenne Experiments
C. Part-time Work
D.

V. EVALUATION : REORGANISATION OF WORKING TIME AND SOCIAL WELL-BEING

Identify, if necessary, on the basis of an inquiry of employers associations' - trade unions which "rules", "practices" should be eliminated or rendered more flexible; or, which rules or practices, constitute a necessary element for safeguarding of health, safety, adequate familial and social life as well of the social rights of workers. Attention will also be paid to ways of introducing new forms.

VI. SHORT BIBLIOGRAPHY

METHOD

1. National Reports of maximum 50 pages double space
Belgium
Denmark
France
F.R. Germany
Great Britain
Greece
Ireland
Italy
Luxembourg
The Netherlands
Portugal
Spain

2. Timing 9 months

LES CONSEQUENCES DES FORMES NOUVELLES D'EMPLOI SUR LE DROIT DU TRAVAIL ET DE LA SECURITE SOCIALE

Yota Kravaritou-Manitakis

SALONIQUE,
AVRIL, 1986

PLAN GENERAL

I. Nouvelles formes d'emploi et changement dans les systèmes des relations de travail

II. Les nouvelles formes d'emploi face au Droit du Travail et de la Sécurité Sociale

III. Le travail atypique provoque une prolifération des normes juridiques : une nouvelle typologie des contrats de travail

IV. Techniques et moyens juridiques

V. Nouveau rôle des négociations et des syndicats

VI. Les objectifs de la recherche

I.   NOUVELLES FORMES D'EMPLOI ET CHANGEMENT DANS LES SYSTEMES DES RELATIONS DE TRAVAIL

L'essor extraordinaire des nouvelles formes d'emploi dans tous les Etats membres, basées sur une relation de travail non orthodoxe par rapport à celle typique, classique et rigide que l'on connaît, a donné naissance à une **prolifération de normes** et à une nouvelle typologie du contrat de travail. Si les nouvelles formes apparaissent dans le contexte de la crise, sous la pression du chômage accru et des nouvelles technologies, pour répondre à la demande des entreprises en faveur d'une souplesse de gestion et d'une main d'oeuvre meilleur marché, les dispositions qui les régissent **ne sont pas** toujours **cohérentes avec les principes qui régissent le droit du travail**. Qu'elles soient pleines d'imagination, qu'elles assurent la "flexibilité" tant désirée par l'entreprise, ces dispositions accordent aux travailleurs une protection moindre que celle prévue par les règles du droit du travail et très souvent les privent des minimas garantis traditionnellement par la Sécurité Sociale.

Or, le Droit du Travail, envahi par les nouvelles formes d'emploi dans tous les Etats membres, est en train de subir des **transformations** plus ou moins importantes suivant le pays. Il se voit en effet obligé d'intégrer un certain nombre de nouvelles formes d'emploi tout en se sentant, en même temps, menacé par la logique différente et souple qui les imprègne.

Avant d'entrer dans cette problématique de l'impact du travail atypique sur le Droit du Travail et de la Sécurité Sociale, il faudrait signaler que ces changements au niveau juridique expriment les <u>mutations plus profondes</u> que subit le système des relations de travail des Etats membres. Ces mutations sont toujours liées aux nouvelles formes d'emploi. <u>Premièrement</u>, parce que celles-ci ont exigé une intervention souvent drastique, soit des syndicats, soit de l'Etat, pour les réglementer, les faire accepter, les consacrer. <u>Deuxièmement</u>, parce que la majorité de ceux qui fournissent leur travail sous des formes nouvelles, appartiennent aux nouveaux groupements sociaux (nouvelles minorités) tels femmes, jeunes, étrangers, étudiants, qui défendent en même temps une autre conception de vie et de travail. C'est dans ce cadre que le Droit du Travail et de la Sécurité Sociale subissent les conséquences des nouvelles formes d'emploi.

II. <u>LES NOUVELLES FORMES D'EMPLOI FACE AU DROIT DU TRAVAIL ET DE LA SECURITE SOCIALE</u>

2.1. <u>Le droit du travail ne couvre qu'une partie des relations de travail atypiques</u>

Par nouvelles formes d'emploi, on entend les formes qui couvrent une <u>relation de travail atypique</u>, à savoir une relation qui n'est pas à durée indéterminée, à temps plein, dans les locaux de l'entreprise.

Certes, dans ce que nous appelons nouvelles formes, on trouve des formes d'emploi déjà connues et depuis longtemps, tels le travail à durée déterminée et le travail à domicile. Ce qui est nouveau est le développement sans précédent et irrésistible de certaines formes de travail atypique dans tous les Etats membres. Ce fait a amené une reconnaissance juridique de certaines formes nouvelles d'emploi, assez timide au début. Il a également amené un changement d'humeur à l'égard du travail atypique. On perçoit un fléchissement des attitudes des syndicats - presque contre eux-mêmes - qui auparavant étaient hostiles à ce type de travail.

En réalité, le droit, dans la mesure où il intervient pour régler les nouvelles formes qui se propagent sans cesse, ne couvre qu'une partie des rapports atypiques : celles-ci fleurissent aussi dans le secteur souterrain du travail noir. Ainsi, malgré l'intervention plus ou moins systématique ou répétée du législateur dans certains pays, comme la France ou la République Fédérale d'Allemagne, il y a des formes nouvelles qui échappent au droit ; il y en a également qui sont illicites. Le sentiment est d'ailleurs largement répandu que, une fois que le droit parvient à régler un rapport de travail, un autre rapport de travail atypique naît aussitôt, échappant aux quelques contraintes prévues par la réglementation.

2.2. Formes nouvelles ayant l'avenir devant elles

On a considéré et on a étudié les formes nouvelles

d'emploi comme des "formes intermédiaires entre l'occupation stable à temps plein et la mise au chômage complet"[1], ce qui est en grande partie vrai. La majorité des formes nouvelles sont d'emploi précaire. La _précarité_ est une de leurs caractéristiques fondamentales. Bien que certaines formes nouvelles, tel le travail _à temps partiel_, appartienne à la catégorie des emplois stables.

Les nouvelles formes d'emploi, malgré l'éventuelle instabilité de la relation de travail qu'elles couvrent, se présentent dorénavant de manière permanente ayant l'avenir devant elles. Le travail atypique n'est que le double du travail typique et ne fait qu'exprimer l'évolution même du Droit du Travail : colloques régionaux et congrès internationaux du Droit du Travail et de la Sécurité Sociale s'en occupent[2].

2.3. Une nouvelle catégorie de travailleurs

Les nouvelles formes d'emploi créent ainsi une _nouvelle catégorie_ de travailleurs dont le _statut_ est _inférieur_ à celui d'un travailleur classique et la protection fort réduite. Dans cette catégorie, entrent plusieurs groupements de travailleurs dont la relation de travail n'est pas toujours bien identifiée, ni bien définie.

Les désavantages les plus connus de cette nouvelle catégorie de travailleurs sont : a) rémunération inférieure à celle que reçoivent les travailleurs de la catégorie classique,

b) protection réduite ou inexistante en cas de licenciement et c) avantages sociaux réduits ou inexistants. Par exemple, ils ne peuvent pas bénéficier des congés et des allocations de vacances ou même parfois d'allocations de maternité (c'est le cas de l'Angleterre) ou des congés de maladie suffisamment longs parce que le type de leur emploi ne leur permet pas de répondre aux exigences de la Sécurité Sociale.

2.4. <u>Erosion de la communauté, diversification des statuts</u>

Le développement des nouvelles formes a provoqué une <u>dichotomie initiale</u> de la communauté des travailleurs de l'entreprise classique. Dans la deuxième catégorie de travailleurs hors entreprise, on trouve souvent plusieurs groupes mal identifiés. Ceci a pour résultat une multiplication des statuts : statut classique, statuts "nouvelles formes" dans leur variété pour ceux qui travaillent dans l'entreprise et statut différent - et aussi variable - pour ceux qui travaillent en dehors de l'entreprise mais pour celle-ci. Les conséquences de cette diversité de statuts et de catégories de travailleurs sont évidentes pour l'exercice des droits collectifs des travailleurs.

2.5. <u>Difficultés pour l'exercice des droits collectifs</u>

Les travailleurs ayant une relation de travail atypique ne sont pas en mesure d'exercer leurs droits collectifs au même titre que les autres travailleurs. Pour des raisons objectives tout d'abord : c'est le cas, par exemple, chaque fois qu'ils sont éloignés des locaux de l'entreprise. Pour des raisons subjectives également : même quand ils travaillent dans l'entreprise, ils ne sont souvent pas à même de participer à la défense des intérêts collectifs. La précarité de leur situation peut en être une explication.

On sait que le développement des nouvelles formes d'emploi et d'autres raisons aussi ont conduit à un affaiblissement des organisations syndicales en dehors et à l'intérieur de l'entreprise. Comme dans la majorité des pays membres, les salariés ayant une relation de travail atypique ne sont pas comptés parmi les effectifs d'une entreprise, celle-ci peut être privée de certains organes de représentation et/ou d'un certain nombre de délégués syndicaux. A souligner aussi les grandes difficultés d'organisation collective pour les travailleurs atypiques qui n'ont pas de lieu de travail stable : l'absence de conventions collectives dans la majorité des Etats membres en est la preuve.

De tous les pays membres, c'est surtout en France et en Italie où l'on constate que des textes juridiques expriment le souci de préservation des droits collectifs pour les travailleurs de relation atypique. Par des textes législatifs dans le premier pays qui prévoient, entre autres, que les salariés ayant une relation d'emploi atypique peuvent être élus comme représentants du personnel et exercer leur mission comme les autres mandataires. Les règles de leurs mandats prédominent d'ailleurs sur celles de leur contrat[3]. En Italie, la reconnaissance des droits collectifs se fait par des dispositions des conventions collectives qui ne se présentent pas sous une forme aussi systématique que la réglementation française. Or, il y a des pays, tel l'Angleterre, qui semblent ignorer tout à fait jusqu'à l'existence de ce problème de l'exercice des droits collectifs par cette catégorie de travailleurs appelés "marginaux"[4].

2.6 Souplesse des formes nouvelles et rigidité des règles classiques : quel est le mal du Droit du Travail ?

En plein développement et envahissantes, les nouvelles formes de travail posent des problèmes nouveaux et sérieux au Droit du Travail et de la Sécurité Sociale, dans tous les pays membres. Si elles se présentent comme de nouvelles formes de travail qui veulent assouplir la rigidité des vieilles formes de travail typiques plus proches du début du 20ème siècle, tandis qu'elles - souples, différenciées, imaginatives - sont plus près du début du 21ème siècle, les difficultés qu'elles créent concernent la suppression de la protection des travailleurs, l'effacement des droits acquis, la discrimination qu'elles engendrent, le principe de l'égalité qu'elles méconnaissent.

Le Droit du Travail étant dans tous les pays de la Communauté - il en est autrement à certains égards aux USA ou au Japon - un droit d'ordre public, élaboré progressivement pour assurer à l'ensemble des salariés une protection minimale, il ne peut intégrer les nouvelles formes que sous la condition qu'elles accordent cette protection minimale. Il est donc faux de penser en termes de "formes nouvelles d'emploi contre Droit du Travail parce que celui-ci fixe des règles communes à toutes les entreprises ou parce qu'il se fonde principalement sur les rapports collectifs du travail"[5]. Le Droit du Travail, le droit capitaliste du travail, est là pour s'adapter aux nouvelles exigences de l'entreprise, en assurant pourtant cette protection minimale à l'ensemble des travailleurs. C'est dans la mesure où cette protection minimale n'est pas assurée par les nouvelles formes que le travail atypique crée des difficultés au Droit du Travail et de la Sécurité Sociale. Par les nouvelles formes, le Droit du Travail évolue, s'adapte, dépasse le carcan des vieilles règles, s'affine, s'enrichit. Il suffit qu'elles ne nient pas sa raison d'être[6], à savoir la protection minimale pour l'ensemble des salariés.

Les réponses données par le Droit du Travail de certains Etats membres montrent clairement cette perspective d'adaptation des règles juridiques aux nouvelles formes[7], bien qu'il s'agisse souvent de réponses incomplètes et éparses. Les problèmes posés par les nouvelles formes d'emploi ne sont pas encore identifiés et élaborés de façon systématique. On est pris de court à plusieurs égards : parfois, le législateur - ou la négociation collective - qui s'est occupé de régler quelques formes nouvelles, tels le travail à temps partiel ou à durée déterminée ou temporaire, se voit obligé de revenir sur la question en un espace de temps très court : il n'avait pas pu prévoir l'ampleur ou l'étendue des problèmes à régler.

III. NOUVELLES FORMES DE TRAVAIL "CAPTUREES" : UNE NOUVELLE TYPOLOGIE DE CONTRAT DE TRAVAIL

3.1. La nouvelle typologie

On observe dans tous les pays membres, qu'ils appartiennent à la famille juridique de common law ou à celle de civil law, que la relation atypique, qu'elle soit ou non réglée par le législateur, connaît une expansion importante et crée une nouvelle typologie de contrats de travail.

Les types de contrat nouveaux - ou parfois types innovés - les plus importants sont communs à tous les Etats membres. Les plus connus sont : le contrat de travail à durée déterminée, le contrat à temps partiel, le travail temporaire avec ses différentes expressions, labour on call, le travail à domicile-télétravail. Les formes les plus officielles et leurs variantes développées en marge du droit se présentent de façon différente dans chaque pays et sont parfois illicites.

Il y a certains pays tels le Royaume Uni, l'Irlande ou les Pays-Bas où on ne trouve ni réglementation légale ou autre des nouvelles formes, ni initiatives en préparation

à cet effet. Ainsi, les problèmes posés par certains types
- même les plus connus - de contrats de travail atypiques ne
trouvent pas de solutions plus élaborées et globales. Or,
il y a d'autres pays membres, telles la République Fédérale
d'Allemagne, la France ou l'Italie, où le législateur s'est
senti obligé d'intervenir pour régler certains contrats de
la nouvelle typologie. Il l'a fait au début comme pour donner une solution de dépannage aux questions suscitées par les
nouvelles formes de travail pour lesquelles il n'était pas
favorable. Mais il a souvent dû revenir peu après sur leur
statut et faire face aux nouveaux problèmes posés entre-temps
par celles-ci.

3.2. Le contrat de travail à durée déterminée

On observe, dans tous les pays, une expansion de ce
type de contrat de travail dont l'utilisation était plutôt
rare et exceptionnelle jusqu'au début des années soixante
dix. Il était aussi mal accepté des organisation syndicales
du fait qu'il prive les travailleurs de certaines dispositions protectrices quant au licenciement et d'autres droits
(ancienneté, conditions d'exercice des droits collectifs).
Or, dans plusieurs pays comme la France, l'Italie ou
l'Allemagne, on constate une sorte de consécration des contrats à durée déterminée par de nouvelles réglementations
juridiques.

3.2.1 République Fédérale d'Allemagne

Le droit allemand, tout en autorisant la conclusion de contrats de travail à durée déterminée[8], imposait en même temps certaines conditions - donc des limites - élaborées par la jurisprudence visant à éviter une utilisation abusive de cette forme contractuelle.

Selon le Tribunal Fédéral du Travail[9], la limitation de la durée du contrat de travail doit répondre à une cause raisonnable justifiée en fait. La notion de cause objective n'est pas définie de façon précise par la jurisprudence. Cette dernière a, cependant, élaboré une série de cas qui sont considérés comme des causes objectives.

On accepte ainsi la conclusion de contrats à durée déterminée, lorsque l'employeur a besoin d'auxiliaires pour remplacer les salariés malades et lorsqu'il a besoin de fixer une période d'essai qui ne doit pas dépasser six (6) mois ; également, dans le cas d'un emploi d'artiste (musiciens, chanteurs, acteurs) ou d'un emploi saisonnier. La cause objective pour justifier ce type de contrats existe aussi en cas de suppression, connue d'avance, des moyens de financement d'un programme de recherche universitaire ou en cas d'engagement d'un professeur par une école qui se trouve dans une situation de diminution permanente de son personnel.

Dans le cas où le motif n'est pas objectivement valable[10] ainsi que lorsqu'il n'est pas possible de déterminer la durée du contrat, ce dernier est réputé conclu pour une période indéterminée[11].

Or, la Beschäftigungsförderungsgesetz (BFG, loi pour la promotion de l'emploi) du 26 avril 1985, a suspendu la jurisprudence précitée provisoirement jusqu'au 1.1.1990[12]. En effet, l'article 1 paragraphe 1 de la loi sur la promotion de l'emploi supprime pendant cette période l'exigence d'une cause objective pour tous les travailleurs qui sont employés dans une entreprise pour la première fois. Dans ce cas, une limitation unique d'une durée qui ne peut pas dépasser dix-huit (18) mois est permise. Pour tous les autres cas, à l'exception d'une nouvelle embauche, les critères élaborés par la jurisprudence doivent être respectés.

La loi sur la promotion de l'emploi favorise de façon générale l'accroissement du nombre de salariés ayant une relation de travail instable et à protection réduite par les dispositions citées et contient, en même temps, d'autres dispositions plus spécifiques dont l'objectif est de favoriser l'embauche dans les petites et moyennes entreprises. Elle prévoit en effet que, dans le cas où l'entreprise est créée depuis moins de six mois et qu'elle emploie moins de vingt salariés, les contrats de travail peuvent être conclus avec une durée de vingt-quatre mois.

3.2.2 France

L'évolution du contrat de travail à durée déterminée en France est très significative[13]. Le principe étant, selon et depuis le Code civil de 1804, qu'on ne peut engager ses services qu'en temps ou pour une entreprise déterminée", c'est d'abord la jurisprudence qui avait trouvé le régime des contrats à durée déterminée et indéfiniment renouvelés. Elle avait assuré aux salariés le cumul de la protection accordée au contrat à durée indéterminée. C'est la loi du 3 janvier 1979 qui introduit pour la première fois une série de dispositions définissant le contrat à durée déterminée. Elle introduit en fait <u>deux catégories</u> de contrats, "par nature" et "de date en date", quel qu'en soit l'objet. La deuxième catégorie de contrats à durée déterminée, qui fut fort critiquée en 1979, est retenue par l'ordonnance du 5 février 1982 et le décret du 26 février 1982 qui réforment de façon significative la réglementation antérieure. Le contrat à durée déterminée est devenu une exception tolérée. Le législateur énumère de façon limitative les cas de recours possibles. Ce n'est qu'en cas d'absence temporaire ou suspension du contrat d'un travailleur, en cas de surcroît exceptionnel et temporaire d'activités, de tâche occasionnelle définie par avance et non durable, d'emplois temporaires par nature, d'accomplissement de formation professionnelle.

Les contrats de travail à durée déterminée doivent être conclus pour une période brève de six ou douze mois au maximum selon le cas. Ils ne peuvent pas être renouvelés. Si les cocontractants ne respectent pas ces règles impératives, le contrat de travail n'est pas nul. Il est requalifié comme contrat de travail typique à durée indéterminée.

Or, même cette réglementation ne paraît plus répondre aux exigences des entreprises et il faudrait s'attendre à une réforme élargissant le critère à ce type de contrat. Les négociations sur la flexibilité qui ont à deux reprises échoué proposaient dans le Protocole sur l'adaptation des conditions d'emploi (point 5, sous le titre "travail différencié") ce nouvel assouplissement.

3.2.3 Italie

En Italie, le contrat de travail à durée déterminée a d'abord été réglé par la loi 230 de 1962 qui n'autorise le recours à ce type de contrat que dans des cas bien précis, limitativement énumérés : travail saisonnier, remplacement de travailleur absent, nature du travail, spectacle. Ses dispositions ont été appliquées par la jurisprudence de façon restrictive, ce qui a amené le législateur à intervenir pour faciliter, dans certains cas, le recours au contrat de travail à durée déterminée[14]. Le nombre de critères est accru. Dorénavant, sur la base des lois n° 918 du 3.2.1978 et n° 598 du 26.11.1979, le recours est possible en cas de surcharge de l'entreprise pour une courte durée dans les branches où l'employeur doit faire face à des périodes de pointe : tourisme, commerce, services. Une loi de 1983 (n° 79) prévoit l'extension de cette autorisation à d'autres branches et une autre loi de 1984 (n° 273) son extension à une catégorie sensible de travailleurs : les femmes.

3.3. Le travail à temps partiel

Le travail à temps partiel connaît un essor considérable dans la mesure où, s'il se présente comme la seule possibilité de s'insérer sur le marché du travail pour certaines catégories de travailleurs, dont les femmes qui représentent environ 90 % des salariés à temps partiel, il correspond en même temps à une demande très élevée de la part des employeurs. La diminution de la durée quotidienne du travail a comme conséquence le fait que les salariés travaillent plus intensément - en principe sans recevoir un salaire plus élevé - et le contrat à temps partiel permet à l'employeur une meilleure gestion de l'emploi. Le résultat en est une cascade de lois qui - dans la majorité des Etats membres - sont adoptées pour circonscrire cette forme de travail atypique qui préexistait sans avoir l'importance dont elle jouit à l'heure actuelle.

3.3.1 Espagne

C'est l'Espagne qui paraît être le premier des Etats membres actuels à régler par voie législative le travail à temps partiel[15]. En vertu de l'article 12 de Statuto de los trabahadores, le travailleur à temps partiel est a) celui qui effectue son travail pendant un nombre déterminé d'heures par jour inférieur aux deux tiers de l'horaire habituel, b) celui qui effectue son travail pendant un certain nombre de jours par an, par mois ou par semaines lorsqu'il s'agit d'un travail d'une durée déterminée qui réapparaît normalement. La loi ne fixe pas de durée de travail minimale. Le contrat à temps partiel doit être conclu par écrit et être enregistré à l'Office de l'Emploi. Les cotisations versées à la Sécurité Sociale sont calculées, selon la loi, en fonction du nombre d'heures ou des jours de travail réels. Par cette disposition, on a introduit une dérogation à la loi sur la Sécurité Sociale selon laquelle il faut toujours cotiser au moins en fonction du salaire minimum interprofessionnel garanti et indépendamment du nombre d'heures de travail effectuées quotidiennement.

3.3.2 France

En France, la législation est très favorable au travail à temps partiel[16]. Cette forme de travail atypique a été réglementé pour la première fois par l'ordonnance n° 82-271 du 26 mars 1982 qui précise les entreprises qui peuvent utiliser le travail à temps partiel, les salariés qui peuvent travailler à temps partiel ainsi que la forme et le contenu du contrat. Elle réglemente aussi les conditions de durée du travail à temps partiel. Le travail ne peut pas dépasser un plafond hebdomadaire ou mensuel égal aux 4/5èmes de la durée légale ou conventionnelle du travail. Si la loi fixe la durée maximale, aucune durée minimale n'est imposée. Par la réglementation du travail à temps partiel, les règles générales sont écartées en ce qui concerne les cotisations de la Sécurité Sociale ou le calcul des effectifs[17].

Ainsi, les cotisations payées pour deux salariés à mi-temps ne seront pas supérieures à celles payées pour un salarié à plein temps si la somme des deux salaires à mi-temps est égale au salaire d'un temps plein. Quant à la durée minimale, signalons quand même la disposition qui permet aux salariés désirant bénéficier des prestations sociales d'exiger de l'employeur un nombre d'heures suffisant (cumul de deux ou plusieurs emplois à temps partiel) pour pouvoir couvrir les exigences de la Sécurité Sociale.

Les salariés à temps partiel bénéficient de tous les droits collectifs reconnus aux salariés à temps plein. Ils peuvent voter et se faire élire aux élections des délégués du personnel et des comités d'entreprise. Ils sont pris en compte dans les effectifs de l'entreprise mais au prorata du rapport entre les horaires inscrits au contrat de travail dans l'établissement, si elle est inférieure, dans le cas où la durée de travail est inférieure à 20 heures par semaine ou 80 heures par mois. Les entreprises jouissent d'une grande liberté dans la répartition du temps de travail, sur la journée, la semaine, le mois ou des périodes encore plus longues. Une autre forme de travail atypique a également vu le jour : le travail alterné. Il est organisé par les compagnies aériennes : le personnel navigant qui le souhaite peut travailler un mois, se reposer le mois suivant, reprendre le travail pour un ou deux mois. Si cette solution est en marge des dispositions sur le travail à temps partiel, elle utilise sa logique et elle n'est pas illicite. Or, des problèmes se créent à propos du calcul des effectifs ou du paiement des cotisations qui peuvent se compliquer aussi du fait que les salariés - comme convenu - ne reçoivent ni rémunération pendant le temps où ils ne travaillent pas, ni indemnité quelconque.

3.3.3 République Fédérale d'Allemagne

En R.F.A., le recours au travail à temps partiel est très avantageux pour l'employeur. Tout en travaillant de façon plus intensive que le travailleur à temps plein, le salarié à temps partiel obtient, en raison de sa faible représentation sur le plan syndical, un salaire souvent inférieur à celui correspondant à la durée de son travail[18]. Privé des indemnités pour les heures supplémentaires, en vertu de la jurisprudence dominante du Tribunal Fédéral du Travail[19], celui-ci est d'autre part exclu de l'assurance vieillesse et maladie ainsi que de l'assurance chômage, lorsque la durée de son travail et éventuellement son salaire sont inférieurs à un seuil expressément cité par le Code social (Sozialgesetzbuch, IV)[20].

Bien qu'elle vise à rendre plus attrayant le travail à temps partiel, la loi sur la promotion de l'emploi de 1985 n'a guère amélioré le sort des travailleurs[21]. Cette loi dispose certes, dans le paragraphe 2 alinéa 1, l'obligation pour l'employeur de traiter les salariés à temps partiel comme les salariés à temps plein,"sauf si des raisons objectives justifient un traitement différent". Reconnu depuis longtemps par les tribunaux, ce principe ne fut pas accompagné d'une réglementation spécifique de la question de la discrimination des femmes, quoique celles-ci représentent en RFA 90 % des travailleurs à temps partiel. La loi laisse d'autre part aux tribunaux la détermination des raisons objectives susceptibles de justifier un traitement différent en permettant ainsi des altérations du principe de l'égalité de traitement entre travailleur à temps partiel et travailleur à plein temps[22].

La loi sur la promotion de l'emploi apporte en revanche une atténuation considérable aux problèmes posés par une forme spécifique de travail à temps partiel, à savoir le partage d'un poste de travail (job sharing).[23]

Cette figure contractuelle impliquait l'obligation pour le travailleur qui partage un poste de fournir la totalité du travail en cas d'absence de son partenaire. La loi précitée a mis fin à cette obligation sauf si celle-ci a fait l'objet d'un accord contractuel précis ainsi que dans le cas de nécessité urgente de l'entreprise. Dans ce dernier cas, le travailleur n'est contraint au remplacement que si cela peut être raisonnablement exigé de lui.

En cas de licenciement ou de démission de l'un des partenaires, l'employeur pouvait d'autre part licencier l'autre pour embaucher une nouvelle équipe. D'après la loi de 1985, un tel licenciement est nul, l'employeur ayant exclusivement le choix de muter le travailleur.

3.3.4 Italie

Jusqu'à très récemment, en Italie, le travail à temps partiel n'était encouragé ni par les organisations syndicales ni par le législateur. Le nombre des travailleurs ayant un contrat à temps partiel se limitait surtout aux petites et moyennes entreprises. La base légale de ces contrats était le principe d'autonomie contractuelle et le droit au libre exercice du travail. Or, comme la demande pour ce type de contrat a augmenté fortement pendant les dernières années de la part d'un certain nombre de grandes entreprises, une loi nouvelle a été promulguée qui réglemente ce type de contrat (273/1984)[24]. Les travailleurs qui souhaitent travailler à mi-temps doivent s'inscrire et indiquer le type et l'horaire du travail. Les conventions collectives qui, en Italie, réglementent en détail le travail à temps partiel doivent prévoir les conditions exactes suivant lesquelles le contrat à temps plein peut devenir un contrat à temps partiel. Les travailleurs à temps partiel sont comptés parmi les membres du personnel et jouissent des droits accordés par la Sécurité Sociale proportionnellement au temps de travail fourni.

3.4. Le travail temporaire

Le travail temporaire, une nouvelle forme en expansion également, dans certains pays comme l'Espagne[25], la Grèce et l'Italie[26] - dans ce pays depuis très récemment -

provoque la méfiance et n'est pas acceptée : les entreprises de travail temporaire sont interdites. La loi espagnole, "Lo statuto de las trabahadores", dans son article 43 n°1, est claire : "il est interdit de recruter ou d'engager des travailleurs pour les louer ou les céder temporairement à une entreprise."

On y rencontre cependant le prêt de personnel sous formes diverses qui ne sont pas toujours clairement définies. C'est également le cas au Royaume Uni quant au "loan of worker" qui n'est pas très utilisé, mais qui est pratiqué parfois entre cols blancs, par exemple professeurs, et pour certains cas de travailleurs qualifiés[27]. Or, même dans ces pays et malgré les interdictions, on trouve quelques sociétés qui fournissent du personnel pour l'organisation de congrès et de réunions ou des travailleurs spécialisés dans l'hôtellerie et des services similaires. Elles travaillent malgré les interdictions.

Tout à fait différent est le régime du travail temporaire dans des pays comme la République Fédérale d'Allemagne, la France ou la Belgique où il est accepté et réglementé par la législation. Dans les deux premiers, le travail temporaire a fait l'objet de réglementation pour la première fois en 1972 et en Belgique, de manière provisoire, en 1976.

Le droit allemand[28] - qui connaît aussi le prêt des travailleurs à titre exceptionnel et provisoire par son employeur pour une entreprise tierce - autorise l'activité des entreprises de travail temporaire à partir de 1972 par la loi sur le louage du personnel (Arbeitsnehmerüberlassungsgesetz). Celle-ci règle, entre autres, les rapports entre les entreprises en question et les travailleurs temporaires d'une part, les rapports entre les travailleurs précités et les entreprises utilisatrices d'autre part. Cette législation est complétée par la très récente loi sur la promotion de l'emploi qui prolonge la durée de placement des travailleurs temporaires de trois à six mois pour tout placement réalisé avant le 1er janvier 1990. Elle lui apporte aussi deux autres modifications en mettant en dehors de son champ d'application le louage au sein de groupes de sociétés ainsi que le louage au sein de la même branche industrielle destinée à éviter la mise au chômage partiel et les licenciements.

En France[29], le travail temporaire que le législateur avait admis au début comme une solution de dépannage et de courte durée a connu une telle expansion que l'ordonnance n° 82-131 du 5 février 1985 a été adoptée pour limiter cette forme de travail précaire. Elle prévoit une limitation des situations dans lesquelles une entreprise a le droit de recourir à un travail temporaire soit que le contrat de mise à disposition et le contrat de travail temporaire sont des contrats à durée déterminée ou de courte durée et elle prévoit aussi des sanctions civiles pour frapper les entreprises en cas de fraude. Des propositions ont été élaborées pour la révision de cette réglementation qui a entraîné une réduction importante du travail temporaire. Il existe d'autres contrats relation quelconque avec le régime des allocations de chômage ? Sous quelles conditions ? Le travail "on call" est traité de façon différente d'un pays à l'autre. En Belgique, ce type de travail atypique n'est pas licite. Aux Pays-Bas[30] comme le législateur n'est pas encore intervenu pour régler les nouvelles formes d'emploi qui, là comme ailleurs, fleurissent, la jurisprudence propose et élabore des solutions fort intéressantes et pleines d'imagination. Dans le cas du travail "on call", on peut distinguer deux types de contrats de travail. Dans le premier contrat, le travailleur est mis à la disposition de l'employeur : il s'agit plutôt d'un pré-contrat. Le deuxième contrat existe au moment où le travailleur est embauché pour effectuer le travail demandé par l'employeur et il s'agit là d'un contrat d'emploi normal. Or, en pratique, ces deux contrats "se fondent" pour donner le "min-max contrat" qui peut procurer un travail dont la durée peut aller de 0 à 40 heures par semaine. L'existence de ce contrat pour le travail "on call" ne résout pas les problèmes de "l'attente" et d'un travail d'une durée tellement réduite qu'il ne permet pas aux travailleurs "on call" - dans ce cas aussi, il apparaît que la majorité se compose de travailleuses - de bénéficier des "minima" accordés par le Droit du Travail et de la Sécurité Sociale.

3.6. Réglementation du travail flexible : KAPOVAZ

Si, dans tous les pays, de nouvelles réglementations

de travail basées sur la logique de la flexibilité et des besoins des unités économiques auxquelles se soumettent les salariés, sont découvertes sans cesse au niveau de l'entreprise, nous ne trouvons en revanche que très peu de textes législatifs qui réglementent le travail flexible proprement dit.

Le législateur de la République Fédérale d'Allemagne, dans la <u>loi sur la promotion de l'emploi</u> (BFG)[31], s'occupe de l'horaire de travail variant selon les besoins de l'entreprise (Kapazitätsorientierte Arbeitszeit ou "KAPOVAZ") qui crée divers problèmes aux travailleurs[32]. En effet, l'incertitude sur le temps d'emploi oblige ceux-ci à être de façon permanente à la disposition de l'employeur, ce qui les empêche d'organiser leur temps libre (protection de la personnalité du salarié) et de conclure éventuellement un autre contrat de travail à temps partiel afin d'obtenir un revenu correspondant à leurs besoins.

Dans le cas où le travailleur doit fournir ses prestations en fonction du volume de travail du moment en cas de "KAPOVAZ", la BFG impose trois obligations[33]. a) Le contrat de travail doit déterminer la durée du travail. Il ne s'agit donc pas de "travail sur demande". b) Le salarié n'est obligé de travailler que seulement dans le cas où il est prévenu quatre jours à l'avance. Dans le cas contraire, le salarié n'est pas tenu d'effectuer sa prestation de travail, sauf s'il le veut bien et s'il veut en même temps conserver son emploi. c) Le travailleur ne peut pas être appelé pour des périodes de travail très brèves : chaque prestation de travail doit avoir une durée d'au moins trois heures consécutives.

3.7 Travail à domicile et ses formes nouvelles : le télétravail

Ce type de travail était déjà connu et réglé d'une façon plutôt rudimentaire dans les pays membres. Or, le recours au travail à domicile devient de plus en plus important et crée de nouveaux problèmes juridiques[34]. Dans quelques pays, comme la France et l'Allemagne, les travailleurs à domicile sont assimilés aux salariés. Or, les conditions de travail de cette catégorie - lieu de travail, le domicile éloigné de l'entreprise, pas de surveillance de l'employeur dans l'exercice du travail, autodétermination de la durée des horaires et du temps de travail - les rapprochent des indépendants[35]. D'un autre côté, le travailleur à domicile, qui est privé de toute possession de capital, est employé à la demande et pour le compte de l'employeur. Si une telle demande cesse, les travailleurs à domicile ne sont pas couverts par les allocations chômage. En réalité, si le nombre de travailleurs à domicile augmente, ils se trouvent dans une situation de plus en plus précaire. Le caractère isolé du travail à domicile - ainsi peut-être que la mentalité d'indépendance qui le caractérise - prive les travailleurs de la possibilité de s'organiser de façon collective[36] pour revendiquer la protection élémentaire accordée aux autres catégories de travailleurs. Les problèmes à résoudre sont relatifs à leurs statuts, aux conditions de travail, à la Sécurité Sociale.

A part les travailleurs qui quittent l'entreprise pour effectuer le même travail à domicile (textile) sous d'autres conditions, c'est le _télétravail_ qui fait réapparaître avec éclat cette vieille forme de travail : travail non industriel, non manuel, il se voit couvert, dans la majorité des pays, par la vieille réglementation du travail à domicile malgré des différences substantielles : le contrôle par exemple exercé par le bureau central du travail effectué à domicile.

3.8. Questions posées également au niveau communautaire

Les relations de travail atypiques soulèvent quelques questions qui peuvent être débattues aussi au _niveau communautaire_. Va-t-on, par la "différenciation", accepter la discrimination parmi les différentes catégories de travailleurs ? Sinon, comment la différentation peut-elle être basée sur l'égalité, principe garanti dans tous les ordres juridiques des Etats membres ? Comment assurer l'égalité du traitement par exemple en ce qui concerne les droits de Sécurité Sociale ? Comment fixer les critères de l'_égalité proportionnelle_ par rapport au travail fourni de façon "différentielle" ? Faut-il fixer des minima ? Peut-on fixer un pourcentage du volume du travail destiné au travail dans chaque entreprise ? Les travailleurs de l'entreprise concernée ont-ils leur mot à dire sur le travail atypique et les travailleurs qui le fournissent axés sur leur propre travail ? Ces questions peuvent-elles être négociées par les partenaires sociaux au niveau de l'entreprise ?

IV. MOYENS ET TECHNIQUES JURIDIQUES D'ADAPTATION

4.1 Moyens classiques

L'adaptation du Droit du Travail aux nouvelles formes d'emploi dans les Etats membres, c'est-à-dire l'assouplissement des règles applicables à la relation de travail, "cette adaptation aux besoins de l'entreprise ou flexibilité"[37], varie d'un pays à l'autre selon les caractéristiques propres du Droit du Travail et des relations professionnelles[38].

Dans la mesure où l'on peut décrire cette adaptation de façon générale, on peut dire qu'elle s'exprime au début et tout d'abord par la jurisprudence qui se sent forcée de modifier quelque peu les règles rigides de protection de la relation de travail. Cela peut être le cas, par exemple, des critères élaborés par la jurisprudence allemande sur le contrat à durée déterminée. Vient ensuite l'intervention législative notamment dans les ordres juridiques où le droit d'ordre étatique occupe une place prépondérante dans l'ensemble des règles du Droit du Travail, laquelle est de plus fondés également sur une relation triangulaire et dont l'objet est de fournir des prestations plus complexes que de la simple force de travail. Ainsi on trouve en France le contrat de sous-traitance, le contrat de services ou le contrat de renting. Il est souvent difficile de tracer les limites entre ces contrats et la simple fourniture de main d'oeuvre, à but lucratif. On trouve des cas pareils également dans les autres Etats membres : en matière de travail temporaire, le licite frôle sans cesse l'illicite.

3.5. "Labour on call" : les problèmes du travail "à la demande"

Le travail "à la demande" est une autre forme de travail atypique qui crée une pléthore de problèmes juridiques. Le travailleur potentiel se met à la disposition de l'employeur qui peut l'appeler à n'importe quel moment. Ce type de travail qui n'a pas la sympathie des syndicats se propage dans quelques branches de l'industrie, du commerce, des services, des transports aériens, de l'hôtellerie et du tourisme.

Un des problèmes spécifiques que cette catégorie de travailleurs rencontre est d'être dans l'attente sans être appelé ou d'être trop peu appelé pour travailler. Qu'en est-il de ce temps d'attente, qui peut être trop long ? Doit-il recevoir une "rémunération minimale" du fait qu'il est à la disposition de l'employeur ? Peut-on envisager une en plus utilisée. On pourrait citer à cet égard la loi française du 3 janvier 1979, la première loi sur le contrat à durée déterminée. L'adaptation se fait aussi par voie de négociations collectives et la conclusion de conventions et d'accords collectifs au niveau national. Cela peut être le cas de la Belgique et la convention collective interprofessionnelle du 13 février 1981 sur la durée du travail[39].

Or, cette voie d'adaptation est également et principalement suivie - ceci vaut pour tous les Etats membres - au niveau des entreprises. D'ailleurs, vu les problèmes créés par le contexte économique de la crise mais aussi la "docilité" des travailleurs ou/et l'affaiblissement ou même l'inexistence des organisations syndicales d'entreprises, les accords d'entreprise élaborent et expriment toutes les formes de "règles d'adaptation" qui peuvent cependant être en contradiction avec les principes généraux du Droit du Travail (exemple extrême : le droit à l'emploi dans une entreprise qui peut être exercé soit par la femme, qui est déjà employée, soit par son mari, à la place de celle-ci dans le cas où il venait à se trouver sans emploi[40].

4.2. Nouvelles voies

Mais cette adaptation du Droit du Travail aux nécessités nouvelles se réalise parfois par des techniques et des processus tout à fait nouveaux pour l'élaboration classique du Droit du Travail, comme dans le cas de la voie italienne des lois négociées.

Nous connaissons certes la voie de la programmation sociale ou des conventions collectives (accords interprofessionnels) telles que nous les avons déjà rencontrées dans des pays comme le Royaume Uni (the social contract), la France, la Belgique, l'Espagne. Dans ce dernier pays, depuis 1980 déjà, le Droit du Travail a pu apporter quelques nouvelles réponses au moyen des accords nationaux tripartites tels l'Acuerdo National sobre Empleo de 1981, le pacte de la Montcloa de 1982 ou l'Acuerdo Economico y Social de 1984. Or, en Italie, il semble se développer un nouveau processus de réglementation dans la mesure où l'Etat n'assure plus seulement le cadre dans lequel les négociations se déroulent en les encourageant et qu'il n'intervient pas en tant que tel pour signer l'accord, mais dans la mesure où il participe aussi aux négociations en tant que partie privée, en tant que troisième partie égale aux deux autres et que c'est à ce titre aussi qu'il signe la convention collective. Il s'agit alors pour l'Italie d'une nouvelle convention collective au niveau national qui ne fixe pas le minima, comme c'était le cas auparavant, mais bien le maxima suivant le principe de la non renégociation, au niveau de l'entreprise, des questions traitées au niveau national. Il s'agit d'une nouvelle voie conventionnelle qui, si elle ne réunit plus toutes les organisations syndicales - comme ce fut le cas en 1983 avec l'accord Scotti[41] - permettra au gouvernement italien socialiste de promulguer un décret qui reprend l'essentiel de l'accord de 1985[42] et, en ce qui concerne ce qui nous intéresse, elle conduit à l'assouplissement des conditions d'embauche ou de la réglementation du travail à temps partiel.

4.3. Le problème de la hiérarchie des sources

Si le marché du travail "reste toujours dominé par les principes juridiques du capitalisme"[43], il n'empêche que le Droit du Travail doit évoluer selon le nouveau contexte économique et les besoins des entreprises, ce qui fait naître de nouveaux problèmes et des solutions éloignées d'une certaine idée que l'on se faisait de lui, tel le problème de la hiérarchie des sources.

Une convention collective peut-elle déroger vers le bas, in pejus ? Dans quelle mesure peut-elle porter atteinte à la protection minimale garantie par des dispositions légales ? Il est clair qu'en Italie, compte tenu des évolutions récentes, la conception et la fonction de la convention collective changent. Pourtant, cela ne paraît pas être le cas en République Fédérale d'Allemagne où la convention collective doit selon l'opinion dominante de la doctrine toujours être plus favorable aux salariés.

Mais, si la conception d'une convention collective, l'idée dominante qui la veut plus favorable aux salariés, est le résultat d'un passé culturel, comment peut-on déterminer sa relation avec les lois et le contrat individuel du travail ? Sur la base de quel critère ? Quel est le contenu de "plus favorable" dans l'état nouveau des choses ? Rien n'assure que la convention collective en tant que source de normes qui s'impose au contrat individuel continue à être toujours plus favorable et "a priori préférable" pour les salariés à notre époque[44]. Quelle est donc la nouvelle hiérarchie des normes qui se dessine et le contenu de son critère.

Quelles sont les techniques qui permettent l'annulation de la vieille logique ? On a vu que le moyen le plus drastique est l'intervention du législateur qui peut méconnaître les critères élaborés par la jurisprudence, en édictant de nouvelles règles, plus souples encore, au nom toujours de l'amélioration de l'emploi. Mais les conventions collectives ne se prêtent pas moins à l'adaptation des dispositions aux réalités économiques : quelle peut être leur étendue ? Où se situe le <u>noyau dur</u> du Droit du Travail auquel elles ne peuvent pas toucher ?

Et, finalement, quel est le rôle des organisations syndicales dans ce procédé d'adaptation ou de transformation du Droit du Travail ?

V. <u>NOUVEAU ROLE DES NEGOCIATIONS ET DES SYNDICATS</u>

5.1. <u>La négociation : vers de nouvelles conquêtes</u>

Il est hors de doute que le rôle de la négociation

collective change dans tous les pays. Une redistribution de fond semble-t-elle se préparer, mais aussi se faire entre la part du Droit du Travail fixée par la loi étatique et celle forgée par les négociations ?

Certes, dans tous les pays membres et dans les pays de l'Europe en général, le rôle de la législation est prépondérant - ce qui n'est pas le cas aux USA où prédomine, dans le Droit du Travail, le corps des conventions collectives. Aussi important que soit le rôle des conventions collectives dans les pays membres, et notamment au Royaume Uni[45], en Italie, en Irlande et au Danemark, celles-ci sont toujours axées sur le corps du droit étatique avec pour objectif depuis quelques années non plus simplement d'améliorer ce dernier, mais de le modifier et d'empiéter sur son terrain. Ces nouvelles virtualités - ou peut-être nécessités - pour la négociation collective et les conventions collectives en Europe[46] soulignent le rôle qui incombe aux syndicats dans ce "remodelage" du Droit du Travail.

Il faudrait notamment mentionner les conventions collectives des organisations syndicales qui agissent au niveau national, certes sans méconnaître celles dont le champ d'action se situe au niveau de l'entreprise, où, cependant, la négociation ne se fait pas toujours par l'intermédiaire des syndicats. En effet, à ce niveau, les employeurs préfèrent souvent les comités ou le conseil d'entreprise - dans les pays où existe un double organe de représentation du personnel (en France par exemple). Il se crée d'ailleurs de nouveaux syndicats, tels les syndicats autonomes en Italie qui se distinguent bien des organisations syndicales "classiques", qui négocient au niveau national les questions de l'emploi et ses formes nouvelles.

5.2. Syndicats et négociations

Comment les organisations syndicales, d'un côté "surprises" par les contraintes imposées aux travailleurs par l'évolution économique et technologique et, de l'autre, engagées dans le processus de redéfinition de leurs stratégie et objectifs, se sont-elles comportées à l'égard du développement des nouvelles formes d'emploi et des questions qui touchent à la flexibilité ? Leur comportement et leurs propositions concrètes tels qu'ils se sont manifestés lors des négociations - que ces dernières aient abouti ou non - diffèrent sensiblement d'un pays à l'autre[47].

A première vue, les syndicats les plus efficaces paraissent être les syndicats italiens, allemands, belges et espagnols.

Les syndicats allemands, les plus combatifs, malgré leur idéologie traditionnelle, conservatrice et intégrationniste, qui les distingue fort des syndicats français, italiens ou belges[48], ont pu mener la lutte la plus acharnée dans la Communauté sur la réduction du temps de travail qui est aussi liée à l'aménagement du temps de travail[49].

Si les syndicats italiens se trouvaient aux antipodes

des syndicats allemands de par leur idéologie - lutte des classes - et de par leur pratique - confrontation dans les relations de travail -, ils semblent aujourd'hui être assez proches de ceux-ci. Tout d'abord par les initiatives qu'ils ont prises pour mieux faire face, entre autres, aux nouvelles formes d'emploi, abandonnant le fameux "garantissmo" en vue d'établir le nouveau système de "contrôllo"[50]. Dans ce contexte, les solutions qu'ils ont proposées et les règles qu'ils ont établies par voie de négociation au niveau national ne traduisent plus tellement une idéologie anti-intégrationniste. Au contraire, c'est l'établissement du système de "néocorporatisme" dans les relations de travail. Dans ce cadre, les syndicats italiens ont estimé nécessaire de "porter atteinte" aux droits acquis des travailleurs - au nom de la protection du <u>bien suprême</u> qu'est l'emploi -, ce qui paraît être moins acceptable pour les syndicats allemands[51].

Mais il faudrait signaler aussi deux autres différences fondamentales. Les organisations syndicales italiennes <u>parti-cipent</u> - aussi par la voie des accords nationaux précités de 1983 et 1985 - à l'exécution du pouvoir d'Etat : si les syndicats renoncent partiellement aux dispositions légales de protection, ils ont leur mot à dire dans le domaine de la politique fiscale et sociale (accord <u>Scotti</u> 1983). De plus, l'assouplissement des règles qui régissent la relation de travail "ne signifie pas un recul vers une autorité unilatérale et arbitraire de l'employeur"[52]. Il signifie plutôt que la protection est dorénavant contrôlée par les organisations syndicales dans le système italien "néocorporatiste" des relations de travail. En République Fédérale d'Allemagne par contre, la protection semble toujours être assurée d'abord par la législation et la voie étatique[53].

5.3. <u>Un rôle nouveau pour les syndicats</u>

Si, parmi les syndicats des pays membres, ceux de la République Fédérale d'Allemagne et de l'Italie paraissent être les syndicats les plus forts ayant quelques objectifs à proposer face à la crise économique et à leur propre crise, leur intervention sur la réglementation des nouvelles formes d'emploi est différente et révèle, pour le cas italien, un <u>changement profond</u> de leur rôle, bien qu'encore mal défini ou plutôt pas très bien compris[54].

Ce changement est également perçu en France, en dépit du fait que les négociations sur la flexibilité n'aient pas abouti[55]. Une des questions importantes négociées était le travail "différencié" : travail à durée déterminée, travail temporaire, travail à temps partiel, travail à domicile. L'échec des négociations paraît souligner le besoin d'une autre politique syndicale globale.

Si les organisations syndicales ne peuvent qu'accepter les nouvelles formes de travail, qui, inévitablement, réduisent le nombre des travailleurs jouissant des droits acquis et conquis par les luttes syndicales pendant les décennies passées et accroissent celui des salariés précaires et des pseudo-indépendants - au nom aussi de l'idée qu'il vaut mieux être travailleur précaire que chômeur -, elles doivent d'un autre côté obtenir elles-mêmes d'autres avantages importants pour les travailleurs (condition indispensable pour que la base les soutienne). Des avantages qui ne soient pas éventuellement calculés selon la logique classique des accords collectifs, mais qui soient plutôt liés à une <u>redéfinition du rôle des syndicats</u>[56] <u>dans la société nationale</u> ainsi qu'à une redéfinition de leur pouvoir de négociations dans la perspective de changement social.

VI. LES OBJECTIFS DE LA RECHERCHE

L'objectif principal de la recherche est d'étudier l'impact du développement des nouvelles formes d'emploi au niveau des normes juridiques dans le Droit du Travail et le Droit de la Sécurité Sociale.

Pour atteindre ce but, on essaiera de <u>présenter la nouvelle typologie des contrats</u>, telle qu'elle résulte de l'apparition des nouvelles formes d'emploi ainsi que l'impact de celles-ci sur a) les conditions de travail des salariés liés par un contrat atypique, b) les droits collectifs de l'ensemble des travailleurs indépendamment de leur qualité de salarié atypique, c) les droits de la Sécurité Sociale, peu importe si les travailleurs atypiques en sont ou non titulaires.

Etant donné que, dans la majorité des Etats membres, les nouvelles formes d'emploi ont fait l'objet de réglementations juridiques, la mise en place de leur typologie nécessitera, outre l'analyse des réglementations, la comparaison de leurs techniques ainsi que des solutions apportées par celles-ci.

Dans le cadre de cette comparaison, on essaiera de confronter les changements juridiques introduits par les nouvelles formes d'emploi entre les pays de la Common law et les pays de la Civil law, tout en faisant la distinction entre les pays germaniques et les pays latins.

En examinant l'efficacité des moyens et des techniques juridiques, utilisées pour adapter le droit classique du travail aux nouvelles exigences de l'économie, on essaiera de plus de mettre en évidence le rôle des organisations syndicales dans ce processus d'adaptation.

La question se posera également de savoir si, compte tenu de l'"atteinte" portée à la protection antérieure accordée aux travailleurs, il se forme dans les Etats membres un Droit du Travail "à deux vitesses" ou bien si le Droit en question garde son "noyau dur" excluant tout assouplissement de ses règles au-delà d'un certain point.

Sachant enfin que "le développement économique n'est pas une fin en soi, mais un moyen d'atteindre un objectif social, à savoir une vie meilleure pour tous et en particulier pour les défavorisés", peut-on trouver, dans les solutions juridiques avancées dans les Etats membres pour régler les nouvelles formes d'emploi, celles <u>qui ne trahissent pas la physionomie du Droit du Travail européen</u>[57], tel qu'il a été forgé à travers le temps ?

NOTES

(1) V. Colloque international, Crise, Maintien de l'emploi et partage du travail, Etudes suisses de droit européen, schweizerische Beiträge zum Europarecht, Georg, Genève 1984. (Colloque de Genève), au colloque de Genève ont été présentés et discutés les problèmes du travail atypique pour la majorité des Etats membres par Däubler, Vogel-Polsky, Olea, Javillier, Ghera, Napier.

(2) Le deuxième thème du 11ème Congrès de la Société Internationale pour le Droit du Travail et de la Sécurité Sociale, qui a eu lieu à Caracas en septembre 1985, était consacré aux "Nouvelles formes et aspects du travail atypiques" (Congrès de Caracas, Vol.II).

(3) V. J. Pelissier, La relation de travail atypique, rapport français présenté au Congrès de Caracas (1985) p.540-541, publié également au Droit Social, juil.-août 1985, p.531 et suiv.

(4) Patricia Leighton, New Forms and Aspects of Atypical Employment Relationships, The Law and Practice in the U.K., rapport anglais au Congrès de Caracas, loc.cit.

(5) On constate que le débat sur la relation entre Droit du Travail et formes nouvelles d'emploi est souvent placé dans des termes faux. V. Raym. Soubie, Après les négociations sur la flexibilité, DS, avril 1985, p.291. V. aussi Les changements des structures économiques en Europe et leurs effets sur les relations professionnelles,

Travail et Société, 1985, p.82-3.

(6) Sur cette proposition de retour des relations de travail à l'époque plutôt chaotique pour celles-ci, avant la naissance du Droit du Travail et quelques tentatives vers cette direction, v. B. Boubli, A propos de la flexibilité d'emploi : vers la fin du droit du travail, Droit Social avril 1985, p.239-240, et Lord Wedderburn, The new industrial relations laws in Great Britain, Labour and Society, vol.10, January 1985, p.46 et suiv. notamment p.58.

(7) V. R. Blanpain, Ajustements structurels et relations professionnelles : aspect du droit du travail, Travail et Société, mai 1985, p.197 et 206. Il reste à bien chercher quelles sont dans les nouvelles formes "les règles de la vie" auxquelles "les règles de la loi doivent s'accorder".

(8) § 620 al.1 Code Civil allemand (BGB) qui prévoit que le rapport de service finit également avec l'expiration de la durée pour laquelle il a été conclu.

(9) Pour une approche globale de la jurisprudence en question, v. Schaub Arbeitsrechtshandbuch, 5 Auflage §39 II.

(10) BAG AP n°16, § 620 BGB contrat à durée déterminée.

(11) BAG AP n°60, § 620 BGB, contrat à durée déterminée. Wd. Däubler in Crise, maintien de l'emploi et partage du travail, loc.cit. p.25, Falkenberg, A typische Arbeitsverhältnisse in der B.R.D., rapport allemand au Congrès de Caracas.

(12) M. Iöwisch : Das Beschäffigungsförderungsgesetz 1985, Betriebs Berater, p.18- 1985, W. Däubler-Martine Friant : un récent exemple de flexibilisation législative : la loi allemande pour la promotion de l'emploi du 26 avril 1985 (A paraître à la revue française Droit Social)

(13) V. J. Pelissier, La relation de travail atypique, rapport national français au congrès de Caracas, loc.cit., J.C. Javillier, op.cit. p.135, D. Marchand, Des juristes débattent de la déréglementation..., Bulletin d'Informations Sociales-BIS, 2/85, p.197-98.

(14) V. parmi d'autres E. Ghera, Crise, maintien de l'emploi et partage du travail, Colloque de Genève, loc.cit., p.185 et suiv. même, Diritto del Lavoro, Caccucci Editori, Bari 1985, p.323 et suiv., G. Guigni, Les tendances récentes de la négociation collective en Italie, Revue internationale de travail, sept.-oct. 1984, p.649-650.

(15) M. Alonso Olea, Crise, maintien de l'emploi et partage du travail, loc.cit., p.95-96.

(16) V. J. Pelissier, La relation de travail atypique, rapport français présenté au congrès de Caracas, loc.cit. p.531 et suiv., J.C. Javillier, Crise, maintien de l'emploi et partage du travail - France, Colloque de Genève, loc.cit. p.126 et suiv.

(17) V. J. Pelissier, loc.cit. p.533.

(18) W. Däubler, in Crise, maintien de l'emploi et partage du travail, loc.cit. p.126 et suiv.

(19) BAG, Betriebs Berater, 1977 p.596, v. également critiques de la doctrine : Schaub Arbeitsrecht Handbuch Vol.I § 44 III 2., W. Däubler, Das Arbeitsrecht 2. 2ème éd. Reinbeck 1981, p.407.

(20) Selon le § 8 al.1 n°1 du Code social I IV, les travailleurs à temps partiel occupés moins de 15 heures par semaine et dont le revenu est inférieur à 390 DM par mois ne sont pas soumis à l'assurance maladie et à l'assurance vieillesse, tandis que les travailleurs occupés moins de 19 heures par semaine sont exclus du régime assurance chômage.

(21) M. Iöwisch, Beschäftigungsförderungsgesetz, Betriebs Berater 1985, op.cit., W. Däubler-M. Friant, op.cit., note 19. Un récent exemple de flexibilisation législative loi allemande pour la promotion de l'emploi du 26 avril 1985, op.cit.

(22) W. Däubler-M. Friant, op.cit.

(23) Sur les problèmes en question, v. Hoyningen Huene, Rechtliche Gestaltungsmöglichkeiten beim Job Sharing Arbeitsverhältnis, Betriebs Berater 1982, p.1240.

(24) Ed. Guera, Diritto del Lavoro, op.cit. p.315-6, et rapport au Colloque de Genève, loc.cit. p.182-183.

(25) V. le rapport espagnol de M.-A. Olea au Colloque de Genève, loc.cit., p.99-101.

(26) V. Ed. Guera, Diritto del Lavoro, op.cit. p.317 et suiv., même, rapport au Colloque de Genève, loc.cit., p.187-188.

(27) V. Patr. Leighton, Forms and Aspects of Atypical Relationship, the Law and practice in the United Kingdom, Congrès de Caracas, loc.cit., p.313-314.

(28) V. W. Däubler, La crise..., loc.cit., p.29.

(29) V. J.C. Javillier, rapport français au Colloque de Genève, loc.cit., p.143 et suiv., J. Pelissier, La relation de travail atypique, rapport au Congrès de Caracas, loc.cit. p.528-529.

(30) V. Chr. Dienand, New Forms and Aspects of Atypical Employment Relationship, rapport néerlandais au Congrès de Caracas, loc.cit., p.28 et suiv.

(31) W. Däubler, Crise, maintien de l'emploi et partage du travail, loc.cit.

(32) Hoyningen-Huene, Rechtliche Gestaltungsmöglichkeiten beim Job Sharing. Arbeitsverhältnis, Betriebs Berater 1982, p.1240.

(33) Article 4, al.2 BFG.

(34) V. le débat développé au Colloque de Genève sur "les formes intermédiaires entre le travail stable à plein temps et le chômage complet", surtout les interventions de Däubler et J. Vandame, p.303 et suiv.

(35) Selon Eliane Vogel, "on devait assurer un minimum de couverture sociale sur la base de solidarité, ce minimum n'étant pas calculé selon une règle de proportionnalité", ibid., p.316.

(36) Le recours aux "nouvelles formes de travail" limite ou même peut les priver de leurs moyens collectifs

d'expression, par exemple des organes qui représentent et défendent leurs intérêts.

(37) G. Lyon-Caen, La bataille truquée de la flexibilité, Droit Social, déc. 1985, p.801

(38) J.C. Javillier, Ordre juridique, relations professionnelles et flexibilité. Approches comparatives et internationales, Droit Social, janvier 1986, p.56.

(39) V. E. Vogel-Polsky, Crise, maintien de l'emploi et partage du travail, rapport belge, Colloque de Genève, loc.cit., p.80 et suiv.

(40) Pour qu'on puisse déceler toutes ces nouvelles "règles" d'adaptation qui paraîssent fleurir dans les entreprises de petite et moyenne taille, ayant des problèmes pour survivre, il faut des recherches à cet effet. Il en est de même des dispositions nouvelles "créatives" que contiennent les contrats de travail pour un emploi atypique, tels le travail à la demande ou le job sharing, dispositions qui ne sont pas encore reprises par la voie conventionnelle ou législative (il se peut aussi qu'il s'agisse de nouvelles dispositions qui s'affranchissent des obligations juridiques imposées par la législation ou par une convention collective).

(41) Signé du côté des travailleurs par la Confederazione Italiana Sindicati Lavoratori (CISL, prédominance socialiste) et l'Unione Italiana del Lavoro (UIL, prédominance social-chrétienne) tandis que la Confederazione Generale Italiana del Lavoro, de prédominance communiste, ne consentait pas.

(42) La CGIL n'est pas d'accord avec les négociations tripartites centralisées. Elle propose les ajustements du système des relations industrielles pour faire face aux réalités des années 80 à deux niveaux de négociations : au niveau sectoriel et au niveau de l'entreprise, restent pour les négociations nationales tripartites les mesures à prendre pour combattre le chômage, modifier le système fiscal ou de Sécurité Sociale, mais l'indexation devrait se discuter uniquement entre employeurs et salariés.

(43) G. Lyon-Caen, La bataille truquée..., loc.cit. p.809.

(43a) G. Guigni, Les tendances récentes..., loc.cit. p.656-7.

(44) G. Lyon-Caen, loc.cit. p.808.

(45) Bien que nous apercevions en Grande Bretagne au cours des dernières années, c'est-à-dire à partir de la date où le Gouvernement Conservateur arrive au pouvoir (1979), l'adoption d'une nouvelle législation qui "increased legal regulation of industrial bargaining and industrial action", bien que celle-ci "has not... obstructed the continuance and the evolution of voluntary collective bargaining in great measure as the primary source of industrial norms". Il n'est pour autant pas facile de prédire l'avenir de la négociation collective au Royaume Uni, v. Lord Wedderburn, The new industrial relation laws in Great Britain, Labour and Society, vol.10, January 1985 p.46 et suiv. notamment 58 et 59.

(46) V. J.C. Javillier, Ordre juridique, relations professionnelles, loc.cit. p.59. Voy. aussi G.J. Bamber et

R.D. Lansbury, Industrial Relations and technological change : Towards a comparative technology ? Rapport présenté au Congrès européen régional de l'Association Internationale des Relations Industrielles, Vienne 25-27 sept. 1984 et K. Tapiola, La négociation, ce qu'elle peut et ne peut pas faire, B.I.S 2/85 p.206-7.

(47) Sur l'objet des négociations à mener par les syndicats en Europe vu par l'oeil patronal, v. J.J. Oechslin, Travail et flexibilité : le point de vue des employeurs, B.I.S., 2/85 p.203-5.

(48) V. sur la problématique belge face aux évolutions, F. Janssens, Belgique-La bataille salariale est une page largement tournée, B.I.S. 1/85 p.2-5.

(49) V. entre autres F. Kessler, La réduction de la durée du travail dans la métallurgie allemande et ses conséquences sur les autres branches industrielles, Droit Social, déc. 1985, p.850 et suiv., F. Furstenberg, La réglementation de la durée du travail en R.F. d'Allemagne, Travail et Société, vol.10, n°2, mai 1985, p.141 et suiv.

(50) G. Guigni, Il diritto del lavoro negli anni '80 in Giornale di diritto del lavoro e di relazioni industriale, 1982, p.373 et suiv., même, Prospettive del diritto del lavoro per gli anni 80, 1983, p.3 et suiv. et Les tendances récentes de la négociation collective en Italie, loc.cit., Runggaldier, Tendances actuelles du droit du travail italien, Droit Social, déc.1985, p.856 et suiv., T. Treu, Recent development of Italian Labour Law, Labour and Society, January 1985, p.27 et suiv.

(51) Selon W. Däubler, "une remise en cause trop brutale des acquis sociaux pourrait engendrer des oppositions incontrôlables et ébranler la fonction des syndicats en tant qu'agents de régulation sociaux". Il s'agit peut-être aussi de questions délicates de processus. En R.F.A., "le législateur a choisi de favoriser la souplesse de la gestion du personnel au détriment de la protection des salariés", loc.cit.

(52) V. Runggaldier, Tendances actuelles, loc.cit. p.859-60.

(53) En ce qui concerne le rôle des syndicats et des Betriebsräten dans les entreprises allemandes sur les mêmes questions, seule une enquête pourrait nous indiquer les réponses.

(54) Dans tous les pays, on observe un abaissement des effectifs syndicaux et du taux de syndicalisation, notamment au Royaume Uni, en France, aux Pays-Bas. Parmi les explications avancées, se trouve l'importante croissance des services au détriment de l'industrie et le nombre de plus en plus grand des femmes employées à l'égard desquelles la politique des syndicats n'est point attrayante par rapport à leurs propres revendications. Elles n'occupent d'ailleurs pas, dans les organisations syndicales, des postes de responsabilité. V. les changements des structures économiques en Europe et leurs effets sur les relations professionnelles, Travail et Société, vol.10, n°2, mai 1983, p.178. La "modernisation" de ces appareils devait prendre en considération, certes, la catégorie

"femmes salariés" qui sont les grandes "consommatrices" du travail atypique. Mais cela ne paraît pas suffire : ils devraient exprimer les intérêts de tous les groupements sociaux, des nouvelles minorités parmi lesquelles se trouvent aussi les femmes.

(55) G. Bellier, Après l'échec des négociations sur la flexibilité, Droit Social 1985, p.79 suit., R. Soubie, Après les négociations sur la flexibilité, Droit Social, loc. cit., p.95 suiv./221 et suiv.

(56) Dans les pays où il existe plusieurs organisations syndicales dont l'idéologie diffère, il est beaucoup plus difficile de définir une nouvelle politique syndicale commune. On sait le mal qu'ont les syndicats communistes tant en Italie qu'en France et en Espagne également à signer les accords qui traitent de la flexibilité et du travail atypique.

(52) V. Introduction du Directeur du B.I.T., Rapport sur l'Evolution du Monde du Travail, Genève 1985, v. aussi la position de O. Clark in La flexibilité du marché du travail : les deux faces du phénomène, B.I.S. 3-4 1985, p.40 : "Il ne faudrait surtout pas conclure... qu'il faut procéder à une révision radicale des mesures sociales adoptées ces dernières décennies, même si les progrès ainsi réalisés ont entraîné des rigidités regrettables dans le fonctionnement du marché du travail. Il faut plutôt, en toute objectivité, chercher à analyser chaque cas où le manque de flexibilité semble porter préjudice

à l'efficacité de la main d'oeuvre en tenant compte à la fois de la valeur sociale et du coût économique".

NEUE WEGE DER ARBEITSORGANISATION

Erfahrungen aus selbstverwalteten Betrieben
Acht Thesen

Lothar Gretsch

Institut für Sozialforschung
und Sozialwirtschaft e.V.

SAARBRÜCKEN
APRIL 1986

These 1

Die Entwicklungstendenzen neuer Formen der Arbeitsorganisation in herkömmlichen Betrieben und in selbstverwalteten Betrieben werden von gänzlich unterschiedlichen Ausgangsbedingungen geprägt. Während herkömmliche Betriebe die Neugestaltung der Arbeitsstrukturen von einem bereits realisierten hohen Funktionsniveau ihres sozio-technischen Betriebssystems aus in Angriff nehmen, beginnen selbstverwaltete Betriebe vom "Nullpunkt" aus, ihre Arbeit hin zu funktionsfähigen, geordneten Arbeitsverhältnissen zu organisieren und zu strukturieren.

These 2

Die klassischen Formen einer Flexibilisierung der Arbeitsorganisation im Sinne der Aufhebung arbeitsbedingter Restriktionen und der Schaffung humaner, persönlichkeitsförderlicher Arbeitsbedingungen, wie dies mit den Konzepten der Aufgabenvergrößerung und Aufgabenbereicherung, der kollektiven Aufgabenerweiterung und Arbeitsplatzrotation beabsichtigt ist, werden primär im Rahmen hochentwickelter Betriebsstrukturen verwirklicht. Unter dem Primat einer möglichst optimalen Verwertung aller eingesetzten Produktionsfaktoren verfolgt der herkömmliche Betrieb das Ziel, mit Hilfe der neuen Formen der Arbeitsorganisation einen höheren Nutzungsgrad des Produktivfaktors Arbeitskraft zu erreichen, ohne die Funktionsmechanismen betrieblicher Herrschaftsstrukturen, wie sie sich für die Beschäftigten in den vielfältigsten Formen und Techniken sozialer Kontrolle und Disziplinierung niederschlagen, außer Kraft zu setzen. Diese neuen Formen der Arbeitsorganisation lassen sich daher nur bedingt als analytische Kategorie auf den Bereich selbstverwalteter Betriebe übertragen.

These 3

Selbstverwaltete Betriebe sind bestrebt, durch die Einführung kollektiver Eigentums- und Verfügungsrechte den strukturellen Widerspruch des Verhältnisses von Kapital und Arbeit und die daraus resultierenden gegenläufigen Interessen aufzuheben. Die Verwertung von Arbeitskraft geschieht nicht mehr unter herkömmlichen betrieblichen Herrschaftsstrukturen, sondern vollzieht sich durch die Neutralisierung der Kapitalmacht in einem Prozeß kollektiver Selbstbestimmung. Die Entwicklung der betrieblichen Sozialbeziehungen und die Aufarbeitung von Konflikten bilden eine unabdingbare Voraussetzung für die Verständigungsprozesse, in denen die sozialen Normen und Regeln des Betriebes, die Gestaltung seiner Struktur sowie die zumutbaren und leistbaren Beiträge seiner Mitglieder festgelegt werden. Die sozialen Beziehungen, wie sie sich in der Sozialordnung des Betriebes manifestieren, erlangen die Tragweite eines eigenständigen Produktivfaktors. Die gesellschaftspolitisch intendierte Modellhaftigkeit des selbstverwalteten Betriebes erwächst gerade aus dem Selbstverständnis einer emotional und sozial stabilisierten Organisationsform, die die komplexe Subjektivität ihrer Mitglieder in einem funktionsfähigen System zu integrieren vermag.

These 4

Der Entwicklungsprozeß alternativer Arbeitsformen in selbstverwalteten Betrieben ist von der Wirkungsweise der geschilderten Vergesellschaftungsprinzipien und -mechanismen abhängig. Davon ausgehend, daß auch in selbstverwalteten Betrieben der hohe moralökonomische Anspruch einer uneingeschränkten Aufhebung von Arbeitsteilung als Erscheinungsform entfremdeter Arbeit nicht zu verwirklichen ist, kommt dem mit der Verteilung und Gestaltung von Arbeitsaufgabe und Arbeitsinhalt korrespondierenden Handlungsspielraum entscheidende Bedeutung für den inneren Zusammenhalt des Betriebes zu. Der Handlungsspielraum ist dabei als Resultante von Tätigkeits-, Entscheidungs-, Kontroll- sowie Interaktionsspielraum zu sehen und nicht als reine Addition von Freiheitsgraden zu verstehen, sondern als Ganzheit zu begreifen. Durch das Zusammenwirken der unterschiedlichen Dimensionen sind synergetische Effekte zu erwarten, die summativ nicht erfasst werden können. Gerade die Möglichkeiten und Anforderungen der sozialen Dimension, ausgedrückt im Interaktionsspielraum, sind entscheidend für die Entwicklung von sozialer Kompetenz. Für die Beurteilung der Handlungsspielräume in der Praxis selbstverwalteter Betriebe ist der Umfang des Interaktionsspielraumes daher maßgebend. Der Dequalifizierung durch weitreichende Formen der Arbeitsteilung entgegen zu wirken, wird Qualifizierung durch die Arbeit im Sinne der Erweiterung und der fortlaufenden Einübung von Handlungskompetenz explizit zum Ziel alternativer Arbeitsgestaltung.

These 5

Der selbstverwaltete Betrieb als emotional und sozial zu stabilisierende Organisationsform im Sinne eines sozialen Experiments trifft auf defizitäre Ausgangsbedingungen, die seine sozialen und ökonomischen Binnenstrukturen nachhaltig beeinflussen.
Zu diesen Ausgangsbedingungen zählen:
- erschwerte Möglichkeiten der Kapitalbeschaffung auf dem öffentlichen und

privaten Kapitalmarkt und damit verbundene geringe Kapitalausstattung
- geringer Technisierungsgrad sowie Einsatz veralteter Technikstrukturen, womit Formen der Arbeitsintensivierung verbunden sind, die weit über das gesellschaftspolitisch intendierte Maß an Substituierung von Kapital durch Arbeit hinausreichen
- erhebliche Defizite hinsichtlich der formalen und realen beruflichen Eingangsqualifikationen der Mitarbeiter
- z.T. milieubedingte Sozialisationsdefizite hinsichtlich des Rekrutierungspotentials (Immer mehr Interessenten aus sozial benachteiligten Schichten drängen in den Selbstverwaltungsbereich, ohne mit den Erfordernissen kommunikativen Handelns jemals in Berührung gekommen zu sein)

These 6

Der Entwicklungsverlauf selbstverwalteter Betriebe ist durch unterschiedliche Phasen geprägt, die jeweils typische Problemlagen im Spannungsverhältnis zwischen sozialer und ökonomischer Handlungsrationalität repräsentieren. Während in der Gründungsphase die Umsetzung der Projektidee neben realen Erfordernissen unternehmensrechtlicher und betriebswirtschaftlicher Art von dem Versuch der prozesualen Klärung und Verstetigung der betrieblichen Sozialbeziehungen und Sozialordnung bestimmt wird, treten in einer anschließenden Phase der ökonomischen Konsolidierung Rentabilitätserfordernisse und Funktionszwänge des Marktes, auf den hin der Betrieb sich orientiert, in den Vordergrund und überlagern die an sozialer Handlungsrationalität ausgerichteten Ordnungsmomente des selbstverwalteten Betriebes.

These 7

Es bestehen zwei divergierende Bewertungsstandpunkte hinsichtlich der politischen Reichweite selbstverwalteter Betriebe. Die sozial- und beschäftigungspolitische Perspektive geht davon aus, daß der alternativ-ökonomische Sektor vorrangig ein soziales Lern- und Experimentierfeld darstellt, das neue, effizientere Formen der alternativen Selbsthilfe einüben und modellhaft erproben soll, das aber aufgrund nicht zu beseitigender ökonomisch-struktureller Defizite einer ständigen Alimentierung und Subventionierung mittels sozialstaatlicher Instanzen bedarf. Dagegen betont eine wirtschafts- und gesellschaftspolitische Perspektive die mögliche Aufhebbarkeit struktureller Defizite durch die Setzung zukunftsweisender wirtschafts- und gesellschaftspolitischer Akzente, - insbesondere die Schaffung wirtschaftsdemokratischer Strukturen -, um die Marktfähigkeit selbstverwalteter Betriebe herzustellen und ihren Bestand als soziales und ökonomisches Experiment zu sichern.

These 8

Der Versuch einer ökonomischen Stabilisierung des selbstverwalteten Betriebes führt häufig dazu, die Dimension des Betriebes als soziales Experiment zu konterkarieren. Die betrieblichen Muster, die in einem breiten Spektrum zwischen den beiden Extremen "Scheitern" oder "Anpassen an herkömmliche Betriebsstrukturen" existieren, müssen bestimmte Rahmenbedingungen im Bereich der betrieblichen Sozialbeziehungen sichern, wenn sie als soziales und ökonomisches Experiment überleben wollen:

- Gewährleistung kollektiver Absprachen über die Gestaltung und Durchführung der betrieblichen Abläufe (sowohl bzgl. übergeordneter betrieblicher Zielsetzungen als auch der konkreten Gestaltung des Arbeitsvorganges)
- Gewährleistung der Eigenqualifizierung durch die Arbeit im Sinne der Erweiterung von kognitiver und sozialer Kompetenz als konstitutive Bestandteile von Handlungskompetenz
- Gewährleistung einer Sicherung persönlichkeitsförderlicher Arbeitsgestaltung durch die Erweiterung von Handlungsspielräumen in den drei Dimensionen Tätigkeits-, Entscheidungs- und Kontroll- sowie Interaktionsspielraum

LIFESTYLE, ECONOMIC STRUCTURE AND TIME USE

Jonathan Gershuny

School of Humanities & Social Studies
University of Bath

BATH, MARCH 1986

Abstract

Keynesian demand stimulation policies are largely discredited as means of countering unemployment. It nevertheless seems strange to have persistant unemployment in societies in which human needs still go unsatisfied. There is a mismatch between the conditions of life in Europe, and the structure of European economies.

"Conditions of life", or "lifestyle" are very difficult to measure; official statistics largely ignore those areas of life which do not have direct connections with "the economy". Yet, this paper will argue, it is precisely "lifestyle" which, ultimately, determines the shape of the economy. How is "lifestyle" to be measured? The most straightforward indicator is the population's use of time.

The paper reports on the progress of an empirical attempt to describe the change in lifestyle, and its relation to change in economic structure, through the analysis of time budget data from a number of different countries. It outlines a new socio-economic accounting system through which changes in time use patterns might be linked to change in final demand and labour supply -

enabling us to explore such issues as the consequences of shorter work time, or alterations in educational or retirement provisions, for levels of employment. Such a new system of accounts might be used for developing alternative "time use" policies for stimulating employment.

J I Gershuny
University of Bath
March 1986

Lifestyle, Economic Structure and Time Use

1. Time Use and Underconsumption.

It is easy to forget the paradoxical nature of unemployment. On one hand we have people, with skills and capacities, having at least the potential for the production of useful goods and services, not doing so (and also unused plant and service facilities). On the other, we have unmet needs, people living in want. There are no doubt good economic reasons for this mismatch; risks of inflation, threats to national balances of trade, fears of the diversion of resources in unproductive directions. But nevertheless there is a puzzle here: surely there must be some way of organising matters better?

Such feelings of puzzlement form the basis of a currently rather unfashionable diagnosis of our present economic ills - "underconsumption". The most familiar variant of this view is that promoted by Keynes. He suggested that we reformulate the puzzle. Supply does not always create its own demand: the economy may reach equilibrium at a level of _effective_ demand (ie wants _plus_ the ability to pay) insufficient to provide jobs for all those who want them - even though there is plenty of _in_effective demand still in the society, and underutilised resources.

The solution to the problem then follows naturally. We render the ineffective demand effective, expand aggregate demand, by putting money in the poorest pockets, or (in Keynes' sarcastic proposal) by burying currency in milk bottles down unused coalmines for unemployed miners to recover, or by useful public works, as in the American New Deal, or as a 1960s economist suggested, by scattering banknotes from a helicopter. We will then experience the virtuous operation of Kahn's multiplier, whereby those newly employed by the increased expenditure (or those further enriched by it) themselves spend a proportion of their consequent earnings, stimulating further jobs and more wealth, until we reach full employment. Demand expands to stimulate its own supply, a reversal of Say's law.

Unfortunately, our modern experience is that this is an altogether too undiscriminating approach. We can stimulate demand - but we cannot control what people spend their money _on_. People are quite likely to spend their money in ways that fail to generate jobs. Though there is unused capital and labour in the society, the spending pattern generated by the demand stimulation may be such that the unused social resources are inappropriate. Underused steel mills are no help if the extra demand we stimulate is for videorecorders.

Technical change (particularly while there are international imbalences in technological development), and the increasingly international scale of the division of labour, make it quite likely that traditional Keynesian demand stimulation is inappropriate as a national policy tool for stimulating employment. New jobs may emerge, but in Formosa, new wealth as a result of the multiplier, but for high technology entrepreneurs in California. If the economy cannot produce the extra goods or services that are demanded, they may be bought elsewhere - or alternatively the increased demand may directly increase local prices. Keynesian demand stimulation (at least when undertaken by individual national economies on their own) now seems revealed as promoting domestic inflation and foreign exchange problems. We can therefore perhaps no longer pursue Keynes' prescription. But the diagnosis - the puzzle - still remains. We have unused human capacities and unmet human needs: why cannot these be matched together?

Keynes *General Theory* is in fact a special case, and a rather aberrant one, of the underconsumptionist argument. The Keynesian mechanism, in which individuals' spending decisions combine to produce an automatic and balanced return to full employment, may not work. But the underlying underconsumptionist proposition - that, irrespective of the mechanism for generating jobs, there should be no unemployment while there are still unsatisfied human needs - still remains.

Consider. We live our lives alternately consuming and producing. We are born (consuming medical services, generating employment for nurses and doctors and cleaners), are cared for during our infancy and childhood (and producing employment opportunities in various industries and occupations), then we work for money (producing goods and services for others) and take leisure and recreation (using and consuming goods and services). And then we retire from paid employment, perhaps subsequently providing some goods and services for others (our families) on an unpaid basis, and finally, as we age, we progressively require more caring services for ourselves. The precise balance between our roles as consumers of goods and services, and as producers of goods and services, is not in any sense fixed or "natural". There are laws which tell us at which ages we may enter and leave the paid workforce, when we must and when we may consume the services of the educational system. There are public policies which determine the accessibility of leisure facilities (and hence, for example, whether we watch television or go swimming). There may also be laws which tell us how much paid work time we can expect (maximum working week) or how many days holiday per year. Technological change may also affect this balance, as where new domestic technology make it possible for us to produce services within our own households that previously had to be bought from outside them. And money also has an influence; extra money means we can buy more commodities, higher wages may mean that less time is spent in paid employment, more in leisure consumption.

Aggregate demand is the sum of all these different sorts of consumption activities; the labour supply is the aggregate of all of these opportunities and constraints for participation in paid work. We can at any point in time be consuming or producing. By consuming, we provide the opportunity for others to produce; and when we do consume, we are, for the most part, not producing. There is a delicate balance: if we spend too much time consuming, there will not be enough time to produce what we need; if we spend too little time consuming, there is not enough opportunity for production, hence, unemployment.

Of course, we run into the same problem of the inappropriateness of some peoples' production time for other peoples' consumption. The marginal item of consumption is by no means necessarily the end product of the work of the marginal worker - this is precisely the problem with Keynes' prescription: aggregate demand stimulation may stimulate the wrong sort of demand. But money is not the only way of affecting this balance between consumption and production. Consider, for example, the effects of raising the statutory school-leaving age (or precisely equivalent, a mid-life educational sabbatical): on one side there would be a reduction in the part of their lives people would intend to devote to production (ie a reduction in the labour supply), on the other, an increase in consumption (and hence an increase in the demand for labour - more jobs for teachers and ancillary workers).

In this case, the consumption is constrained, to consist of an increase in the consumption of educational services. Constraint is not, however, necessary, only predictability. We know that people with more money in their pockets, spend large parts of it in ways that generate inflationary and foreign exchange presures; this is what stops us stimulating aggregate demand so as to generate employment. Suppose we knew that people with more spare time during the week would spend it in the consumption of local leisure and recreational services. We could then sensibly compensate employers for shorter working weeks without pay reduction, subsidise the construction of local leisure centres - promoting leisure to generate new jobs.

We will return to this sort of policy issue later in the paper. The point for the moment is simply the demonstration of the important effect that lifestyle, conditions of life, has on economic structure. Modern states have a wide range of influences on styles of life, many of them with the potential for affecting the balance between consumption and production activities - and hence unemployment. Keynes' version of underconsumptionism operates on just one influence on lifestyle, household income. We may be able to devise other, and more sophisticated, combinations of economic and social policy which more successfully adjust the balance.

Even to think about such radical policy alternatives, however, requires information that is far removed from the conventional economist's armoury of theory and of national income and expenditure statistics. Economists know about employment and output by industry, household incomes and household expenditure patterns. In order to devise these more sophisticated underconsumptionist (or perhaps we should call them simply "consumptionist") policy instruments, we need information about what goes on outside "the economy". We will need to judge the effects of different sorts of public and private service provisions, of different working time regimes, of new service-providing infrastructures (thinking her particularly of telecommunications), on choices of activities. To make these judgements, we require detailed information on the nature and context of daily activity patterns. We will need information on how people spend their time, we will need theories on the determinants of time use, and we will want accounting structures for integrating the time-use, "lifestyle", data with the more conventional economic data.

There are of course other reasons for collecting and analysing time-use data.

It provides almost the only empirical basis for understanding the sexual division of labour in the home, for example. Insofar as "time budget" studies provide indications of unpaid work, they are invluable sources for economists' attempts to extend GNP calculations to include the value of household production. Time use statistics may also provide very helpful "output" measures for evaluating the performance of service institutions. But this paper will concentrate on the potential application of time-use data in the construction of "consumptionist" socio-economic models, showing the interconnections between lifestyle and conventional economic structure.

2. An International, Intertemporal Comparison of Time Budgets

The only systematic and comprehensive source of data on time use patterns comes from "time budget studies". These consist of large random sample surveys, whose respondents complete "diaries" describing in detail their activities over a period (which varies between surveys between one and seven days). The diaries provide sufficient detail to register the duration of each activity for the respondents' periods of diary keeping, so it is possible to work out a "time budget", a comprehensive set of accounts of time allocation, analogous to the more familiar accounts of the allocation of money over a given period. A large number of such studies have been carried out; Table 1 lists 53 national-scale surveys (either national random samples,or substantial urban samples) from 23 countries - and this is certainly not a comprehensive list. (A more detailed description of the international stock of time budget data may be found in Robinson 1983, and Gershuny 1985.)

Table 1

Time Use Studies in Various Countries

Country

EEC
Netherlands	1975, 1980
Belgium	1965
France	1947, 1958, 1963/4, 1966, 1967, 1974/5, 1984/5
West Germany	1965, 1979, 1979/80
Denmark	1961, 1975
U.K.	1938, 1961, 1971, 1974/5, 1981, 1983/4, 1983/4
Italy	1973, 1979

Other Europe
Austria	1981
Switzerland	1979
Norway	1971/2, 1980/1
Finland	1979
Sweden	1981/2

Eastern Europe
Poland	1965, 1978
East Germany	1965
Czechoslovakia	1965, 1979/80
Hungary	1963, 1965, 1976/7
Yugoslavia	1965
Bulgaria	1970/1, 1976/7
Soviet Union	1980

Far East
South Korea	1981
Japan	1960, 1965, 1970, 1975, 1980

North America
Canada	1971, 1981
U.S.A.	1965, 1975/6

Near East
Israel	1970

This very large fund of survey material does not however mean that the patterns of time use, and of change in time use over historical periods, are well understood either internationally or even nationally. Any time budget data is very difficult to collect and use. The preparation of the data involves restructuring the raw survey material in a much more fundamental way than in a conventional questionnaire - the activity sequences described by respondents ("I got up at 7.15, then I...) must be translated into a closed set of categories, and aggregated into activity totals (490 minutes of sleep, 80 minutes eating etc). And then, since the range of possibilities for even one individual's activities is very wide, and there are a large range of different sorts of people (varying as to sex, family position, age, occupation, income, class) with quite different activity patterns, the task of describing lifestyle in even one society at one point in time, is a very complex and exacting one.

And there are further, and particularly serious, problems which plague attempts to use the fund of survey data described in Table 1 for comparative purposes. While the Table 1 surveys share a common core of methodology - the use of a diary format to record activity sequences which are subsequently aggregated into totals of time spent in activities - time budget surveys may nevertheless differ from eachother in a number of ways.

1   They may cover different parts of the population: most, though not all, place upper and lower limits on the age of respondent; some surveys are concentrated exclusively on urban (or more rarely, rural) populations. The sampling methodology (random, stratified or quota), and the nature of the sampling frame (household or individual) also

varies. Apparent differences in results between surveys may be the spurious consequences of such differences in research strategies and techniques.

2   The design of the diary is by no means standard. Diaries may be collected using natural language (ie the respondents' own descriptions of activities in their own words), or in fixed and precoded activity categories. They vary in length, between a day and a week; some involve a series of non-sequential days (eg one work day, and one non-work day). They may be completed by an interviewer after the diary period, or by the respondent during the period. Some diaries are now collected through the medium of telephone interviews.

3   The activity classification scheme may vary, so that categories such as "domestic work" mean different things in different surveys. However, in the mid-1960s there was a multinational comparative dataset collected under the auspices of UNESCO (Szalai 1973), and the coding scheme used in this exercise (while deficient in some important respects) has come to be used as a sort of de facto international standard, and many of the more recent surveys listed in Table 1 can be compared through this coding system.

4   A large amount of contextual information on the respondents is necessary to make sense of the time-use data. There is no standard list of the sorts of ancillary variables that should be collected for a time-budget survey, nor of the coding categories for these variables. Thus, for example, a country with no substantial

urban/rural disparities, may omit some geographical variables which are indispensible to the understanding of conditions in other countries.

Despite the scope and importance of these problems, it is nevertheless possible to make some progress, both in the comparison of time use patterns over historical periods, and between countries. The difficulties listed above mean that, to be effective, attempts to make comparisons involve a return to the raw data, reconstructing and reconstituting variables, so as to arrive at a "lowest common denominator" across the various surveys. This exercise is certainly not possible for all the surveys in Table 1, since (apart from the enormous size of such a task) the data may be lost or inaccessible, or organised in such a way as to be incomparible across time or between countries.

Such a task is currently being undertaken, at the University of Bath, for seven countries, and a total of 15 surveys (Netherlands, 1975, 1980; Denmark 1961, 1975; UK 1961, 1974/5, 1983/4; France 1965, 1975; Norway 1971, 1980; Canada 1971, 1981; USA 1965, 1975). Almost all of this material has now been received (only one survey, from France in 1975, is missing) and most of it has been processed (the reworked Canadian and USA data will become available at the end of April 1986); in addition, new studies are currently underway in the Netherlands, Denmark, France and the USA, which it is hoped will be added to the Archive in due course.

3. Change in Lifestyles, 1960s to 1980s

Using this material, it will be possible to put together a quite unique account of how patterns of life have been changing over recent decades in developed economies. We shall return to the question of how to link this lifestyle data to evidence on the structure of the formal economy, so as to explore the possibilities for the construction of "consumptionist" policies. But before doing so, let us briefly consider the evidence of social change that has emerged at this intermediate point in the research project.

Table 2 presents a very preliminary view of the pattern of change which emerges from the 12 surveys which have so far been processed. The first section of the table gives the average minutes per day spent in three major categories of activity - paid work, unpaid work (in a broad sense including childcare, shopping and gardening as well as routine domestic tasks), and leisure (the residual time is devoted to sleep, personal toilet and non-sociable eating).

There are, at this level of data presentation, no clear patterns of change, instead a rather confused picture, in which the time use averages, and the changes in them, differ between countries. Indeed, in the one case where we have three surveys of the **same** country, even the directions of change alters between the decades - domestic work in Britain appears to decrease through the 1960s, and then increase again during the 1970s.

In fact this confusion is not particularly surprising. Three quite different sorts of change are conflated in this one table. First, there are differences in the biases in the composition of the samples; most of the surveys, for example, contain to a varying degree a disproportionate number of women, since

TABLE 2   Work and Leisure in 7 Countries

	Paid Work			Domestic Work			All Leisure			All Work		
	1960s	1970s	1980s	1960s	1970s	1980s	1960s	1970s	1980s	1960s	1970s	1980s

Average minutes per day

Netherlands		164	165		219	226		418	400		383	391
Denmark	247	245		152	134		409	417		399	379	
UK	262	254	216	209	188	210	311	339	383	471	442	426
France	294			242			246			536		
Norway		236	228		250	227		312	346		486	455
Canada		234			208			362			442	
USA	292			209			326			501		

Sex Effects

MEN

Netherlands		118	131		-116	-129		13	17		2	2
Denmark	59	84		-92	-71		21	0		-33	13	
UK	131	109	61	-118	-103	-78	2	4	22	13	6	-17
France	137			-143			11			-6		
Norway		110	73		-115	-75		14	16		-5	-2
Canada		109			-114			19			-5	
USA	131			-122			-1			9		

WOMEN

Netherlands		-85	-82		84	83		-9	-11		-1	1
Denmark	-59	-85		92	73		-21	0		33	-12	
UK	-119	-102	-45	105	96	59	-2	-4	-17	-14	-6	14
France	-115			120			-10			5		
Norway		-104	-67		109	69		-13	-15		5	2
Canada		-83			86			-15			3	
USA	-119			110			+1			-9		

Employment Effects

FULL TIME

Netherlands		186	185		-108	-110		-39	-36		78	75
Denmark	144	158		-57	-57		-52	-62		87	101	
UK	185	167	169	-118	-107	-89	-36	-17	-54	67	60	80
France	139			-105			-25			34		
Norway												
Canada		133			-90			-30			43	
USA	113			-80			-29			33		

PART TIME												
Netherlands		-39	-34		62	74		-16	-36		23	40
Denmark		-17			60			-40			43	
UK	-92	-87	-45	69	41	89	-19	-17	-49	-23	-46	44
France	-45			43			-4			-2		
Norway												
Canada		-26			9			5			-17	
USA	35			-16			34			19		

NOT EMPLOYED												
Netherlands		-44	-77		56	38		17	20		12	-39
Denmark	-144	-180		57	50		52	83		-87	-130	
UK	-257	-244	-143	161	163	77	58	44	55	-96	-81	-66
France	-284			213			53			-71		
Norway												
Canada		-221			151			51			-70	
USA	-288			203			69			-85		

women seem less disinclined than men to keep diary-type records. Samples like the 1983/4 UK survey, in which women comprise almost 60% of the respondents, will tend to overestimate the amount of domestic work, and underestimate the amount of paid work, insofar as women tend to do more domestic and less paid work than men do. And where the extent of the overrepresentation differs between samples, there will emerge a totally spurious appearance of a difference in average time use. Second, there are real changes in the composition of the population over time. One component of the change in paid work over the three decades covered by Table 2, is the increase in the proportion of the population falling into the category of "employed women". This will have the effect of increasing the overall amount of paid work in the society, and also, (since employed women tend to do less housework) decreasing the amount of unpaid work. Third, there are actual changes in behaviour over time. Particular sorts of people have particular behavioural tendencies - these also influence the average time statistic, thus a further component in any reduction of time spent in domestic work, might be that particular "sorts of person" actually do less at a later point in history than at an earlier.

In order to establish how time use has actually changed in a population, it is necessary to eliminate the effects of the first category, sample biases, and then distinguish between the second two, between changes in the <u>composition of the population</u> on one hand, and in the <u>behaviour of particular population subcategories</u> on the other.

The second part of Table 2 shows some examples of the effects of belonging to particular population subcategories, in the twelve surveys. We see, for instance, that men in the Netherlands in 1975 did 118 minutes more paid work than the average, 116 minutes less domestic work and 13 minutes more leisure (also, since the length of the day is the same for men and women, presumably they slept 15 minutes less than the average). The women by contrast did 85 minutes less paid work, 84 minutes more domestic work, and 10 minutes less leisure than the average. (The overall average is skewed towards the womens' totals and away from the men's because of the overrepresentation of women in the sample.) Figure 1 plots the broad patterns of change for men and women from the Table 2 data.

Here we see a very substantial degree of stability. The signs of the effects are, with only a very few exceptions, constant across all the surveys for each population category. The men in each of the surveys do more paid work than women, the women all do more unpaid than men, and with just one apparent exception, the women all have marginally more leisure time than men (this may however reflect a systematic underrepresentation of men's leisure time, in that breaks during paid work time tend not to be reported in time diaries). Employed people all have substantially less leisure than non-employed.

There is nothing very surprising here (though it is satisfying to have our expectations of society so clearly mirrored in empirical evidence). What makes this sort of analysis useful is that it tells us which sorts of social characteristics make a difference in the determination of time use patterns - and hence, which sorts of characteristics we have to try to hold constant when we try to distinguish change in behaviour from change in social composition. When we apply this sort of technique to the surveys in our archive, three distinct sorts of social characteristic emerge as particularly important: sex, employment status, and (having a major effect on women's time use but not on

Figure 1   Broad Change in Time Use 1961 - 1984

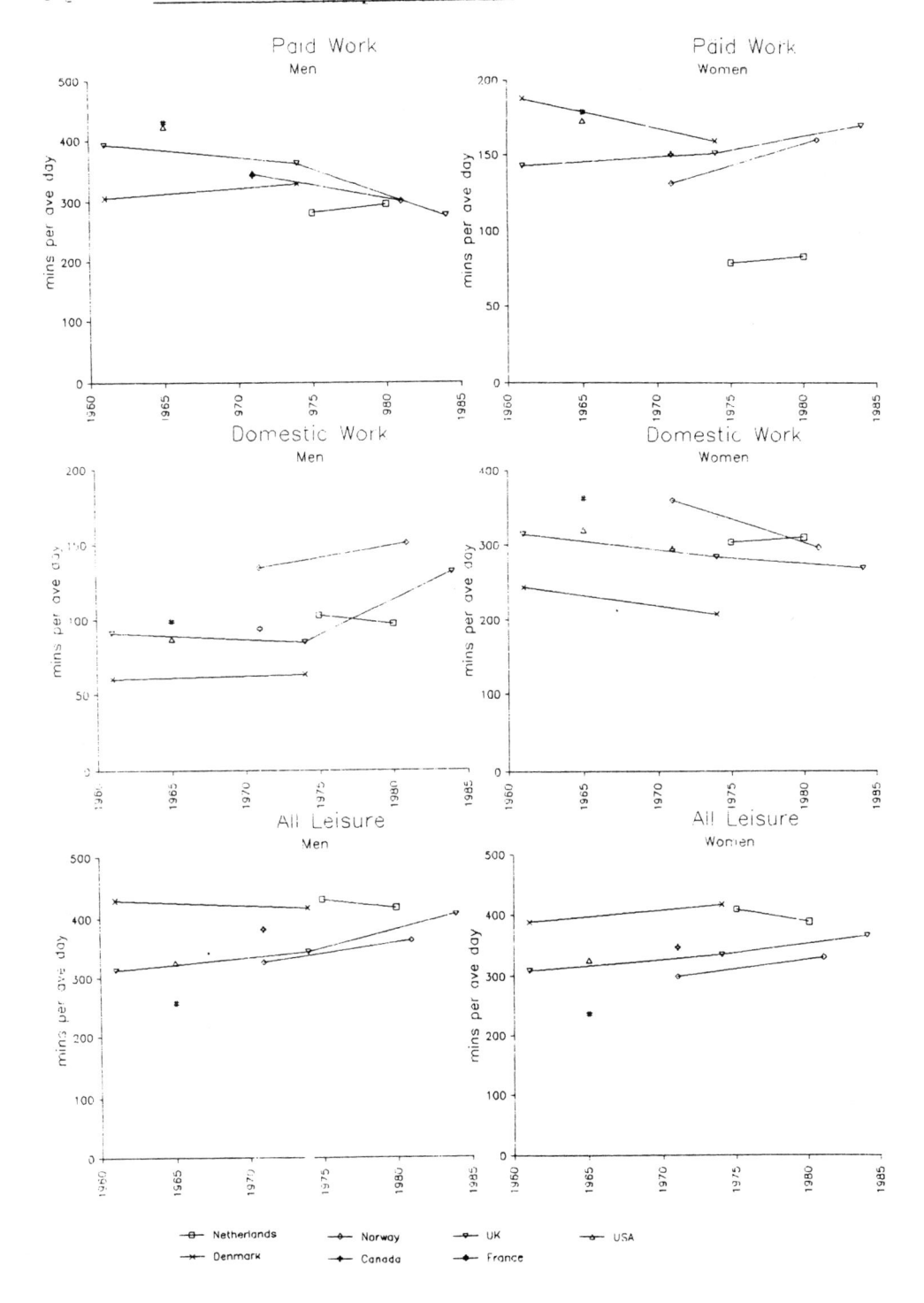

men's) family status - particularly, the age of the respondents' youngest child.

To identify changes or differences in behaviour, then, we must break down the sample into the subgroups defined by these three social characteristics. This work is currently underway, and a flavour of the results can be acquired from Figure 2, which shows change in various categories of domestic work in Britain, controlling for sex and employment.

These figures in fact show the elasticity of time in various domestic activities with respect to the amount of paid work carried out by the respondent. We have divided up the samples into groups according to hours of work, and then (since there are a large number of such categories and the numbers of respondents in each category are small) averaged the amount of unpaid work in each category with that of the adjoining categories.

Look first at the women's housework category. For each of the three surveys (1961, 1974/5 and 1983/4) there is a clear negative slope; the marginal minute of paid work substitutes for, depending on the position and the year, something around half a minute a minute of routine domestic work. This observation is at the root of the widely remarked phenomenon of the "dual burden" - women who take on paid work do not have an adequately compensating reduction in their burden of unpaid work. What has not been previously remarked, however, is the difference between the succesive surveys. Category by category, at each level of paid work, the domestic work time for women in 1974/5 was <u>some 50 to 100 minutes per day less than in 1961</u>. This is a clear change in "behaviour", and very probably results from the diffusion of

Figure 2   Domestic Work Elasticities 1961 - 1983/4

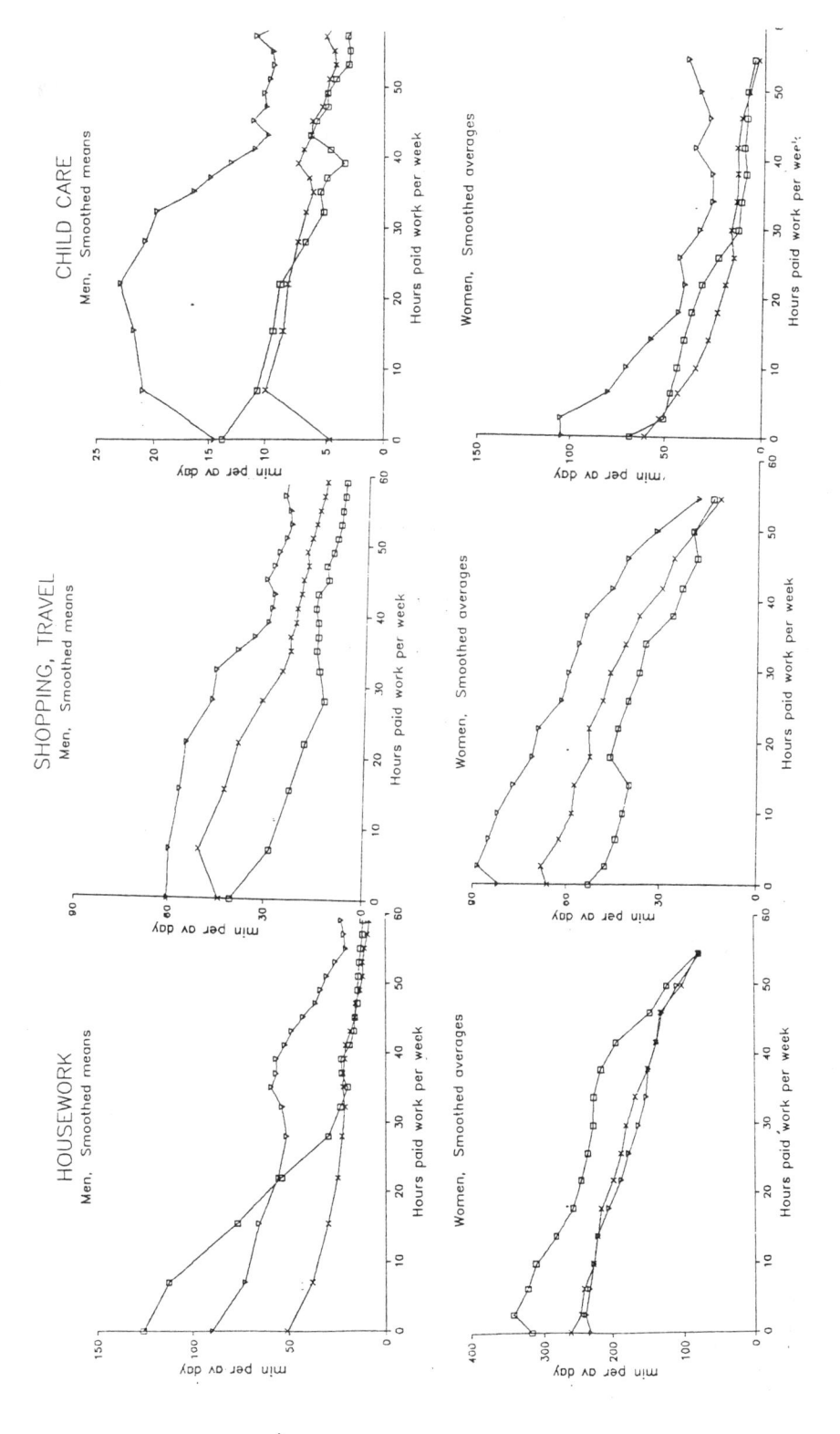

domestic equipment (washing machines, vacuum cleaners, electric cookers, central heating) into households over the period; more productive capital equipment in the household, hence more efficient domestic production, and less domestic work time. Over the latter period, the change was, though in the same direction, very much smaller - perhaps most British households had acquired the most productive sorts of domestic equipment by the mid 1970s.

The equivalent set of curves for men is superficially more complicated. There seems to be an enormous drop in the domestic work time of men employed for less than 30 hours per week. This is in fact a compositional effect: in 1961, with full employment and a relatively buoyant economy, a large proportion of the few men not employed or working short hours were doing so voluntarily, because they had heavy domestic responsibilities (probably care of old people or children), whereas in 1975 the much larger number of men in this group also included a large number of involuntarily unemployed and underemployed, with much less heavy domestic responsibilities.

So for comparative purposes we can ignore the steeply rising portion of the 1961 curve. With this exclusion, what we now see is almost the inverse of the pattern of change for women. The portions of the 1961 and 1974/5 curve above 30 hours of work show virtually no change whatsoever. But the whole curve shifts bodily upwards from 1974/5 to 1983/4. Men working 35 to 45 hours per week at their jobs, increased their routine domestic work time by about an hour per day between 1974/5 and 1983/4. There cannot be a technological explanation for this - it presumably reflects an ideological change, a change in social norms with respect to men's domestic work.

Turning to the shopping and domestic travel elasticities, we find essentially the same trends for men and women. At each level of work involvement the amount of time devoted to shopping and associated activities has increased throughout the 1960s and 1970s. The explanation here presumably has to do with the spatial reorganisation of retail and other service facilities. Local shops are replaced by remote supermarkets, small schools by large distant ones - in both cases these changes lead to improvements in efficiency in terms of cost reductions in "the economy" while increasing the personal time costs imposed on individuals' acting outside the economy. There is also a fair degree of consistency between the sexes in the child care category. In both cases, child care time remains pretty much constant for most paid-work categories between the 1961 and 1974/5 surveys and then rises markedly between 1974/5 and 1983/4; this rise cannot be explained in compositional terms, since the average number of children per household fell over this period - and in fact the increase in childcare time is highly concentrated in households in which the youngest child is below school age. People seem just to spend more time with their children.

So, once we control for sex and employment, and look at some slightly more detailed activity categories, quite clear and easily explicable patterns of social change emerge. In the example discussed above, we have seen some technologically induced change (reduction in women's work time 1961 to 1974/5), some change related to the development of new social norms (increase in men's housework 1974/5 to 1983/4), other developements related to change in spatial organisation (shopping), and, presumably, simple change in tastes (childcare).

When we look at British leisure in these more disaggregated terms, we again find rather straightforward patterns of change. Overall, most groups had between 30 minutes and an hour per day more leisure in 1983/4 than they did in 1961 (and this does not include the unemployed). The majority of this extra leisure is spent out of the home, in sports, walking, going to restaurants and drinking establishments (though the data shows the expected decline in cinema- and theatre-going. Most interestingly, while television-watching has increased over the period, the increase is entirely at the expense of listening to the radio - time spent in "passive" leisure (watching television, listening to radio, tapes and records) has actually declined over the two-and-and-a-half decades covered by surveys.

We find, in Britain, (even excluding unemployed people from the analysis) a reduction in paid work, and in unpaid work for women; a (small) redistribution of domestic labour between the sexes; an overall increase in leisure time, and that increase being taken mainly in sociable activities outside the home; home leisure activities moving proportionately away from the passive consumption of broadcast entertainment. Equivalent analyses are in progress for the other six countries in the archive; Given the cross-national similarities in the trends seen in Figure 1, we anticipate that broadly similar conclusions will emerge from the international comparisons.

4. Determinants of Change in Time Use Patterns

The analysis of the time budget survey material will tell us a great deal about _how_ time use has changed. But (since the arguments outlined in the first section of this paper involve purposeful intervention in the change), it is clearly also important that we discover why time use patterns change. We need to develop some theoretical basis from which we may argue that a particular change in circumstances will lead to particular changes in behaviour. We need to be able to say that, for example, particular technological innovations such as home shopping, or particular changes in social organisation such as shorter working weeks, will lead to more out-of-home-leisure consumption (and hence more jobs).

There is a substantial economic literature on the determinants of time allocation, producing sophisticated and elegant mathematical models (eg Becker 1965, Gronau 1979) - which are altogether rather hard to apply to the sort of data we have been discussing. They are, in most cases, rather narrowly concerned with the determinants of labour supply, disregarding the complex choices between different sorts of unpaid work and leisure. And their basic assumptions, of self-knowledge, rationality, and knowledge of alternative available courses of action and theier consequences, are deeply implausible. Familiarity with the complexity of behaviour demonstrated by the time use data, does not encourage belief in the economic theory of time.

There is however the basis of a more satisfactory theoretical framework for understanding the processes of determination of lifestyle, deriving from the work of Swedish geographers, studying time in the 1960s (Carlstein, 1977). The starting point of this work is the observation that all human activities are located both in time and space, and that activity sequences are constrained by the geographical locations of, and temporal restrictions on, particular activities.

The "time geographers" see households as having "activity programmes" - lists of tasks that are expected to be carried out out by or on behalf of the household over a period - and what we might think of as "household work and leisure strategies" - sets of expectations of which activities are to be carried out by which household members. Over time, strategies may be modified without altering programmes (eg change in the domestic division of labour) and the programmes themselves may change - perhaps as a consequence of strategic change (as where the size of the household wash decreases as the husband takes over responsibility for it from the wife). Activities are characterised by their geographical locations ("stations"), by their duration, and by any temporal constraints that apply to them (eg pub or shop opening hours, clocking-on times).

This simple set of concepts constitutes a powerful tool for interpreting the process through which activities are determined. Consider the example in Figure 3. Let us suppose that the household contains a couple and a preschool child. The woman of the household is presently not working but has been offered a job in a factory. The job would require her to clock-on at at 9.15 in the morning. The current household strategy has the woman

Figure 3   The Swedish Time   Geography

Terminology - Activity stations
 - Geographic constraints, distances, speeds
 - Temporal constraints - times of day for acts
 - Activity norms - household programmes
   - gender division of labour

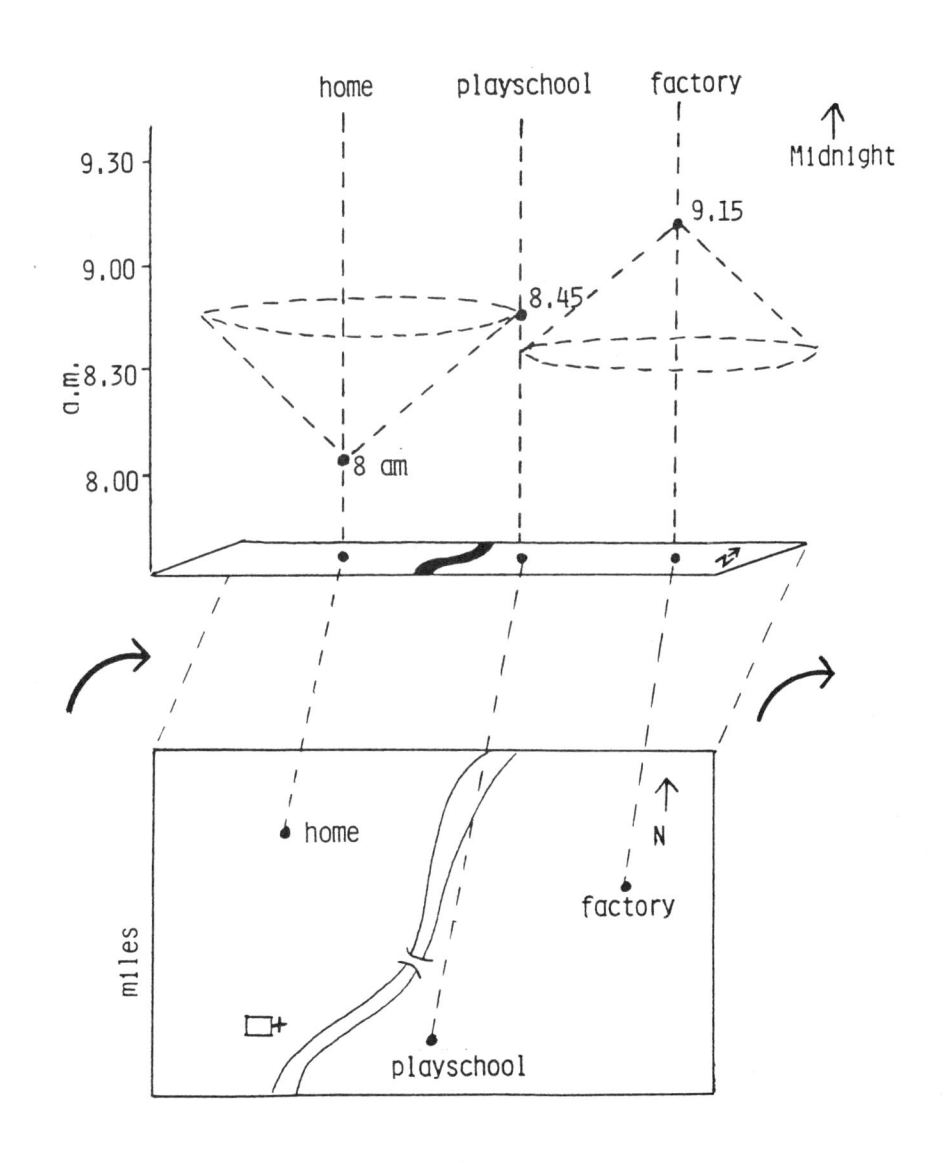

responsible for weekday daytime child care; how is the child to be cared for if she takes the job?

There is a playschool across the river, which opens at 8.45 in the morning. The cone drawn on Figure 3 with its apex at the station marked "home" shows the limit of places that someone leaving home at 8 am can reach at any given point in time (the slope of the sides of the cone is proportional to the maximum speed of transport available - the faster the transport, the more places can be reached at any point in time, and hence the flatter the cone). If the woman leaves home at 8.00 am she can (just) deliver the child at the playschool at 8.45. The cone with its apex at the factory shows, for various points in time, the geographical limits of the area from which the factory can be reached by 9.15 am. If the woman is at the playschool at 8.45 she cannot then get to the factory in time to clock on at 9.15. Does the domestic division of labour (the household "strategy") change - if the tempero-spatial constraints on the man are less severe, perhaps it becomes his job to deliver the child. Or perhaps it is possible to pay some other person to do this. Or perhaps the constraints and complications are such that the woman simply does not take the job.

This is clearly the correct framework for thinking about change in time use. The historical changes that we find in the time budget data must clearly reflect the interplay of habits and preferences with changing options and temporal and geographical constraints. Some of the raw material for developing these explanations are to be found in the the time budget surveys themselves. Most time-budget surveys contain some ancillary information about the geographical locations of activities - some (eg the Canadian material) contains rather detailed information of this sort. And the diaries themselves contain data on the start and finish times of activities. Part at least of the change in time use over time can be explained simply by changes in constraints (eg increases in domestic travel time explained by the increasing distance to shops and schools).

But this only gets us part of the way. We need to understand how households discover new options, how possibly conflicting preferences for alternatives are negotiated among household members. We need to understand the _process_ through which changes in households' opportunities and constraints are translated into new patterns of behaviour. These requirements take us beyond the possibilities of the time-budget data, towards a more experimental approach.

One rather promising option (which emerges from transport planning research) is the use of structured time-use decision-making "games" (Jones, Dix and Heggie, 1983). The experiment faces actual households with hypothetical changes in their circumstances, and traces the consequences. The experimenters gather a household together, and plot the week's activities of each household member on a rectangular board, one side of which is marked with a set of stylised "stations" (workplace, shops, schools etc.), the other with the hours of the week, and a set of coloured wooden blocks representing different activities. They then introduce a perturbation - in their case, a change in the transport system, but for our purposes this could as well be an offer of shorter working hours, or a part time job, or a teleshopping terminal - for a member of the household, and then simply observe the process through which the household adjusts to it.

So the husband, let us say, is offered an hour's reduction to his workday. What will he do? "I'll go down the pub." "But there's the laundry to collect, Tuesdays." "You promised me I could go to Judo/Ballet/Scouts if the car was available." "Gran wants to come and visit." What *does* he do? Buy a new washing machine? Ferry the kids? Work an hour's overtime instead? The experimenters watch the process of negotiation, and the outcome, and draw conclusions as to what might happen if the hypothetical option were to be offered in real life. The transport researchers were dealing with actual proposals for new bus services, and were therefor able to see what the real-life outcome was. It appears that the game did pretty well model the actual outcomes.

The historical time use data will certainly get us some part of the way to understanding the impact of prospective social or technical innovations on lifestyle. But we will need to integrate the insights we gain from this work, with evidence gained from experiments - from small scale controlled "laboratory" experiments such as the time use game described here, and also from larger scale social "field" experiments, the "wired cities", four-day working weeks, remote working and home shopping experiments which are at present underway all over the world.

5. Lifestyle and Economic Structure.

Lifestyle is a rather vague and general term - in this paper we have adopted a rather specific meaning for it. It has been used to mean "a household's pattern of allocation of time to various activity over a given period" (so that "a society's lifestyle" is used as shorthand for the mix of patterns of time use adopted by the various households in that society.).

The intention of this paper is to demonstrate the interconnections between lifestyle and economic structure (and the connections between changes in lifestyle and changes in the balance between labour supply and labour demand). The reason for adopting such a very specific, time allocation based, definition of lifestyle, is that it enables us to make extremely direct empirical links with the economic structural variables. We can divide time use into three categories of activity - paid work, unpaid work, and consumption/recreation (with sleep as a residual). Of these, the paid work time-use category corresponds precisely to the labour supply to the formal economy, while each of the detailed categories of unpaid work and leisure consumption activities have direct complementarities with items of final expenditure or final Government service outputs.

Thus, the "blue book" statistics on employment of workers in particular occupations, correspond to the time budget data of paid work done by respondents in those particular occupational categories; time spent in cafes in the survey data corresponds to expenditure on restaurant services in the "blue book" statistics; hours spent at school correspond to the (notional) output of the educational system; time spent washing dishes, to money spent on washing-up sponges and washing-up soap - and so on. We can, in short, draw up a comprehensive table of associations, of identities and complementarities, between, on one side, inputs and outputs to and from "the economy", and on the other, categories of time use.

The set of correspondences summarised in Figure 4b, is the basis for a system of socioeconomic accounts which relate lifestyle and economic structure. Each time use category requires a particular set of inputs of goods and services from the formal economy. Washing clothes, for example, requires washing machines, soap powder, repair and maintenance services and so on.

At a particular historical juncture we know (from the time budget statistics) how much time is spent by the society in

Figure 4a Time Use and Conventional Economic Models

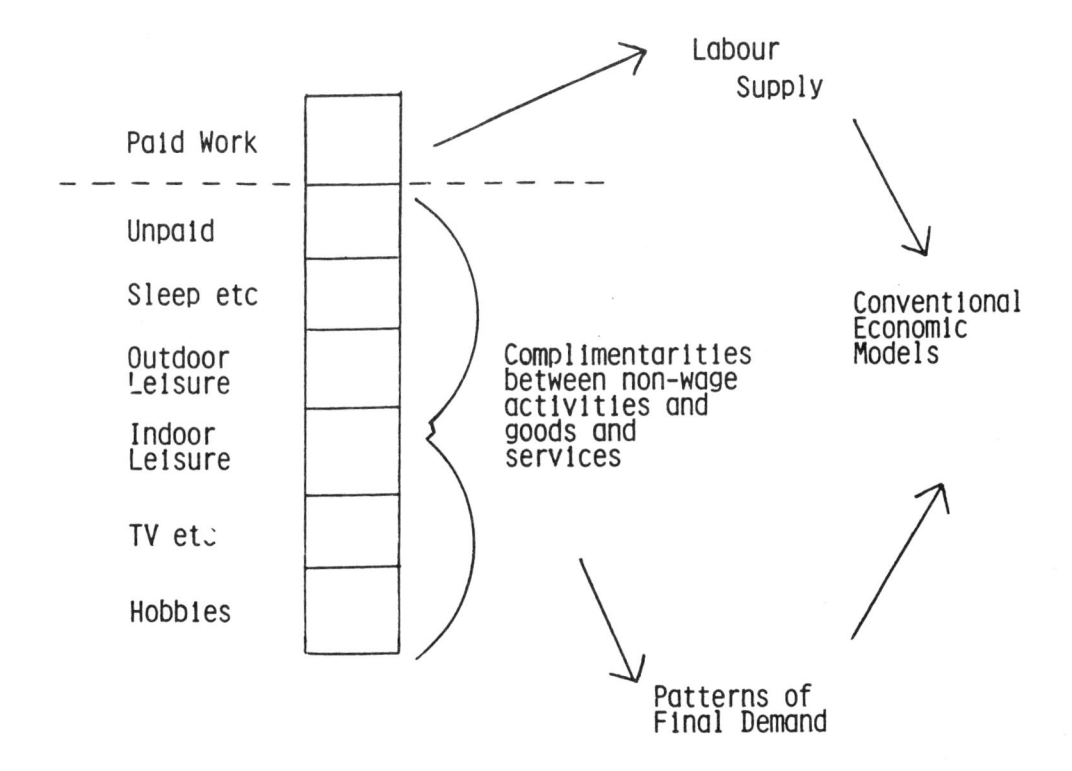

```
Paid Work         ──────→  Labour
─ ─ ─ ─ ─ ─ ─ ─              Supply
 Unpaid                          │
                                 ↓
 Sleep etc
              } Complimentarities   Conventional
 Outdoor        between non-wage     Economic
 Leisure        activities and       Models
                goods and
 Indoor         services             ↑
 Leisure                             │
                     ↓               │
 TV etc           Patterns of
                  Final Demand
 Hobbies
```

Figure 4b   Time Use and Consumption

COMMODITY INPUTS TO HOUSEHOLD (CONSUMPTION CATEGORIES)

FUNCTIONS/PURPOSES		Equipment Capital	Materials	Intermediate Services	Final Services	Public Services
BASIC	HOUSING FABRIC	House purchase tools	Fuel, paint	equip. repair	decorating etc.	Pub. Utilities
	HOUSE FITTINGS	Furniture, cleaning equip.	Cleaning materials	Repair domestic equip.	Domestic services	Welfare services
	CLOTHES	Clothing, washing m/c	Soap etc.	Repair	Laundry cleaning	Welfare
	FOOD	Cookers, fridge	Food etc.	Repair	Restaurant services	Welfare services
RECREATION	EAT, DRINK, OUT	–	–	–	Restaurant services	–
	OUT, SPECTATOR	–	–	–	Spectator activities	Cultural services
	OUT, PARTICIPANT	Sports Equipment	–	Repair	Fees, subscriptions	Sporting facilities
	AT HOME, PASSIVE	TV etc; records etc.	–	–	–	–
	..., READ & WRITE	Books, papers	Stationery	–	–	–
	PLAY, HOBBIES	Toys, games etc.	–	–	–	–
	GARDENING, PETS	Tools	Pet food, Plants	–	–	–
	HOLIDAYS	Caravan, second home	Maintenance	–	Hotels	–
MAINTENANCE	TRANSPORT	Car purchase	Petrol, oils	Repairs, Insurance	Transport, postal servs.	Roads etc., subsidies
	MEDICAL	–	Drugs	Health Insurance	Medical fees	Health services
	OTHER PERSONAL	–	Cosmetics, toilet, soap	–	Hairdressing, manicure	Social services
	EDUCATION	–	–	–	School fees	Educ. services
	SECURITY, ADMIN. LAW	Security equipment	–	–	Security services	Pub. Admin., security

ACTIVITIES (TIME USE CATEGORIES)

Mainly Production	Mainly Consumption
"Odd jobs"	Sleeping, visiting entertaining talking
Housework child-care shopping etc.	
Washing, cleaning repair of clothes	
Food preparation, washing up	Eating, drinking
–	Clubs, Pubs. Restaurants
–	Cinema, Theatre, excursions etc.
Sports coaching	Playing sports, walking
–	Watching TV, listening to music
–	Study, computer, reading
Sewing, knitting	Games & passtimes
Gardening, pet Care	Relaxing
–	Leisure travel
Domestic, work travel	In bed sick, at doctor's, hospital
Personal hygiene	Personal services
Voluntary tutoring	At school, classes

clothes-washing, and (from the domestic expenditure statistics) how much money is spent on each of the goods and services input to the process. We can establish coefficients of relationship between these phenomena: we can say that, for example, so many (million) minutes spent in clothes-washing, correspond to so much money spent on soap powder. The official economic statistics register the whole output of the economy. The time budget data covers all the time use of the society. So the output of the economy can be comprehensively "explained" in terms of categories of time use (with the exception of goods and services exported); and the "consequences" of time use can be mapped in terms of final consumption, and hence ultimately employment (or else imports, and hence employment elsewhere).

These coefficients of correspondence do of course change. We saw previously that routine domestic work had declined overall in Britain between the early 1960s and the mid 1970s, and assumed that this change was associated with an increase in the household stock of equipment; each minute of housework was associated with <u>more</u> expenditure on domestic equipment in 1975 than in 1961. So, there are in fact two sorts of change over historical periods: change in the society's allocation of time between the various consumption and production activities; and change in the consequence of particular patterns of time allocation for the pattern of final demand.

The socio-economic accounting model outlined here is undoubtably extremely crude (though in principle not noticably cruder than some of the standard operations of national income accounting). And crude though it may be, it would nevertheless provide us with something that conventional economic modelling does not — a framework for thinking about the impact of changes in lifestyle on economic structure.

What has been written so far constitutes the specification for a very extensive research programme. It calls for the collection of historical series of estimates of societies' patterns of time use. It calls for the development of theories of the determination of time-use patterns. And it proposes a framework for integrating national time-use data with conventional national income accounts, to produce a new system of socio-economic accounts. The reason for proposing this research program is that it may reveal new policy options; it provides us with a new, "consumptionist" framework for integrating various streams of social and economic policymaking — into what we might think of as a "time use policy".

6. Time Use Policy.

In the first section we dismissed the Keynesian version of consumptionism as too indiscriminate. We cannot simply stimulate effective demand, if consumers opt for patterns of expenditure which do not have the desired effect of producing jobs. The aim of the "time use" approach to policymaking is simple (though not the practice): to search for areas of life in which job-generating consumption activities may be <u>directly</u> stimulated through public policy.

We can guess at some of the essential elements of such a time use policy; these are illustrated in Figure 5. There are three main planks. First, policies for the reduction of the length of the working life. These might include raising the school leaving age, adding to requirements for post-school training or education of young people, and extending provisions for further and higher education for adults and the retired. Adult workers might be offered the option of taking mid-career sabatical leave, either for educational or for recreational purposes. In addition to earlier retirement, older workers could be offered the option of a more gradual phased withdrawal from full time employment, with long periods of leave interspersed with full time work in the final years of employment.

As Figure 5 suggests, these measures would have two different sorts of consequences. Directly, they lead to a reduction in the number of people needing jobs, since they constitute the removal of substantial parts of particular age cohorts from the labour force. Indirectly, they lead to an increase in the demand for labour. In some cases this increase in labour demand is quite straightforward - raising the school leaving age increases the

Figure 5 Time Use Policy and Unemployment

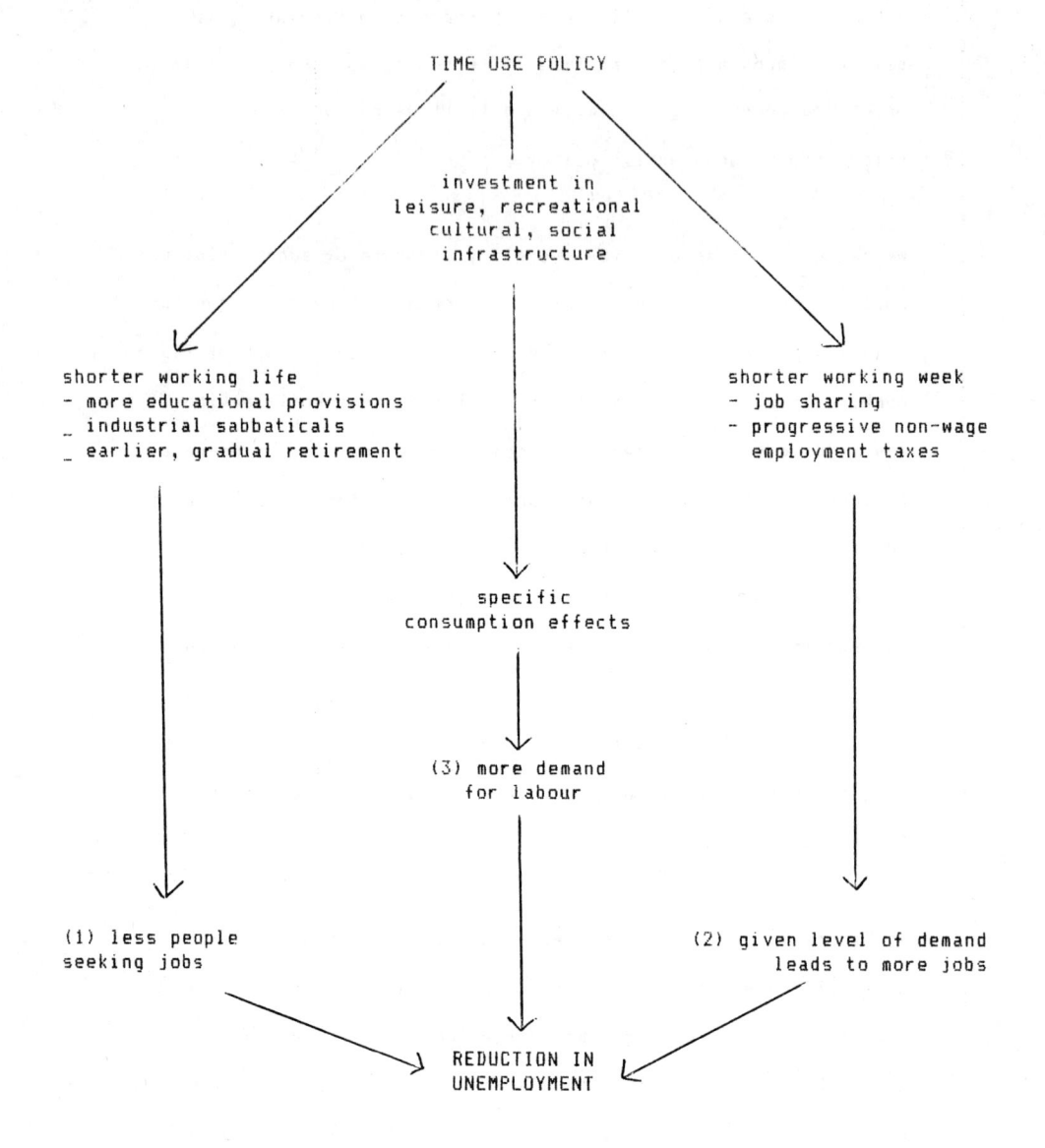

```
                          TIME USE POLICY
                         /       |       \
                        /        |        \
                                 investment in
                              leisure, recreational
                                cultural, social
                                 infrastructure
                        ↙            |            ↘
   shorter working life              |              shorter working week
   - more educational provisions     |              - job sharing
   - industrial sabbaticals          |              - progressive non-wage
   - earlier, gradual retirement     |                employment taxes
           |                         ↓                       |
           |                     specific                    |
           |                consumption effects              |
           |                         |                       |
           |                         ↓                       |
           |                   (3) more demand               |
           |                      for labour                 |
           ↓                         |                       ↓
   (1) less people                   |              (2) given level of demand
       seeking jobs                  |                  leads to more jobs
            ↘                        ↓                      ↙
                              REDUCTION IN
                              UNEMPLOYMENT
```

demand for teachers. In others – the increase in demand for leisure or informal work facilities by early retirees for example – the consequence is more difficult to predict.

The second plank of such a time use policy is the promotion of a shorter working week, with the aim of encouraging job sharing. Policy instruments here include the provision of legal rights for employees to demand part-time work, public subsidies to employers operating job-sharing schemes, and technical help in implementing them. But probably the most important element of public policy here will be the reduction of the current disincentives – mostly fiscal – to shorter time working. Employers who must pay non-wage benefits on a per capita, flat rate, basis, have an incentive for limiting the number of their employees; converting these payments to a progressive system based on total weekly incomes would encourage job sharing.

The consequences of such policies are again twofold. Job sharing means that a given level of demand for labour yields more jobs. The shorter working hours again mean a change in the pattern of final demand, in the direction of providing more employment in the production of leisure related goods and services. But in neither case are the consequences very clear: a given reduction of hours cannot be expected to translate itself into an exactly proportional increase in the number of jobs; nor is it clear exactly what are the uses to which the extra free time will be put.

The third major element in this programme would be investment in the new facilities and infrastructural provisions demanded by people with extra non-work time. A proportion of the investment in new entertainment facilities could certainly be provided by the market. But new educational establishments, sports and similar recreational facilities, cultural institutions, parks and access to the countryside would all come more naturally into the ambit of public provision. Of course, the balance between the different sorts of leisure provision would depend on what people wish to do with their extra free time.

By now two things should be emerging. On one hand, there may be very substantial scope for the application of the sort of integrated social time-use policy I have been outlining. The possibility of such an approach to the problem of mass unemployment must be admitted. On the other hand, everything written so far is speculation; we have only the vaguest of understandings of the social mechanisms which would govern the implementation of these lines of policy and determine their consequences. A great deal of social research is required if we are to be able to evaluate the practical feasibility of this approach.

We can list the main areas of uncertainty with respect to the three mechanisms for reduction in unemployment listed in Figure 5. In some cases a body of research material does already exist. Mechanism 1 (reduction in the number of people seeking jobs) requires substantial intergenerational transfers, in the the form of additional educational and pensions provisions. A certain amount of evidence on the determinants of the willingness to make such transfers is to be found in the literature on the economic and social psychology of altruism.

Mechanism 2 (job sharing through shorter working hours) raises the issue of what Samuel Brittan (1981) has called the "lump of labour fallacy" - the marginal productivity of the last few weekly hours of work may be very low (as suggested by the less-than-proportional loss of output during the three day week period in the UK in 1974), so that a substantial reduction in the working week could generate a rather less than proportional increase in the number of jobs. Some German estimates suggest that with a 5 hour per week reduction, the "replacement ratio" might be substantially greater than .5 (Schettkat 1984). There is also the question of how the reduction in working time would be financed. If there were no wage compensation (ie if the wage decreased in proportion with the work week), then the strategy would be in effect a job-sharing tax - we would then be returned to the empirical question of the degree of the community's economic altruism. And if there were to be wage compensation, the issue of whether this would be inflationary would depend on exactly what people do with their extra free time. (An extended review of the literature on the consequences of shorter working weeks is to be found in Cuvillier 1984.)

This brings us back to the central issue in this paper. Mechanism 3 (the specific consumption effects of extra free time) is a field of almost entire ignorence. Some very preliminary suggestions are just now emerging from the results of time budget research , but so far we know very little. Yet this is the crucial issue for the underconsumptionist argument. If extra leisure time leads to an increase in participation in activities which require the purchase of commodities that are produced by the local economy, then working time reduction is a viable strategy for reducing unemployment.

The proposition is that increased leisure time may generate new jobs. We will probably find from the multinational comparative data analysis that this proposition is at least consistent with the historical evidence - that economic growth and full employment are associated with declining hours of work. But for the time use policy to be translated into a plausible, implementable, form, we need to go further. Just as a successful application of a Keynesian demand stimulation policy depended on estimates of the population's Marginal Propensity to Consume (ie its propensity to spend its income rather than save it) so our time use policy depends on our estimates of our population's propensity to spend its marginal leisure time in particular activities.

Extra money in European consumers' pockets may, _ceteris paribus_, mean more jobs in Korea. If we knew that extra money, _combined with_ extra free time, would be spent in purchasing services in the local economy, then it would make sense to stimulate effective demand _and_ subsidise shorter working hours. It is the attempt to influence, or direct, or constrain, marginal consumption towards those commodities which provide employment, which distinguishes the "time-use" version of consumptionism from Keynes'. We shall need to work hard at developing the sorts of theory, and acquiring the data, that we need for predicting (and for influencing) precisely how people use their extra leisure time.

REFERENCES

GS Becker — "A Theory of the Allocation of Time", _Economic Journal_ 239 Vol LXX, September 1965.

S Brittain — _How to End the Monetarist Controversy_, Hobart Papers 80, London, Institute of Economic Affairs, 1981

T Carlstein — () in Carlstein, Parkes and Thrift, _Timing Space and Spacing Time_ London, Edward Arnold. 1977

R Cuvillier   The Reduction of Working Time, Geneva, Internaltiona Labour Office, 1984.

JI Gershuny   Developing a Multinational Time-Budget Archive University of Bath, Mimeo, 1985.

R Gronau   "Leisure, Home Production and Work: The Theory of the Allocation of Time Revisited" Journal of Political Economy, 85, 1977

PM Jones, MC Dix, MI Clark and IG Heggie
                  Understanding Travel Behaviour, Aldershott, Gower 1983.

J Robinson   Free Time in Western Countries University of Maryland, Survey Research Centre, 1984

R Schettkat   Generale Arbeitszeitverkurzunq: Gesamptwirtshaftliche Kosten und Beschaftigungswirkungen, Discussion Paper ILM/LMP 1984.2, Wissenschaftszentrum, Berlin 1984.

A Szalai   The Use of Time, The Hague, Mouton, 1974

Tentative conclusions and further work

Tentative conclusions and further work

by Françoise Piotet and Eberhard Köhler

La première série des travaux exploratoires engagés à l'initiative de la Fondation européenne et le Colloque qui s'est tenu à Bruxelles le 25 avril 1986 ont permis:

- de mieux cerner les axes principaux de recherches nécessaires à une meilleure compréhension des problèmes et des questions liés à ces nouvelles formes d'emplois;

- de voir comment réorienter la problématique de certaines recherches pour en rendre les résultats plus opératoires;

- d'éliminer et ce n'est pas là un mince mérite, les fausses questions ou les faux problèmes.

Plusieurs questions sont apparues qui sont de nature diverse et qui nécessiteraient des travaux d'envergure différente.

La liste de ces questions qui n'est certes pas exhaustive, devrait permettre de faciliter les choix en fixant des priorités.

Il semble que l'on puisse ordonner ces questions et recherches autour de deux grands axes:

I - <u>Le ou les constats</u>

II - <u>Les conséquences et les alternatives</u>

I - <u>LE CONSTAT</u>

1) Quelle est la réalité de ces formes nouvelles d'emploi?
    Plusieurs approches ont été proposées pour appréhender ce problème.

- La première, de type plutôt micro-économique, s'est attachée à développer une première esquisse de la stratégie des entreprises en matière d'emploi: stratégie du "noyau dur" et de "la périphérie", la périphérie étant représentée par le travail temporaire, l'intérim, les contrats à durée déterminée, le temps partiel et le développement de la sous-traitance.
Quelle est l'extension de ce modèle?
Quels types d'entreprises touche-t-il?
Quels secteurs sont concernés : tous - quelques-uns?

- La seconde, complémentaire de la précédente, repose sur une approche que l'on pourrait qualifier de macro-économique et macro-sociale.
Elles consisterait d'abord à essayer, dans un premier temps, d'identifier en stocks, les effectifs concernés par chacune de ces formes "atypiques d'emplois", et d'approfondir l'analyse en partant des salariés concernés par ces formes d'emplois.

- Quelles sont les caractéristiques de ces salariés, et en ont-ils? Autrement dit, ces formes atypiques d'emplois touchent-elles de manière aléatoire l'ensemble de la population active ou au contraire sont-elles réservées à certaines catégories spécifiques de la population? Les femmes, les jeunes, etc...

- Ces catégories, si elles existent, sont-elles condamnées à ces emplois atypiques? Ces emplois sont-ils des voies de passage vers des emplois relevant du noyau dur? Il s'agirait donc là d'analyser des flux et non plus des stocks, les recherches conduites dans ce sens ayant pour objectif la mise à jour de segmentation dans le marché du travail.

- Les deux précédentes approches reposent sur des problématiques dont une des hypothèses fondatrices repose sur l'adaptation des entreprises à des contraintes environnementales essentiellement économiques.
Une troisième approche est proposée qui s'appuie sur l'offre technologique et son évolution. Les recherches déjà engagées par la Fondation sur le travail à distance, associé au développement de l'informatique, seront sans nul doute riches d'enseignements.

2) Si les questions précédentes ont pu être posées, c'est qu'elles se fondent sur des discours et des pratiques qui sont déjà à l'oeuvre.

Le débat actuel sur la flexibilité a été sous-jacent à l'ensemble de nos travaux. Les termes en sont largement connus. Les discussions du seminaire soulignent toutefois l'intérêt d'un approfondissement de ce sujet.

Au-delà des distorsions médiatiques, quelles sont les propositions concrètes des acteurs concernés: organisations syndicales et patronales, aussi bien que pouvoirs publics?

Ces propositions entraînent-elles un consensus fort ou bien existe-t-il des divergences? Quel est le degré d'adhésion des différentes "bases" aux propositions de leurs représentants?

Les propositions concernant la flexibilité sont d'origine institutionnelle. Quelle est l'appréciation à l'égard des différentes composantes des formes nouvelles d'emplois, de la population active, opinions et comportements des salariés nécessitent massivement une investigation particulière déjà entamée sur un point particulier qu'est le télé-travail. Une exploration beaucoup plus fine devrait être conduite sur les autres formes d'emplois et en particulier sur la sous-traitance et son développement qui revêt semble-t-il aujourd'hui, des caractéristiques spécifiques.

Une réponse partielle à ces questions, partielle parce que portant sur un point déterminé, est déjà apportée par la recherche conduite sur l'évolution de la législation et des négociations portant sur l'aménagement du temps de travail. Dans la présentation qui en a été faite, au-delà même des éléments d'informations essentielles qu'apporte cette recherche à la connaissance des réalités et des pratiques, émerge une question fondamentale ayant trait au niveau de négociation. Cette question n'appelle pas une recherche qui se poserait uniquement en termes techniques, mais elle renvoie au problème soulevé par la flexibilité, qui est celui de la régulation sociale, des arbitrages nécessaires entre intérêts particuliers et intérêt général, mais aussi du court et du moyen long terme. Cette question est donc, dans le sens précis du terme, une question politique que des recherches spécifiques doivent pouvoir éclairer.

II - LES CONSEQUENCES ET LES ALTERNATIVES

Au-delà donc d'un constat dont l'élaboration est en elle-même fort complexe, la Fondation a suscité les premières recherches exploratoires mais aussi les premiers éléments de problématique de recherches possibles sur les conséquences des formes nouvelles d'emplois sur certains segments de la société, mais aussi sur les individus eux-mêmes.

1) Il s'agit d'abord d'une recherche comparative sur l'évolution ou le bouleversement du droit du travail et de la sécurité sociale, confrontés à la flexibilité.

   Quels sont les éléments de régulation à maintenir?

   Quels sont les aménagements à apporter pour éviter le risque du développement d'une société anomique?

   Quels droits pour quelles protections?

   Comment, aujourd'hui, doivent s'articuler, lois et négociations?

2) Il s'agit ensuite de recherches à conduire en vue de mieux comprendre les conséquences à court et moyen terme de ces formes nouvelles d'emplois sur l'organisation sociale et la vie familiale. A partir des conséquences déjà constatées ou à constater - positives ou négatives - il s'agirait pour ces recherches de pouvoir éclairer et orienter les politiques d'accompagnement ou de correction: politiques de logement, d'urbanisme, aussi bien que politiques fiscales ou d'aménagement du territoire...

   Dans ce sens, la Fondation soutient une recherche particulièrement originale sur une meilleure connaissance de l'allocation du temps au sein des familles afin d'en déduire des politiques efficaces de développement de la demande intérieure susceptible de générer des emplois.

   Dans tous les cas, les recherches à conduire devraient s'attacher à examiner l'ensemble des avantages et des inconvénients aussi bien pour l'entreprise que pour la collectivité, à court et à moyen terme, des formes nouvelles d'emplois.

3) Au-delà de leurs conséquences collectives, celles-ci ont aussi sans doute un impact important sur les individus, impact de nature très diverse, aussi bien physiologique que psychologique: apparition de nouvelles zones de liberté,

mais aussi développement du stress, de nouvelles maladies, d'accidents du travail pour certains de ces emplois, etc.

Recherches difficiles car de nouveaux équilibres sont sans doute à trouver entre les aspirations à plus de liberté et d'autonomie et la capacité des individus à gérer celles-ci sur le moyen et long terme. Les pistes déjà amorcées sur le travail "isolé" devraient sans doute être étendues en même temps que des investigations nouvelles sur "les théories des besoins" pourraient utilement éclairer les recherches conduites sur le cadre social ou sociétal.

L'ensemble des chercheurs ont souligné les difficultés à saisir une réalité extraordinairement mouvante. On ne peut par exemple que faire des hypothèses sur les conséquences actuelles du télétravail à domicile, tant le nombre de personnes concernées est peu nombreux.

Faut-il pour autant attendre que cette forme de travail soit largement répandue pour en analyser les conséquences et tenter de corriger celles qui sont néfastes?

Les formes nouvelles d'emplois sont-elles une réponse conjoncturelle d'adaptation ou au contraire préfigurent-elles une organisation nouvelle et durable de l'entreprise?

Comment développer leurs effets positifs et dès à présent, analyser et prévoir leurs effets pervers pour essayer de les corriger?

C'est bien à ces questions que les recherches à engager doivent tenter de répondre, sachant, en paraphrasant VALERY, que nous ne sommes pas dans un monde fini, mais dans un monde incertain qui rend les recherches en sciences humaines particulièrement difficiles.

III - A practical way forward

In the course of the discussion at the Colloquium on 25 April, 1986, it became clear that there was a great desire and a great need for **quantification** of the problematique. At present, practically all parties concerned - the two sides of industry as well as the citizens of the European Community in general - have to rely to a great extent on speculation about possible trends regarding the spread of "atypical" forms of work and activity, i.e. away from the "standard" pattern of full-time permanent work. As long as nobody knows how real and how extensive these trends are, and why they are occuring at all, uncertainty will persist regarding the need for concern and the possibility of corrective, protective, or constructive positive action by the various actors, be they parliaments, governments, employers, or unions, that have a legitimate concern in this matter.

In order to shed more light on the reality of the situation, the European Foundation has initiated work which may lead ultimately towards the establishment of an experience and attitude survey regarding the desirability or otherwise of the development of "atypical" forms of work and activity.

The main aims of such a survey will be to collect quantitative and qualitative data on questions such as:

- to what extent are new forms of work and activity practised in comparison to more traditional "work pattern";

- what are the reasons for their development;

- to what extent do these forms of work fit into existing legal frameworks and collective agreements and what modifications, if any, are desirable, or respectively

- to what extent are the social partners and the governments/parliaments active in accommodating new arrangements within the framework of collective agreements and social security legislation;

- to what extent do the "users", i.e. employers and employees, of new forms of work and activity perceive the benefits and/or disadvantages of these arrangements;

- to what extent does a greater choice of work patterns meet the economic and social needs and aspirations of employers and employees and of society in general.

Some of the questions posed may be - at least partially - answered once some of the ongoing research will be finalized and the results will have been analyzed and interpreted. Among those currently running projects which will be finalized later in 1986 and early in 1987 is the work done by the two teams headed by Professor Blanpain and by Prof. Kravaritou, respectively. Other issues seem satisfactorily and relatively exhaustively covered by existing work (cf. Epstein on job sharing, Ochs and Gretsch on alternative cooperative enterprises, or the body of knowledge already assembled on telework), so that further research into these areas seems not to be imminently necessary. However, an informed watch will be maintained over any developments which may happen in the future. Different emphases on certain issues will be pursued through different projects within the total framework of the European Foundation's research programmes. For example, the study of cooperative undertakings (1986/87 programmes of work), particularly in Spain, Portugal, France and other relevant Member states will be distinct from the approach taken by Gretsch and Ochs in the paper which is part of this documentation.

Also, the ongoing analysis of existing time-budget data which the Foundation is undertaking with Prof. Gershuny will continue to provide quantitative and qualitative data that should go a long way towards explaining what changes have taken place historically and cross-nationally in the use of time, in particular also changes in the ratio between working time and other time.

However, many questions will remain to be researched; therefore, the second meeting of the Foundation's Advisory Committee on 27 June, 1986, came to the unanimous conclusion to move towards the preparatory phase of a survey project. During this phase, the European Foundation will need to clarify the following questions:

- which groups need to be included in the survey? Employers, unions, employees, social security experts, legal experts, politicians, and/or who else?

- how big should be the sample sizes for each group? Should they be weighted, structured or random samples?

- if they are to be structured, which structure should be introduced? By sector, by country, in which countries, etc.

Once these basic questions have been clarified, it will be possible to

- develop appropriate research instruments for each group, such as survey questionnaires, interview guides, checklists, etc.

- test the research instruments in a pilot phase.

In order to limit the many risks and pitfalls of a methodological and political nature associated with attitudinal and experience survey research, it was the Advisory Committee's opinion that a technical working group should be set up to deal with the technical questions. The results or progress of this working group would frequently be related back to the original Advisory Committee which is more political in nature by virtue of the unions', employers' and government representation on it. In this way, through a dynamic and constant interchange of knowledge between the two groups, a satisfactory and acceptable research design should emerge, one that will yield the most important and most useful data. The work of the technical working group will commence late in 1986/early in 1987.

Annexes

ANNEX I

Europäische Stiftung zur
Verbesserung der Lebens-
und Arbeitsbedingungen

Fondation Européenne
pour l'amélioration des
conditions de vie et de travail

European Foundation
for the Improvement of
Living and Working Conditions

Neue Arbeits-
und Tätigkeitsformen

Nouvelles formes
de travail et d'activités

New Forms
of Work and Activity

COLLOQUIUM/COLLOQUE 25.4.1986

**Centre Albert Borschette,
36 rue Froissart — Bruxelles**

Programme

Chairman: Prof. Dr. Ralf Dahrendorf

09.30 **Welcome**
Dr. Clive Purkiss, Director, European Foundation

Opening statements
—Michael Welsh, MEP, Chairman of the Committee on Social Affairs and Employment of the European Parliament

— Dott. Enrico Kirschen, Chairman, Economic and Social Committee — Section for Social Questions

—Jean Degimbe, Director-General for Employment, Social Affairs and Education, Commission of the European Communities, Chairman of the Administrative Board of the European Foundation

—Prof. Dr. Ralf Dahrendorf, Universität Konstanz, Chairman of the Advisory Committee

10.00 **Presentation of the main problem areas**
Prof. Françoise Piotet, Université Sorbonne, Paris,
Eberhard Köhler, Research Manager, European Foundation, Dublin

Statements of

—UNICE (Union des Industries de la Communauté Européenne)

—ETUC (European Trade Union Confederation)

11.00 **Refreshments**

11.30 **Plenary Discussion**

13.00 **Lunch**

14.30 **Continuation** of plenary discussion and summary of results Prof. Dr. Ralf Dahrendorf

16.00 **End** of Colloquium

Official languages: English, French and German

Programm

Vorsitzender: Prof. Dr. Ralf Dahrendorf

09.30 **Begrüßung**

Dr. Clive Purkiss, Direktor, Europäische Stiftung

Einführende Bemerkungen

— Michael Welsh, MEP, Vorsitzender des Ausschusses für soziale Angelegenheiten und Beschäftigung, Europäisches Parlament

— Dott. Enrico Kirschen, Vorsitzender, Wirschafts- und Sozialausschuß — Fachgruppe für Sozialfragen

— Jean Degimbe, Generaldirektor für Beschäftigung, soziale Angelegenheiten und Bildung, Kommission der Europäischen Gemeinschaften, Vorsitzender des Verwaltungsrates der Europäischen Stiftung

— Prof. Dr. Ralf Dahrendorf, Universität Konstanz, Vorsitzender der beratenden Arbeitsgruppe

10.00 **Vorlage des Problemrahmens**

Prof. Françoise Piotet, Université Sorbonne, Paris,
Eberhard Köhler, Forschungsleiter, Europäische Stiftung, Dublin

Stellungnahmen von

— UNICE (Europäische Industrievereinigung)

— EGB (Europäischer Gewerkschaftsbund)

11.00 **Erfrischungen**

11.30 **Plenardiskussion**

13.00 **Mittagessen**

14.30 **Fortsetzung** der Plenardiskussion und Zusammenfassung der Ergebnisse
Prof. Dr. Ralf Dahrendorf

16.00 **Ende** des Kolloquiums

Offizielle Sprachen: Englisch, Französisch, Deutsch

Programme

Président: Prof. Dr. Ralf Dahrendorf

09.30 **Accueil**
Dr. Clive Purkiss, directeur de la Fondation européenne

Introduction
— Michel Welsh, MEP, président de la Commission des affaires sociales et de l'emploi du Parlement européen

— Dott. Enrico Kirschen, président du Comité economique et social — section des affaires sociales

— Jean Degimbe, directeur-général pour l'emploi, les affaires sociales et l'education des Communautés européennes, président du conseil d'administration de la Fondation européenne

— Prof. Dr. Ralf Dahrendorf, Universität Konstanz, président du Comité consultatif

10.00 **Présentation de la problématique**
Prof. Françoise Piotet, (Sorbonne),
Eberhard Köhler, chargé de recherche à la Fondation européenne de Dublin

Interventions de
— l'UNICE (Union des Industries de la Communauté Européenne)
— de la CES (Conféderation Européenne des syndicats).

11.00 **Rafraîchissements**

11.30 **Discussion plénière**

13.00 **Déjeuner**

14.30 **Suite** de la discussion plénière et synthèse par le Prof. Dr. Ralf Dahrendorf

16.00 **Fin** du Colloque

Langues officielles: anglais, français et allemand

Hintergrundmaterial

Neue Organisationsweisen der Arbeit zur Anpassung an eine veränderte Nachfrage nach Produkten und Dienstleistungen, veränderte Verhaltensweisen und eine anhaltende technologische Entwicklung gekoppelt mit noch nicht dagewesenen Arbeitslosenzahlen zwingen zu einer Neueinschätzung des Arbeitsmarktes und damit einer Neudefinition von Arbeit. Für eine Vielzahl von Personen hat "Arbeit" ihre herkömmliche Bedeutung im Sinne von Vollzeitbeschäftigung gegen Bezahlung verloren.

Zum besseren Verständnis dieser Veränderungen startete die Stiftung 1985 ein Forschungsprogramm über **neue Arbeits- und Tätigkeitsformen.** Dieses Programm untersucht die Art und Weise, in der der Arbeitsmarkt auf diese veränderten Bedingungen reagiert sowie die neuen Arbeitsformen, die zunehmende Beachtung finden und bewertet die Implikationen hiervon. Zu diesen neuen Arbeitsweisen gehören solche, die Flexibilität in die Wohnsituation von Arbeitnehmern einbringen, und zwar in Bezug zu deren Arbeitsplatz sowie jene, die auf einer andersartigen Nutzungsweise von Zeit fußen wie Heimarbeit, Dauerwochenendarbeit, 12-Stunden-Schichtarbeit, Arbeit "auf Abruf" und Telearbeit.

Contexte

Les attitudes, la demande en biens et en services évoluent, l'évolution technologique se poursuit, le chômage atteint un niveau sans précédent. Ces facteurs sont à l'origine de nouvelles formes d'organisation du travail qui nous obligent à repenser le marché du travail et à redéfinir ce qu'est le travail. Pour beaucoup, ce concept a perdu son sens traditionnel d'emploi exercé à plein temps contre salaire.

Afin de mieux comprendre ces phénomènes, la Fondation a lancé en 1985 un programme de recherche **Nouvelles formes de travail et d'activité.** Il a pour thèmes: la réaction du marché du travail au changement, les nouvelles formes de travail qui se répandent et l'évaluation de leurs conséquences. Parmi ces nouvelles méthodes de travail, certaines introduisent un élément de flexibilité en ce qui concerne le lieu de travail, alors que d'autres modifient l'utilisation qui est faite du temps (par exemple travail à domicile, travail permanent de week-end, travail posté de douze heures, travail impliquant l'astreinte à domicile, télétravail).

Background Material

New ways of organizing work to meet changes in demand for products and services, changing attitudes, and continuing technological development, coupled with unprecedented levels of unemployment are forcing a reassessment of the labour market and with it a redefinition of work. No longer for many people does "work" hold its traditional meaning of full-time employment for remuneration.

To understand these changes more fully the Foundation initiated a research programme on **New Forms of Work and Activity** in 1985. It is designed to address the way that the labour market is responding to these changing conditions, to study the new kinds of work which are attracting increasing attention and to assess their implications.

These new ways of working include those which introduce flexibility in where workers live in relation to their work places as well as those which look differently at the way time is used, such as: home-work; permanent week-end work; 12-hour-shiftwork; "on-call" work and telework.

Hintergrund-material

Auch außerhalb des formellen Arbeitsmarktes finden grundlegende Änderungen statt. Je schwieriger es wird, eine bezahlte Arbeit zu finden, desto mehr Personen wenden sich anderen Tätigkeitsformen zu, die gewöhnlicherweise nicht den gleichen Stellenwert einnehmen, wie z.B. gemeinnützige Arbeit, Familienfürsorge usw. In einer Gesellschaft, in der sich der soziale Status lange Zeit aus der Arbeit ergab, benötigen diese Tätigkeiten einer Neubewertung.

Die Stiftung hat dieses Thema bereits aus verschiedenen Perspektiven untersucht. Sie versucht nunmehr, zu einem umfassenderen Verständnis der einzelnen Faktoren zu gelangen und untersucht mögliche nachfolgende Aktionen. Die Untersuchung erstreckt sich auf folgende Bereiche:

- Externe und interne Arbeitsmärke und Beschäftigungs-flexibilität.
- Entwicklung von Job-sharing.
- Entwicklung von Telearbeit.
- Auswirkungen auf Familien und soziale Organisation.
- Psychische Auswirkungen neuer Arbeits- und Tätigkeitsformen.

Contexte

Des changements considérables se produisent également en dehors du marché du travail traditionnel. A mesure qu'il est de plus en plus difficile de trouver un emploi rémunéré, on pratique d'autres formes d'activités auxquelles d'habitude on n'accorde pas la même importance: travaux d'utilité collective, aide sociale, etc. Dans une société comme la nôtre où le statut dépend beaucoup de l'emploi, il est possible que les activités mentionnées doivent faire l'objet d'une réévaluation.

La Fondation a déjà étudié ces problèmes sous plusieurs angles. Elle va maintenant chercher à cerner de plus près les questions soulevées pour ensuite examiner les actions qui pourraient être entreprises. Les recherches se concentreront sur les thèmes suivants:

- Marché interne et externe du travail et flexibilité de l'emploi.
- Évolution de la division du travail.
- Évolution du télétravail.
- Impact sur la famille et la société.
- Impact psychologique de nouvelles formes de travail et d'activité.

Background Material

Outside the formal labour market too, fundamental changes are taking place. As paid work becomes more difficult to find, more people are becoming involved in other forms of activity not usually regarded as having the same value; such as community work, family-care occupations and so on. In a society where status has for long been largely derived from work these activities may need re-evaluation.

The Foundation has already studied this subject from several angles. It will now seek to gain a more comprehensive understanding of the issues involved and will examine what actions could follow. The Foundation's research will look at:

- External and internal labour markets and employment flexibility.
- Development of job sharing.
- Development of telework.
- Impact on families and social organization.
- Psychological impact of new forms of work and activity.

Hintergrundmaterial

- Rechtliche und vertragliche Arbeitszeitbestimmungen.
- Arbeitsrechtliche und sozialversicherungsrechtliche Fragen betreffend neue Arbeits-und Tätigkeitsformen.
- Arbeitsorganisation in kooperativen Unternehmen.
- Sich verändernde Strukturen der Zeitnutzung.

Zu diesen Fragen werden Arbeitspapiere erstellt, die einem beratenden Ausschuß auf einem am 25. April 1986 in Brüssel stattfindenden Kolloquium vorgelegt werden. Dieser **beratende Ausschuß** wurde von der Stiftung zur Unterstützung bei ihrer künftigen Planung in diesem Bereich eingesetzt. Er setzt sich aus Vertretern der Gewerkschaftsbewegung und der Arbeitgeberorganisationen zusammen. Den Vorsitz führt Professor Ralf Dahrendorf (ehemaliger europäischer Kommissar). Das Kolloquium wird von ca. 40 Teilnehmern besucht, und zwar Vertretern der Sozialpartner, Regierungen, europäischen Gemeinschaftsinstitutionen, IAO, OECD sowie unabhängigen Sachverständigen.

Contexte

- Dispositions juridiques et contractuelles relatives au temps de travail.
- Problèmes de droit du travail et de législation sur la sécurité sociale relatifs à de nouvelles formes de travail et d'activité.
- Organisation du travail dans les coopératives.
- Nouvelles modalités de l'utilisation du temps.

Des communications sur ces thèmes seront présentées à un comité consultatif lors d'un colloque qui se tiendra à Bruxelles le 25 avril 1986. La Fondation a constitué ce **comité consultatif** qui l'aide à organiser la recherche dans ces domaines. Il est composé de représentants des syndicats et des organisations d'employeurs, et il a pour président le professeur Ralf Dahrendorf, ancien commissaire européen. Ce **colloque** réunira environ quarante participants représentant les partenaires sociaux, les gouvernements, les institutions de la Communauté européenne, l'OIT, l'OCDE, et des experts indépendants.

Background Material

- Legal and contractual provisions relating to working time.
- Issues in labour law and social security legislation regarding new forms of work and activity.
- Work organization in cooperative undertakings.
- Changing patterns of time use.

Papers on these will be presented to an advisory committee at a colloquium in Brussels, on the 25 April 1986. This **Advisory Committee** was set up by the Foundation to assist its future planning in this area. It is composed of representatives of the trade union movement and employers' organizations and is chaired by Professor Ralf Dahrendorf (formerly a European Commissioner).

The **Colloquium** will be attended by some 40 participants representing the social partners, Governments, European Community institutions, ILO, OECD, and independent experts.

Europäische Stiftung zur Verbesserung der Lebens- und Arbeitsbedingungen

Die Europäische Stiftung zur Verbesserung der Lebens- und Arbeitsbedingungen im Loughlinstown House, Co. Dublin, ist eine autonome Gemeinschaftseinrichtung, die durch eine Verordnung des Ministerrates der Europäischen Gemeinschaften vom 26. Mai 1975 gegründet wurde.

Der Verwaltungsrat der Stiftung setzt sich aus vier Gruppen zusammen, und zwar der Europäischen Kommission, der Regierungen, der Arbeitgeberverbände und Arbeitnehmerorganisationen jedes Mitgliedstaates. Die von der Stiftung durchgeführte Forschung erstreckt sich auf Bereiche wie Schichtarbeit, Arbeitsorganisation, neue Technologie, Lohnsysteme, Verkehr und Pendelverkehr, Verrentung, Erhebungen über Arbeitszeit und Freizeit und eine Vielzahl weiterer Bereiche.

Die Stiftung ist in enger Zusammenarbeit mit einer großen Anzahl von nationalen Forschungsinstituten tätig und unterhält enge Kontakte zu den verschiedenen europäischen und internationalen Einrichtungen, die sich mit der Verbesserung der Lebens- und Arbeitsbedingungen beschäftigen.

Fondation européenne pour l'amélioration des conditions de vie et de travail

La fondation européenne pour l'amélioration des conditions de vie et de travail, située à Loughlinstown House, dans le Comté de Dublin, est un organisme communautaire autonome créé par un règlement du Conseil des ministres des Communautés européennes du 26 mai 1975.

Le conseil d'administration de la Fondation européenne comprend quatre groupes : la Commission européenne, les gouvernements des États membres, les organisations d'employeurs et les organisations de travailleurs de chaque État membre.

La Fondation a déjà entrepris des recherches dans des domaines comme le travail posté, l'organisation du travail, les nouvelles technologies, les systèmes de rémunération, les transports et les trajets domicile-travail, la retraite, le temps de travail et le temps de loisir, et bien d'autres.

La Fondation coopère étroitement avec un grand nombre d'instituts de recherche nationaux et entretient des relations suivies avec les divers organismes internationaux et européens qui s'occupent de l'amélioration des conditions de vie et de travail.

European Foundation for the Improvement of Living and Working Conditions

The European Foundation for the Improvement of Living and Working Conditions in Loughlinstown House, County Dublin, is an autonomous Community body established by a Regulation of the Council of Ministers of the European Communities which came into force on 26th May, 1975.

The Foundation's Administrative Board comprises four groups, namely, the European Commission and the governments, the employers' federations and the trade unions of each member State

Research which has been carried out by the Foundation includes such areas as shiftwork, work organisation, new technology, wage payment systems, transport and commuting, retirement, surveys into working time and leisure time, and many more.

The Foundation co-operates closely with a large number of national research institutes and maintains close contact with the various European and international bodies concerned with the improvement of living and working conditions.

European Foundation for the Improvement of Living and Working Conditions

Loughlinstown House, Shankill, Co. Dublin, Ireland. Tel: (01) 826888 Telex: 30726 EURF EI

ANNEX II

COLLOQUIUM / COLLOQUE / KOLLOQUIA

New Forms of Work and Activity
Nouvelles formes de travail et d'activités
Neue Arbeits-und Tätigkeitsformen

Centre Albert Borschette, 36, rue Froissart, Brussels
25 April 1986

List of Participants / Liste des Participants / Teilnehmerliste

Chairman of the Colloquium **Président du Colloque** **Vorsitzender des Kolloquiums**	Prof. Ralf DAHRENDORF Universität Konstanz Postfach 55 60 D-7750 Konstanz 1
Members of European Parliament **Deputés au Parlement européen** **Mitglieder des Europäischen Parlaments**	Mr. Michael WELSH, MEP, Chairman, Committee on Social Affairs and Employment Watercrook 181 Town Lane Whittle-le-Woods Nr. Chorley, Lancs. PR6 8AG
	Mr. Jean-Paul BACHY, MEP Lotissement Sous-Ligneul Aiglemont F-08100 Charleville-Mézières
	Mr. José CABRERA BAZAN, MEP Placentines, 2 41004 Seville
	Mr. Raphael M.G. CHANTERIE, MEP Eikenlaan 26 B-8790 Waregemirchberg
	Mr. Benedikt HÄRLIN, MEP Im Mehringhof Gneisenaustrasse 2 1000 Berlin 61

European Parliament – Secretariat **Parlement européen – Secrétariat** **Europäisches Parlament – Sekretariat**	Mr. Jean Marie TRIACCA Socialist Group European Parliament 97, rue Belliard B-1040 Brussels
	Mr. Toni HOLENWEGER Groupe Arc-en-ciel European Parliament Plateau de Kirchberg Luxembourg
	Ms. Silvana PENNELLA Groupe communiste 97, rue Belliard B-1040 Bruxelles
	Dr. Maria SOFIANOPOULO European Parliament 97, rue Belliard B-1040 Bruxelles
	Ms. Paola RUSSO European Parliament 97, rue Belliard B-1040 Bruxelles
Belgian Permanent Representation to the EEC **Représentation Permanente de la Belgique auprès de la CEE**	Mr. François VANDAMME Belgian Permanent Representation to the EEC Brussels
Economic and Social Committee **Comité Économique et Social** **Wirschafts-und Sozialausschuß**	Dott. Enrico KIRSCHEN Chairman of Section for Social Questions Economic and Social Committee rue Ravenstein 2 B-1000 Brussels
	Mr. HICK Economic and Social Committee rue Ravenstein 2 B-1000 Brussels

Commission of the European Communities
Commission des Communautés européennes
Kommission der Europäischen Gemeinschaften

Mr. Jean DEGIMBE
Director-General for Employment
Social Affairs and Education
(A/1 05/8)
B-1049 Brussels

Mr. Klaus HARALD KAEDING
Directorate General for Employment
Social Affairs and Education
(A/1 07/24)
B-1049 Brussels

Ms. Gerlinde SCHÖNBERG
Directorate General for Employment,
Social Affairs and Education
B-1049 Brussels

Mr. Werner WOBBE
Commission of the European Communities
DG XII/A/1 - FAST
B-1049 Brussels

Committee of Experts of the European Foundation
Comité d'Experts de la Fondation Européenne
Sachverständigenausschuss

Dr. Reinhold WEIL
Institut für angewandte Arbeitswissenschaft e.V.
Marienburger Strasse 7
D-5000 Köln 51 (Marienburg)

Employer's Representatives
Représentants du Groupe des Employeurs
Arbeitgebervertreter

Dr. Fritz-Jürgen KADOR
Geschäftsführer der Bundesvereinigung
der Deutschen Arbeitgeberverbände
Gustav-Heinemann-Ufer 72
D-5000 Köln 51 (Bayental)

(Member of the Advisory Committee)
(Membre du Comité consultatif)
(Mitglied des Beretenden Ausschusses)

Mr. Cornelius DUBBELMAN
Rabo Bank Nederland
P.O. Box 17100
NL-3500 HG Utrecht

(Member of the Advisory Committee)
(Membre du Comité consultatif)
(Mitglied des Beretenden Ausschusses)

Employer's Representatives
(continued)
Représentants du Groupe des Employeurs
(suite)
Arbeitgebervertreter
(forts.)

Ms. Beatrice VERSCHUEREN
UNICE
Union des Industries de la
Communauté Européenne
Rue de Loxum 6
B-1000 Brussels

Mr. Bernard LE MARCHAND
Secrétaire Général de la FIGED
17 Avenue Edouard Lacomblé
B-1040 Brussels

Ms. Lone LIND
Head of Section
Department for Collective Agreements
Dansk Arbejdsgiverforenong
V. Voldgade 113
DK-1503 Copenhagen

Mr. Christian VAN GENT
Raad van Het Filiaal and Grootwinkel-
bedrijf
Postbus 33
NL-1500 EA Zaandam

Unions' Representatives
Représentants du groupe des Syndicats
Gewerkschaftsvertreter

Mr. François STAEDELIN
Secrétaire
Confédération Européenne des Syndicats
rue Montagne aux Herbes Potagères 37
B-1000 Brussels

(Member of the Advisory Committee)
(Membre du Comité consultatif)
(Mitglied des Beretenden Ausschusses)

Prof. Eliane VOGEL-POLSKY
Institut de Sociologie
Université Libre de Bruxelles
Avenue Jeanne 44
B-1050 Brussels

(Member of the Advisory Committee)
(Membre du Comité consultatif)
(Mitglied des Beretenden Ausschusses)

Union's Representatives (continued) **Représentants du groupe des Syndicats** (suite) **Gewerkschaftsvertreter** (forts.)	Mr. Heinrich FUCHS Deutscher Gewerkschaftsbund (DGB) Postfach 26 01 D-4000 Düsseldorf 30 Mr. Marc SAPIR Confédération Européenne des Syndicats rue Montagne aux Herbes Potagères 37 B-1000 Brussels
Government Representatives **Représentants des Gouvernments** **Regierungsvertreter**	Mr. Hans-Jürgen BIENEK Bundesministerium für Arbeit und Sozialordnung Rochusstr. 1 D-5300 Bonn 1 Mr. Maurice CASHELL Head of Planning and Policy Analysis Unit Department of Labour Mespil Road Dublin 4
OECD **OCDE**	Mr. Oliver CLARKE 2, rue André Pascal F-75775 Paris Cédex 16
International Labour Office **Bureau International de Travail** **Internationale Arbeitsorganisation**	Mr. Raymond GOOSE and Mr. Gérard FONTENEAU Bureau de Liason de l'OIT avec les Communautes Européennes et les Pays du Benelux 40, rue Aimé Smekens B-1040 Brussels
IACT	Mr. Marcel PIERRE Administrateur Général de l'Instutut pour l'Amélioration des Conditions de Travail rue de la Concorde 60 B-1050 Brussels
Fondation Roi Baudouin	Ms. Magda LAMBERT rue Brederode 21 B-1000 Brussels

Researchers
Chercheurs
Forscher

Ms. Joyce EPSTEIN
28 St. Petersbourgh Place
London W2 4LD

Prof. Yota KRAVARITOU-MANITAKIS
Al. Michaelidi 19
Falero-Thessaloniki

Ms. Christina DIMITRAKOU DELIYANNI
25 Martiou 34
Panorama-Thessaloniki

Prof. Françoise PIOTET
8, rue de la Véga
F-75012 Paris

Prof. Roger BLANPAIN
Faculty of Law
University of Leuven
Tiensesstraat 41
B-3000 Leuven

Mr. Otto RENDA
Institut für angewandte Betriebs-
psychologie
Am Espenpfuhl 52
D-1000 Berlin 47

Mr. Nigel MEAGER
Institute of Manpower Studies
Mantell Building
University of Sussex

Mr. Lothar GRETSCH and

Mr. Peter OCHS
Institut für Sozialforschung und
Sozialwirteschaf e.V.
Trierer Strasse 42
D-6600 Saarbrücken

Mr. Wolfgang STEINLE
EMPIRICA
Kaiserstr. 29-31
D-5300 Bonn 1

Researchers	Ms. Ros MORAN
(continued)	Ms. Jean TANSEY
Chercheurs	Irish Foundation for Human Development
(suite)	Garden Hill
Forscher	E.H.B. Box 41A
(forts.)	1 James' Street
European Foundation – Secretariat	Dr. Clive PURKISS, Director
Fondation Européenne – Secrétariat	Mr. Eric VERBORGH, Deputy Director
Europäische Stiftung – Sekretariat	Mr. Eberhard KÖHLER, Research Manager
	Ms. Ann McDONALD, Conference Officer
	Ms. Christine GOLLIN, Secretary

New Forms of Work and Activity: Documentation from a Colloqium, Brussels, April 25, 1986.

Luxembourg: Office for Official Publications of the European Communities

1986 - 339 pp. — 240 x 173 cm.

Multilingual version (En/Fr/De/Es versions to be published at a later date).

ISBN: 92-825-6418-5

Cataloque number: SY-46-86-775-3A-C

Salg og abonnement · Verkauf und Abonnement · Πωλήσεις και συνδρομές · Sales and subscriptions
Venta y abonos · Vente et abonnements · Vendita e abbonamenti
Verkoop en abonnementen · Venda e assinaturas

BELGIQUE/BELGIË

Moniteur belge/Belgisch Staatsblad
Rue de Louvain 40-42/Leuvensestraat 40-42
1000 Bruxelles/1000 Brussel
Tél. 512 00 26
CCP/Postrekening 000-2005502-27

Sous-dépôts/Agentschappen:

**Librairie européenne/
Europese Boekhandel**
Rue de la Loi 244/Wetstraat 244
1040 Bruxelles/1040 Brussel

CREDOC
Rue de la Montagne 34/Bergstraat 34
Bte 11/Bus 11
1000 Bruxelles/1000 Brussel

DANMARK

Schultz EF-publikationer
Møntergade 19
1116 København K
Tlf: (01) 14 11 95
Girokonto 200 11 95

BR DEUTSCHLAND

Verlag Bundesanzeiger
Breite Straße
Postfach 01 80 06
5000 Köln 1
Tel. (02 21) 20 29-0
Fernschreiber:
ANZEIGER BONN 8 882 595
Telecopierer:
20 29 278

GREECE

G.C. Eleftheroudakis SA
International Bookstore
4 Nikis Street
105 63 Athens
Tel. 322 22 55
Telex 219410 ELEF

Sub-agent for Northern Greece:

Molho's Bookstore
The Business Bookshop
10 Tsimiski Street
Thessaloniki
Tel. 275 271
Telex 412885 LIMO

ESPAÑA

Boletin Oficial del Estado
Trafalgar 27
E-28010 Madrid
Tel. (91) 76 06 11

Mundi-Prensa Libros, S.A.
Castelló 37
E-28001 Madrid
Tel. (91) 431 33 99 (Libros)
431 32 22 (Abonos)
435 36 37 (Dirección)
Télex 49370-MPLI-E

FRANCE

Service de vente en France des publications des Communautés européennes
Journal officiel
26, rue Desaix
75732 Paris Cedex 15
Tél. (1) 45 78 61 39

IRELAND

Government Publications Sales Office
Sun Alliance House
Molesworth Street
Dublin 2
Tel. 71 03 09

or by post

Stationery Office
St Martin's House
Waterloo Road
Dublin 4
Tel. 68 90 66

ITALIA

Licosa Spa
Via Lamarmora, 45
Casella postale 552
50 121 Firenze
Tel. 57 97 51
Telex 570466 LICOSA I
CCP 343 509

Subagenti:

Libreria scientifica Lucio de Biasio - AEIOU
Via Meravigli, 16
20 123 Milano
Tel. 80 76 79

Libreria Tassi
Via A. Farnese, 28
00 192 Roma
Tel. 31 05 90

Libreria giuridica
Via 12 Ottobre, 172/R
16 121 Genova
Tel. 59 56 93

GRAND-DUCHÉ DE LUXEMBOURG

Office des publications officielles des Communautés européennes
2, rue Mercier
L-2985 Luxembourg
Tél. 49 92 81
Télex PUBOF LU 1324 b
CCP 19190-81
CC bancaire BIL 8-109/6003/200

Messageries Paul Kraus
11, rue Christophe Plantin
L-2339 Luxembourg
Tél. 48 21 31
Télex 2515
CCP 49242-63

NEDERLAND

Staatsdrukkerij- en uitgeverijbedrijf
Christoffel Plantijnstraat
Postbus 20014
2500 EA 's-Gravenhage
Tel. (070) 78 99 11

PORTUGAL

Imprensa Nacional
Av. Francisco Manuel de Melo, 5
P-1000 Lisboa
Tel. 65 39 96

Grupo Bertrand, SARL
Distribuidora de Livros Bertrand Lda.
Rua das Terras dos Vales, 4-A
Apart. 37
P-2701 Amadora CODEX
Tel. 493 90 50 - 494 87 88
Telex 15798 BERDIS

UNITED KINGDOM

HM Stationery Office
HMSO Publications Centre
51 Nine Elms Lane
London SW8 5DR
Tel. (01) 211 56 56

Sub-agent:

Alan Armstrong & Associates Ltd
72 Park Road
London NW1 4SH
Tel. (01) 723 39 02
Telex 297635 AAALTD G

SCHWEIZ/SUISSE/SVIZZERA

Librairie Payot
6, rue Grenus
1211 Genève
Tél. 31 89 50
CCP 12-236

UNITED STATES OF AMERICA

European Community Information Service
2100 M Street, NW
Suite 707
Washington, DC 20037
Tel. (202) 862 9500

CANADA

Renouf Publishing Co., Ltd
61 Sparks Street
Ottawa
Ontario K1P 5R1
Tel. Toll Free 1 (800) 267 4164
Ottawa Region (613) 238 8985-6
Telex 053-4936

JAPAN

Kinokuniya Company Ltd
17-7 Shinjuku 3-Chome
Shiniuku-ku
Tokyo 160-91
Tel. (03) 354 0131

Journal Department
PO Box 55 Chitose
Tokyo 156
Tel. (03) 439 0124